IMAGES
of America

THE 1910 WELLINGTON DISASTER

On the Cover: Supt. James O'Neill (center) and unidentified men sift through the debris searching for victims and hopefully more survivors. The wreckage was buried beneath approximately 40 feet of snow. (Courtesy of John A. Juleen Collection, Everett Public Library.)

IMAGES
of America

The 1910 Wellington Disaster

Deborah Cuyle and Rodney Fletcher

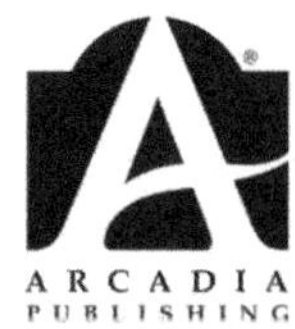

ISBN 978-1-4671-0273-5

Published by Arcadia Publishing
Charleston, South Carolina

Library of Congress Control Number: 2018955296

For all general information, please contact Arcadia Publishing:
Telephone 843-853-2070
Fax 843-853-0044
E-mail sales@arcadiapublishing.com
For customer service and orders:
Toll-Free 1-888-313-2665

Visit us on the Internet at www.arcadiapublishing.com

We write this dedication on the evening of the 108th anniversary of the Wellington disaster. God rest your souls in Heaven, each and every one of you.

Contents

ACKNOWLEDGMENTS

We would like to acknowledge all history lovers, as they work hard to do all they can to preserve and protect our past for future generations to enjoy. Bob Kelly with the Skykomish Historical Society is foremost; without his vast knowledge of and interest in Wellington, this book would not be possible. The Wenatchee Valley Museum was wonderful and supportive of the project; they have an amazing collection. The Northwest Railway Museum was also a great help and has wonderful Wellington links on their website.

Dozens of other individuals went out of their way to help scan photographs and dig up materials, and we are grateful for their valuable time and energy. There are too many of you to list here, but rest assured we appreciate you.

We also acknowledge all of those from 1910 who were involved in fighting the horrific storm and fatal avalanche that night. They put up a good fight, even if they did not win.

And as always, thanks to the friendly and supportive team at Arcadia Publishing, for all they do to preserve and promote local history. Their dedication is infectious, and their endeavor vastly important.

Images appear courtesy of Bob Kelly and the Skykomish Historical Society (SHS), the Library of Congress (LOC), Wenatchee Valley Museum & Cultural Center/Oliver Loch Chapple Collection (WVM), and the John A. Juleen Collection, Everett Public Library (EPL).

All witness statements were taken from the transcript of testimony at the coroner's inquest after the disaster, courtesy of the Washington State Archives.

It is a federal offense to remove any artifacts from the Wellington site. Please respect this law, as leaving artifacts allows others to experience Wellington. We ask that the site remain untouched by trash and graffiti. Thank you.

Introduction

During one of the worst storms in the history of the Cascades, unsuspecting passengers on two Great Northern (GN) trains became trapped in the remote mountain wilderness for almost a week surrounded only by strangers, with the trains perched precariously on the side of a mountain and thousands of tons of snow looming overhead. At night, they tried to sleep, even with the eerie sounds of a nearby avalanche rumbling down the slopes taking everything in its path. Passengers on the Seattle Express No. 25 and the crew of fast mail No. 27 were definitely stuck, with their trains slowly being buried. Each restless day and every long, dreadful night, they patiently waited for the opportunity to move on to their destinations.

What began as a short, guilt-free delay quickly became an absolute nightmare.

One hundred–plus extra people in a small town soon created multiple difficulties for the locals and the Great Northern crew. There wasn't quite enough food to feed everyone. Sanitation became a huge problem very fast. For drinking water, passengers were forced to quench their thirst with melted, dirty snow.

The passengers became irritated, restless, bored, and frustrated. For the Great Northern crew members, they became increasingly difficult to handle and keep calm.

Women prayed and cried. Men smoked and played cards. Children ran through the cars to pass the time. Crew members shoveled snow and worked on broken equipment. Telegraphers struggled with lines that were forever being cut off or, worse, torn down by slides.

The year 1910 would go down in history for some of the worst storms ever experienced in the mountains since 1897, when the Cascades supposedly received 140 feet of snow. This particular night, March 1, the strange weather brought rain, thunder, and lightning after a nine-day blizzard. The windows of the Pullman cars were soon covered up, and the passengers were entombed in a solid mass of snow.

Rev. James Thomson was on board and did what he could to help people. He also conducted a sermon Sunday night to help boost morale. All were singing and praying together for the storm to pass and for their safety from the snow cap high above the trains. Women wished they could wear men's clothing and risk walking out like a small group of men had done earlier—desperately making their way down to the safety of Scenic—a life-risking hike, but much better than being a sitting duck.

Just a few days earlier, at Cascade Tunnel Station, a slide tore down the mountain, destroying a beanery that had accommodated the same trains, taking with it the two cooks who so graciously fed and cared for the passengers before they were stranded at Wellington. The cook Harry Elliker and waiter John Bjerenson were killed instantly, and the beanery completely destroyed.

The passengers heard of this tragedy and became frantic; the avalanche escalated their fears. It was no secret to anyone that their trains had just moved from the exact spot where the avalanche occurred. It could have been they who were killed so quickly. They begged to be returned to the perceived safety of Cascade Tunnel.

But the crews and locals reassured the passengers that there had never been an avalanche in the spot where the trains were now parked. It was thought to be the safest location to remain until the storm passed. And as the crew pointed out, the tunnel was plagued by conditions that were dangerous and unsanitary. Passengers would be forced to trudge through mud all the way to the hotel twice a day for their food, a walk which several disabled passengers would be unable to make. Anyway, there was not enough coal to both move the trains and keep the cars heated. The trains would stay put.

So, the remaining passengers settled in for another long evening. The last lamp was turned off by the porter sometime before midnight, and all the cars were soon filled with snoring. Before they went to bed, many had made the decision to finally leave the stalled trains first thing in the morning, no matter what.

During the night, as the storm raged, the gigantic snow cap (rain-soaked now) was possibly struck by lightning, which loosened its grip from the steep mountain; practically in an instant, most everyone in the trains was dead, crushed by an enormous avalanche a half-mile long, a quarter-mile wide, and 14 feet thick—approximately 10 acres of snow—killing them within seconds.

Asking who was to blame is of no use now; what is done is done. Research proves that everyone concerned was working as hard as they could, performing the best they could, and providing safety for the passengers as well as they could. With snow falling sometimes at the rate of one foot per hour, it is amazing the crews were able to do anything productive at all.

The Great Northern Railway crews were struggling to control the snow nonstop, often working without sleep or food for days. Soaked to the bones in freezing cold weather, with snow up to their armpits, these men worked tirelessly in the hopes of getting the lines open and the trains moving again.

Wellington residents were equally industrious in their efforts—accommodating a few hundred more mouths to feed was no easy task, especially while cut off from the outside world. No trains meant no supplies. Not only were they feeding the passengers and crews, they also had to feed the countless snow-shovelers trying to clear the tracks.

Many lost their lives that night, and those who were lucky enough to survive had to deal with the harrowing rescue efforts. Rumors suggest that men had to rely on shots of whiskey to calm their nerves, warm their bodies, and give them the courage needed to go back into the freezing snow to dig for more bodies.

One

The Heroes of Wellington

There were many heroes throughout the Wellington disaster, all of whom have their place in history. Many recognize the big names like James Hill, the "Empire Builder;" James O'Neill, the Cascade Division superintendent; or even Joseph Pettit, the conductor of the Seattle Express No. 25 who tragically lost his life that morning after he had walked to safety at Scenic but then returned to the stranded passengers.

Yet there were scores of other heroes who remain mostly unknown. Alathea Sherlock, the telegrapher Basil's wife; the engineer Bob Miles's wife; and Mrs. Shelton, wife of the night telegrapher, immediately began tending to the injured in the makeshift hospital they created in the bunkhouse. Alfred Hensel, the only surviving mail clerk, was determined to collect the numerous scattered bags of mail with a broken wrist and collarbone as well as several fractured ribs, although he probably refrained from this. J.J. Mackey and John Wentzel both walked to the closest towns in the waist-high snow to relay the bad news, since the telegraph wires were still down.

Then there were the heroes who dealt with the worst of it all: the men who followed crimson blood trails in the snow to locate, dig up, and wrap the bodies of the dead. The exhausted coroners who had the grisly task of identifying the victims from what little clues survived were champions. The physicians and the countless other unidentified saviors who eagerly made their way to remote Wellington to help are not always named but were extremely important.

Hundreds of snow shovelers, working for pennies a day in the freezing weather, go unnamed in history—many lost their lives that night and were never identified.

Although some have tried, there is no blame needed for this disaster. Everyone fought as hard as possible and made the best decisions they could at the time, but unfortunately, Mother Nature prevailed, and the rest is history.

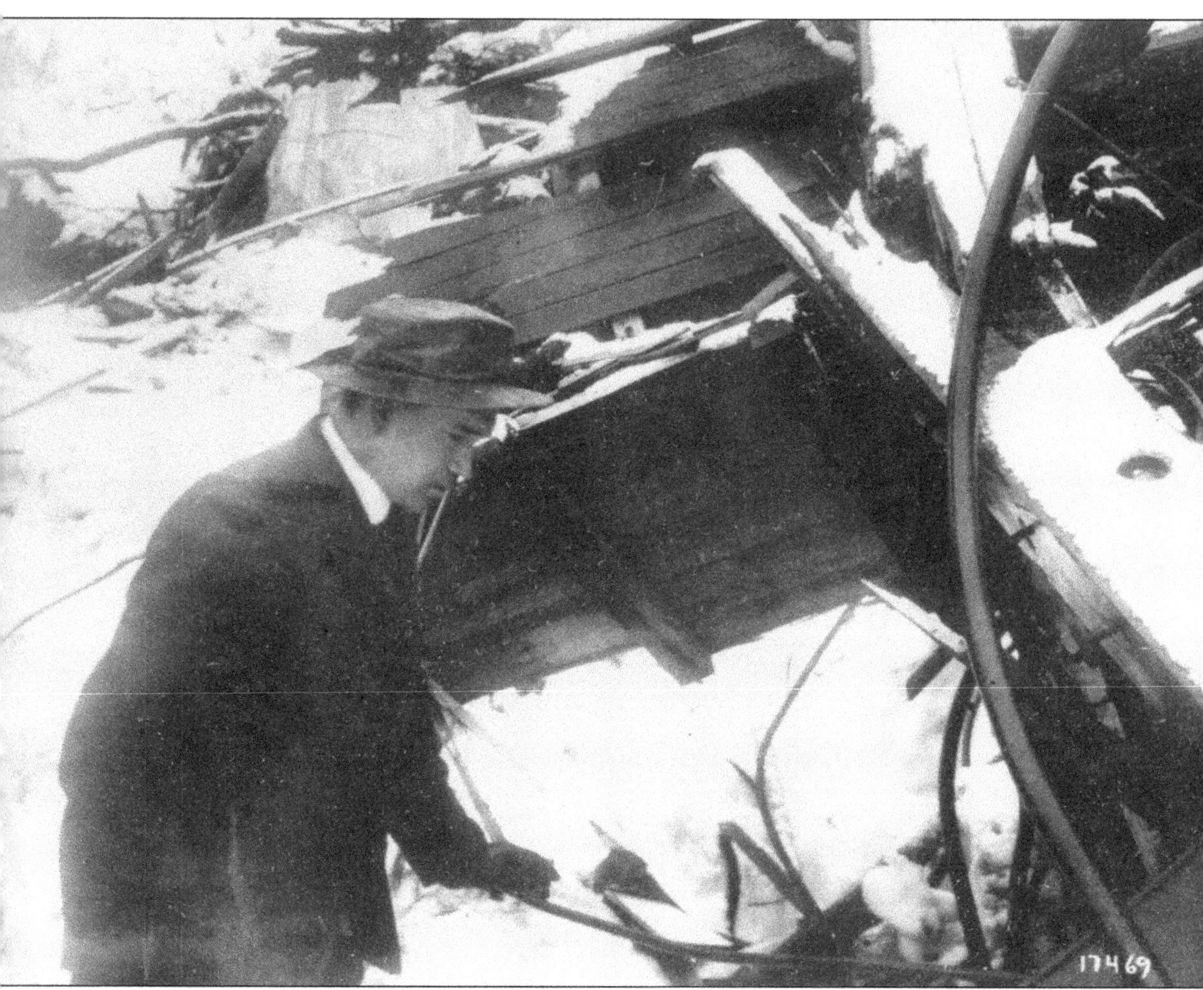

Supt. James O'Neill carefully inspects some wreckage that was swept down into the ravine below the tracks. He had endured fighting the snow for days without sleep or food. He decided to shut the entire Cascade Division down, something he had never done before in his career. O'Neill's father was a section foreman, and young O'Neill started his career at just 13 years old, working as a water boy earning $1 per day. By age 15 he was a brakeman, and by 17, a freight train conductor earning 3¢ per mile. He quickly earned a reputation for keeping his trains on schedule no matter the weather and was nicknamed "the Kid Conductor from Buxton." O'Neill loved to smoke cigars and lived in Everett with his wife, Berenice, and small child Peggy Jane. (Courtesy of WVM, 87-142-6.)

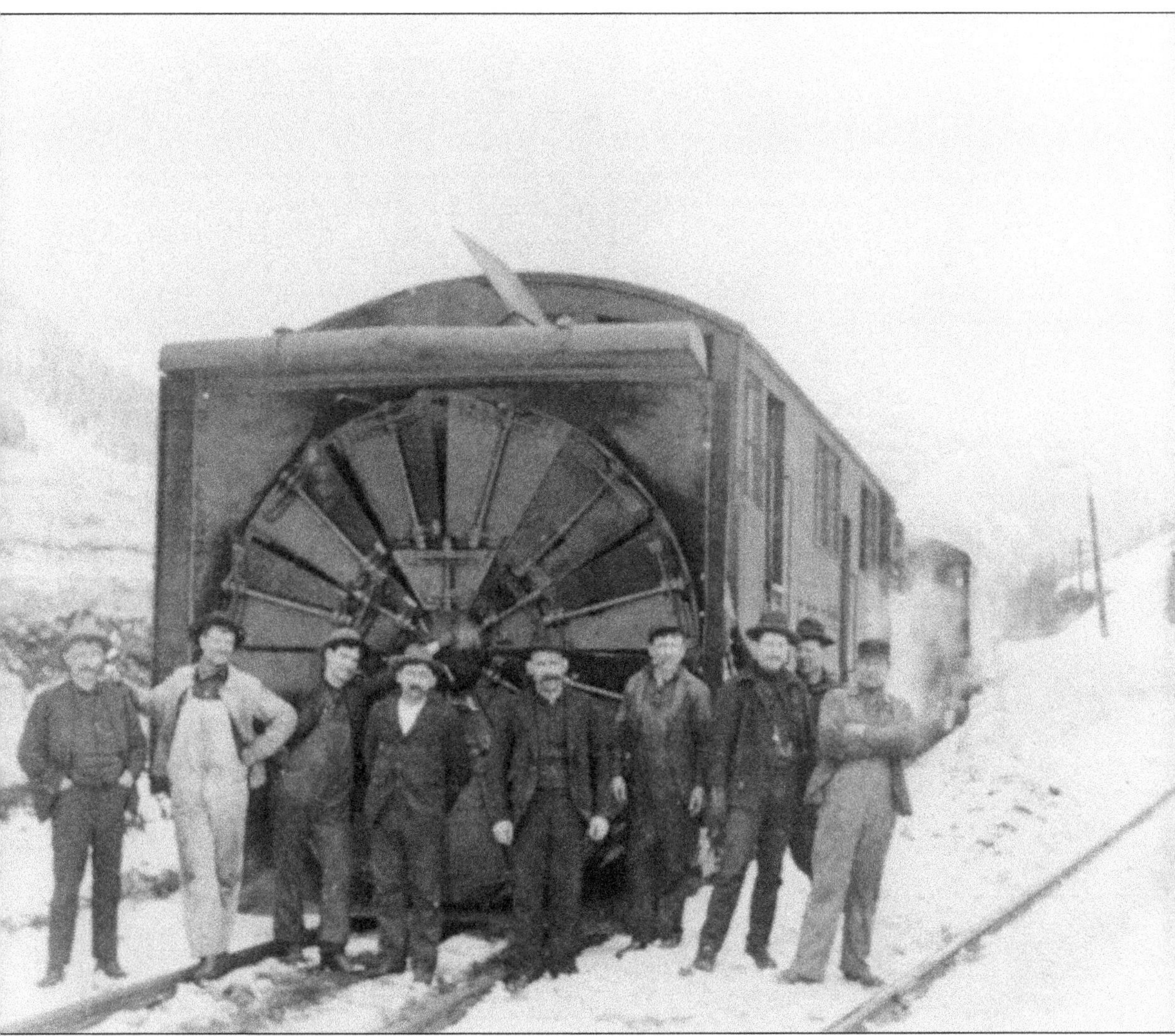

This unidentified Wellington crew poses in front of a rotary snowplow. James O'Neill left Arthur Reed Blackburn, Skykomish trainmaster, in charge at Scenic, which saw temperatures as low as 10 degrees below zero at times. Conductor Homer Purcell was in charge of rotary X807, and these men had to buck through relentless slides over and over again during the storm to clear the tracks. O'Neill later testified, "The rotaries had been working a slide of about fifteen hundred feet long by ten to thirty feet deep . . . we were going back for water and we ran into another slide." The men could not keep up with the slides; as soon as they cleared one, it seemed another one took its place. On Friday afternoon, J.J. Dowling was making his way from Scenic in rotary X808, but even that was becoming a daunting task. (Courtesy of SHS.)

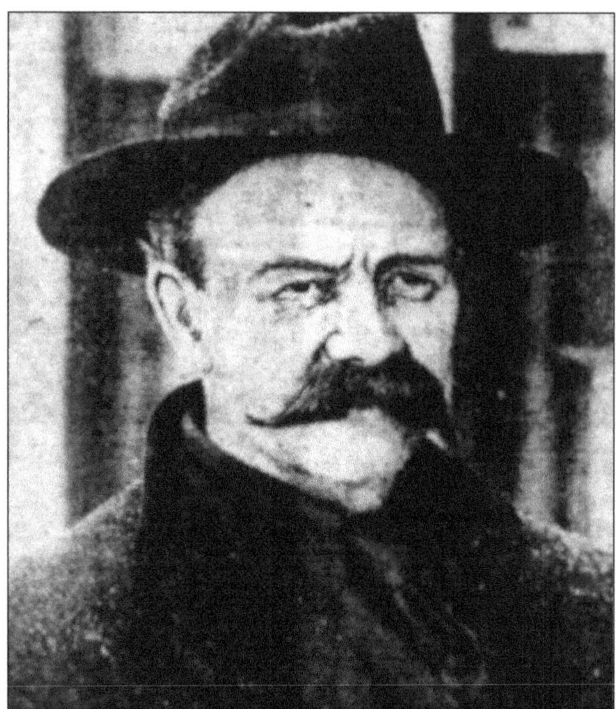

J.J. Mackey walked five miles to Scenic to alert everyone of the disaster, and when he arrived, he was half dead from exhaustion. If O'Neill had been sleeping in his private car at Wellington that night, he could have been killed. Some feared that Mackey risked his life that night walking to Scenic and that his trek was suicide. This image was published on March 5, 1910, in the *Spokane Press*. (Courtesy of SHS.)

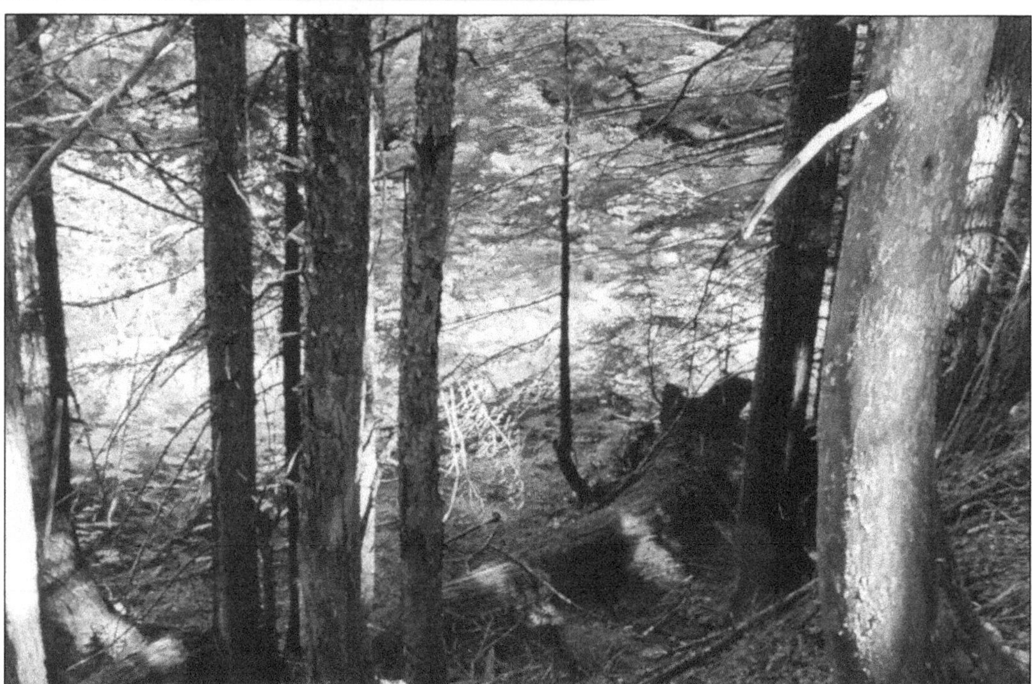

Arthur Blackburn was sleeping in O'Neill's private car that night but survived. As he was pulled from the wreckage, he said, "Look out for the others." Station agent William Flannery helped him, but another slide knocked them both down, and Blackburn rolled into the Tye River. He had been a trainmaster for 16 years. Pictured is the Tye River, where some of the trains came to rest. (Author's collection.)

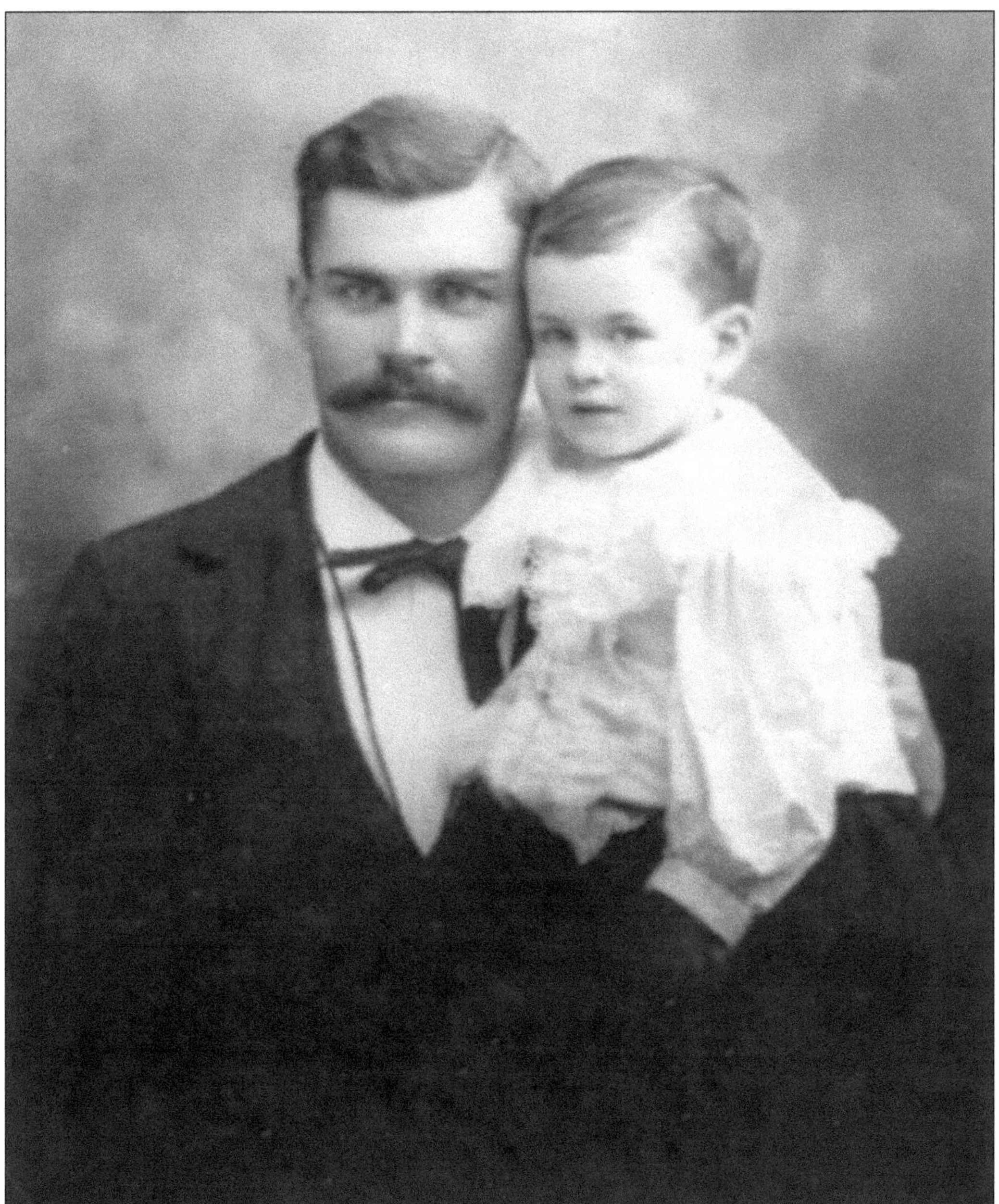

Joseph Pettit was a GN conductor and helped some of the passengers hike to Scenic the day before the disaster. Unfortunately, he returned to the trains and was killed in the avalanche. The baby in the photograph is identified as "Lawrence" and might be Frank Lawrence Pettit, Joseph's oldest son. Pettit was well liked by everyone, as he had a friendly and courteous personality. Henry White, a surviving passenger, testified, "Pettit had gone to the hotel and told them to be prepared to serve an early breakfast . . . he had given all of us our meal tickets so we could get an early start." The passengers could have left that evening, saving themselves, as the tracks were finally almost clear, but most figured it was too late and they would head out early the next morning. Joseph Pettit was the great-grandfather of Kim Rossevelt-Barnett, who helped provide this image. (Courtesy of Verna [Sorlie] and Kim Rossevelt-Barnett.)

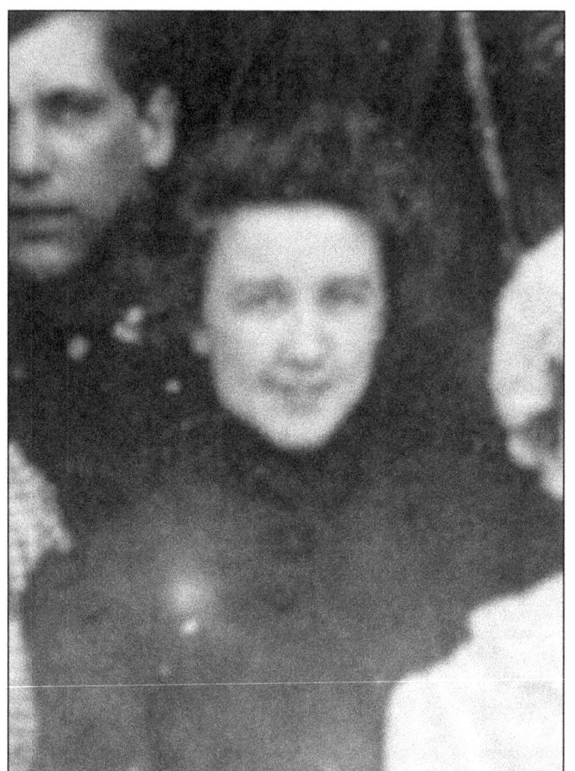

Alathea Sherlock was a true heroine during the tragedy. She turned the bunkhouse into a makeshift hospital. The Sherlocks were from Minnesota and moved to Wellington the year prior to the disaster. Alathea testified, "We were awake and the first we heard was someone yelling 'Everybody up!' and my husband asked, 'What's the matter?' 'The train is down in the ditch!' " (Courtesy of WVM, 87-142-162.)

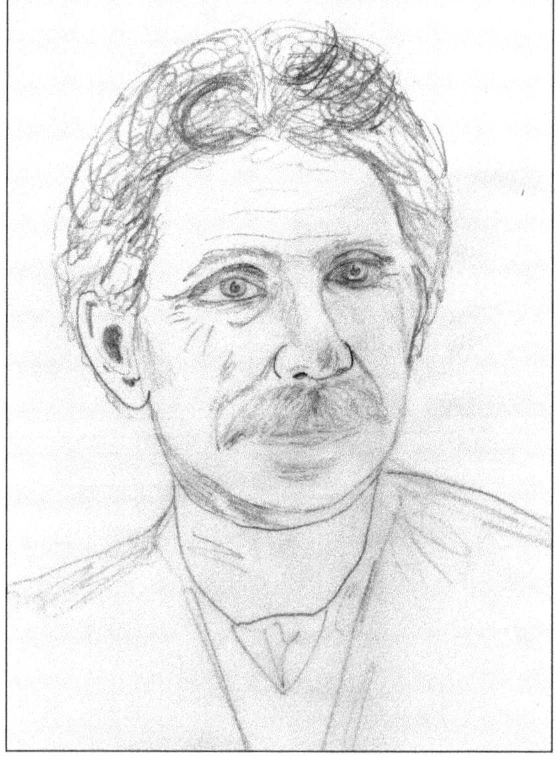

The body of Rev. James Thomas of Bellingham was the 70th to be recovered. The Sunday before tragedy struck, Reverend Thomas led a service in the Seattle Express coach; everyone who attended sang and prayed together, with passengers and crewmen shoulder to shoulder. This image is from the *Seattle Post Intelligencer* of March 5, 1910. (Author's collection.)

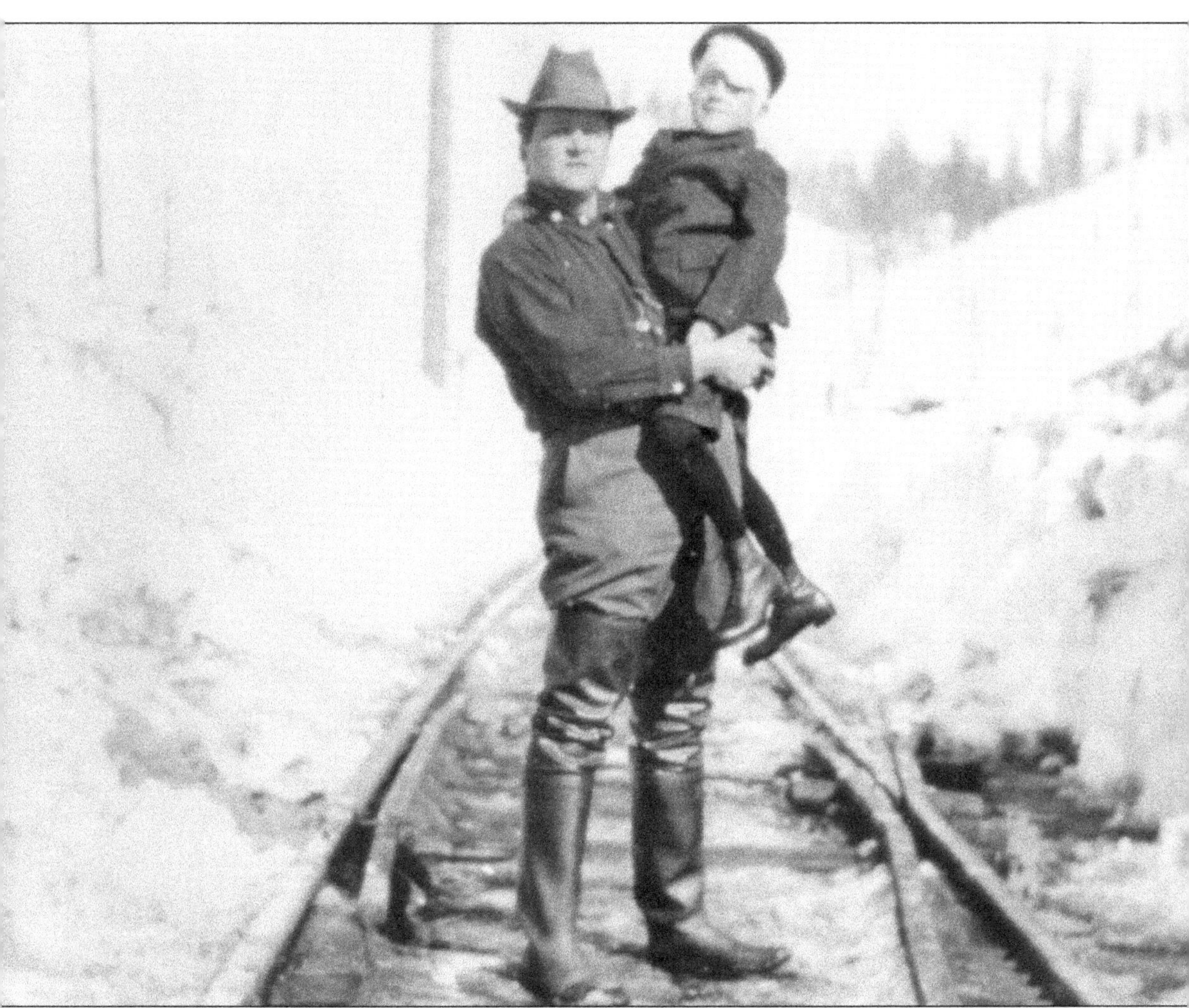

Doctor Stockwell and child survivor Raymond Starrett pose together after the disaster. The boy was found with a splinter in his forehead that Basil Sherlock cut out of him. Stockwell later told reporters, "The train took us only to three miles from Scenic, after walking there we then had a straight climb up of 1,000 feet to the track above through snow varying in depth from 10 to 70 feet . . . we had three more miles to walk along the track to Wellington and we finally got there at 10 o'clock at night." Stockwell, of Monroe, was the first physician to reach the scene and brought two nurses with him, Leonora Tod Hunter and Annabelle Lee. (Courtesy of WVM, 87-142-12.)

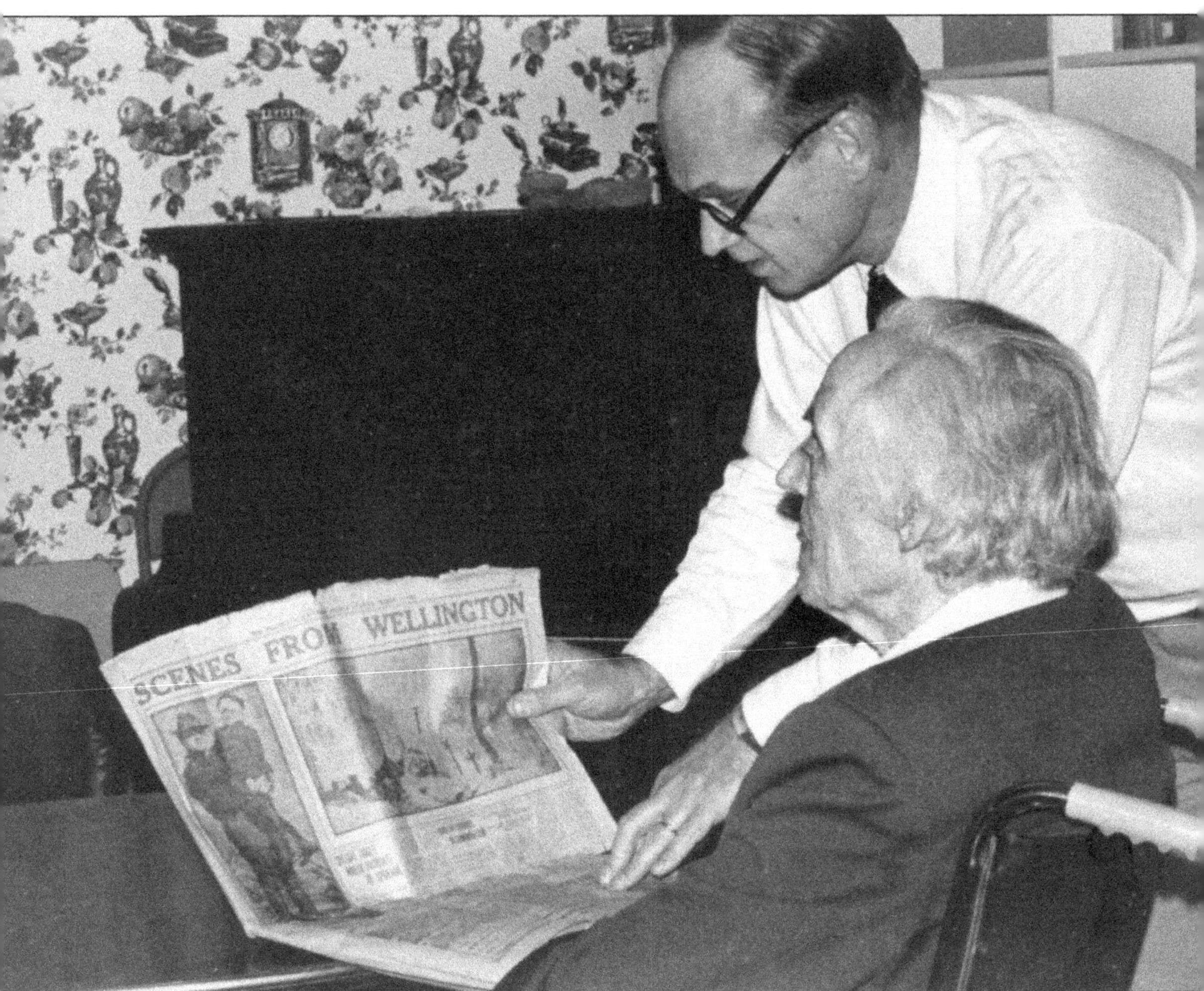

In 1980, Oliver Chapple interviews Raymond Starret (seated), as Starret remembers surviving the disaster at age seven. Dr. A.W. Stockwell took an instant liking to the boy and claimed that if his parents were not found, he would like to adopt him. Telegrapher Basil Sherlock relieved the boy of the big splinter with a clean razor and bandaged him up promptly. William Bailets recalled, "When I went down there the only thing we could find was a little boy with a snag—a big splinter stuck right up through his forehead." Starret bore the scar from the Wellington disaster on his forehead his whole life, a constant reminder of the nightmare. He and the Sherlocks corresponded through cards and letters after they were reunited by a letter written by Basil Sherlock to Starret in 1960. (Courtesy of WVM, 87-142-4.)

April 4th, 1960

Mr. Raymond Starrett,
Route 1 Box 466,
Olympia, Wash.

Dear Raymond :

Am wondering if you would care to know how I met you, over fifty years ago. Beleive you were only a boy of seven years. If so, it will cost you a picture of yourself taken recently with your hat off. Perhaps you wish to forget it. For over fifty years I have . Twenty five of those years were spent working on the grave yard shift 12M to 8 A. M. and when the hands of the clock would point to 110 A.M. on March first, I would shut my eyes and see it all over again.

Last March first our news paper came out with a story in the way of a 50 year annivarsay of the avalanch at Wellington, ash. and since then, cannot get you out of my mind. Perhaps you will not remember me now. About March 3rd 1910 you knew me for I was in the temporary hospital and the nurse brought you in to where I was and said "Here is a young man that has been asking to see you for sometime." I am the one that removed the stick from your head.

Sincerely,

B J Sherlock

On April 4, 1960, Basil Sherlock typed a letter to Raymond Starrett 50 years after the avalanche, explaining that he was the one who removed the splinter from his forehead. The two remained in communication until Sherlock's death. The Sherlocks moved to Wellington on August 25, 1909, and lived in one of the little cottages. Basil and his wife, Alathea, tended to 17 of the injured brought up to the makeshift hospital after the slide. They were both awake prior to the avalanche listening to the thunder and lightning. The snow was so deep, it covered the side windows in their cottage, and they had to board them up so they would not break. Basil Sherlock died on July 20, 1962. (Courtesy of WVM, 87-142-170.1.)

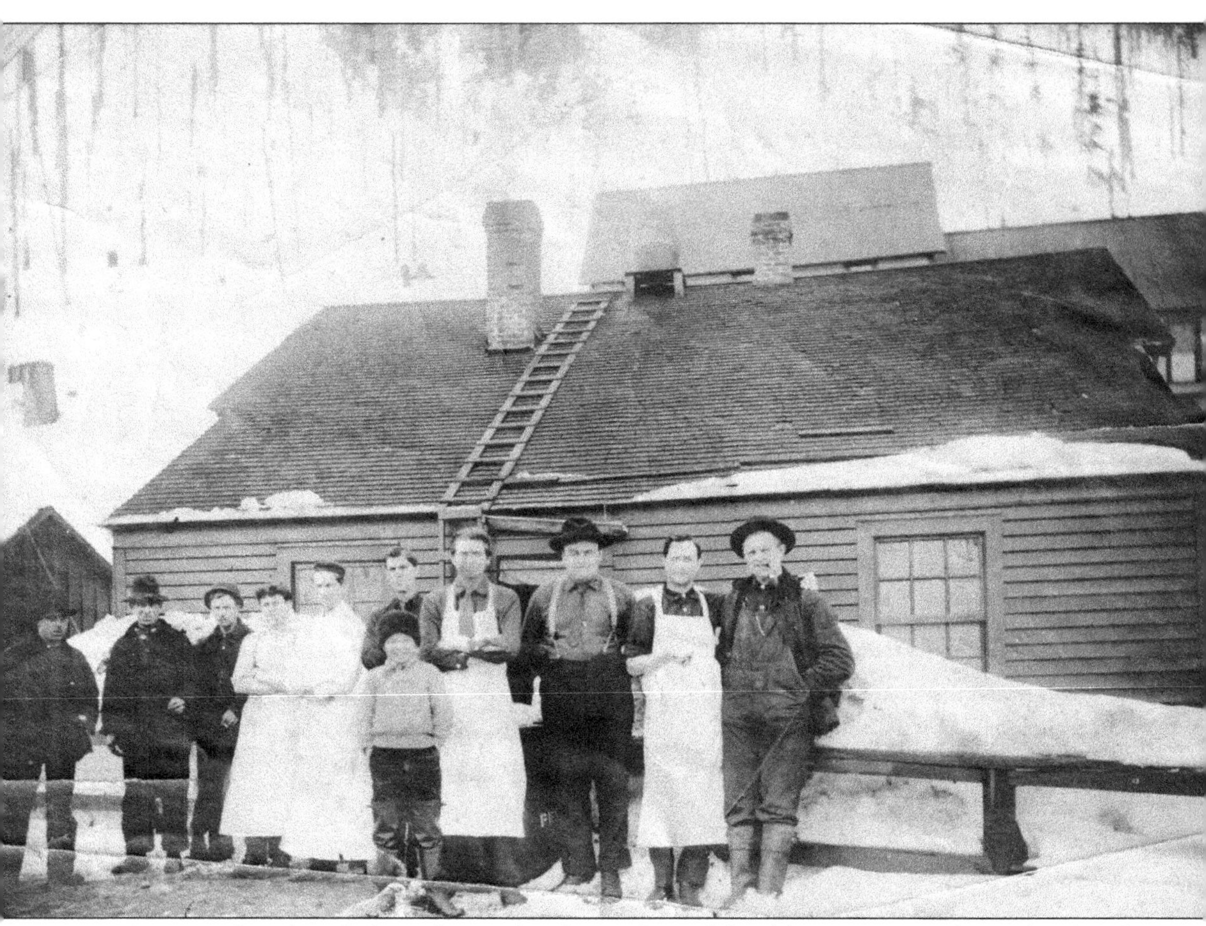

A group of unidentified people stand in front of a cook bunkhouse prior to the avalanche. On Friday, February 25, cook Jon Olson and waiter Henry Elliker both tragically lost their lives when a slide wiped out the beanery at the Cascade Tunnel Station. This devastated the already fearful passengers, as their trains had just been parked at that exact spot for 36 hours before pulling into Wellington. The beanery was described as a single large room with a huge potbellied stove and hand-hewn, grime-streaked tables. Passenger Wertz, who hiked out Monday with Pettit and the group, testified, "I was paying fifty cents per meal for all I ate, and it was pretty steep for a laboring man and I wanted to get out of there." Nothing was left of the wooden beanery except the metal cook stove. (Courtesy of SHS.)

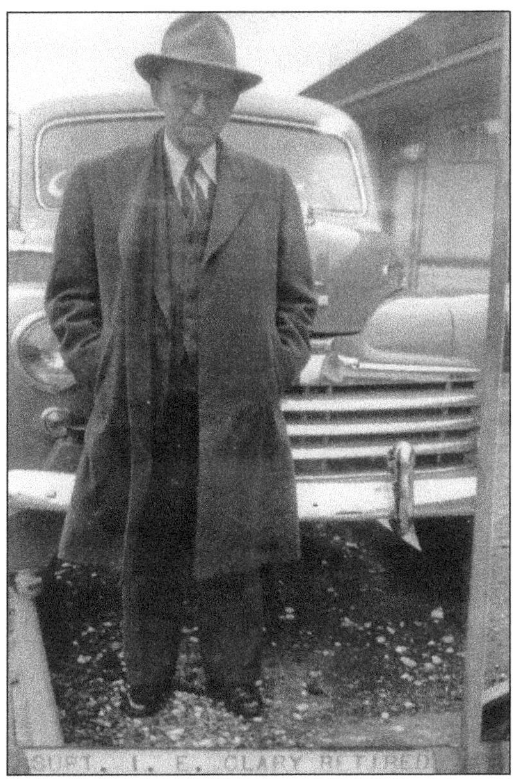

Conductor Ira Clary worked the rotary plows since 1908 and survived the tragedy, along with conductor Homer Purcell. They rescued brakemen Smart and Duncan, and then Purcell risked his life to rescue fireman Kerlee, as the boiler steam collapsed the snow and Purcell fell in. Clary and Duncan pulled Purcell from danger and retrieved Kerlee. (Courtesy of Don Reiling and Seattle Federal Credit Union.)

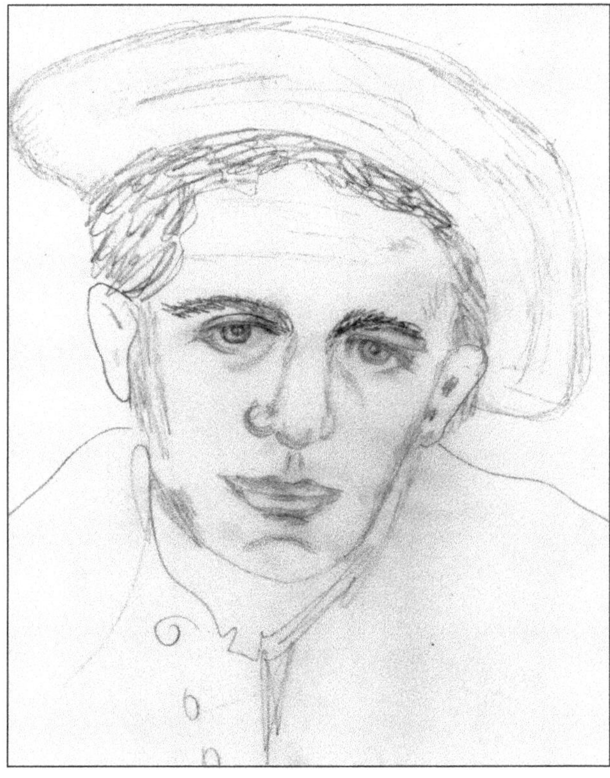

Homer Purcell was a rotary conductor who survived the ordeal. He, Clary, Duncan, and Joe Finn had stayed up playing cards until late and fell asleep just hours before the avalanche. Finn walked back to Wellington to sleep, but the other three slept on the floor of a mail car. This image was published on March 3, 1910, in the *Seattle Star.* (Author's collection.)

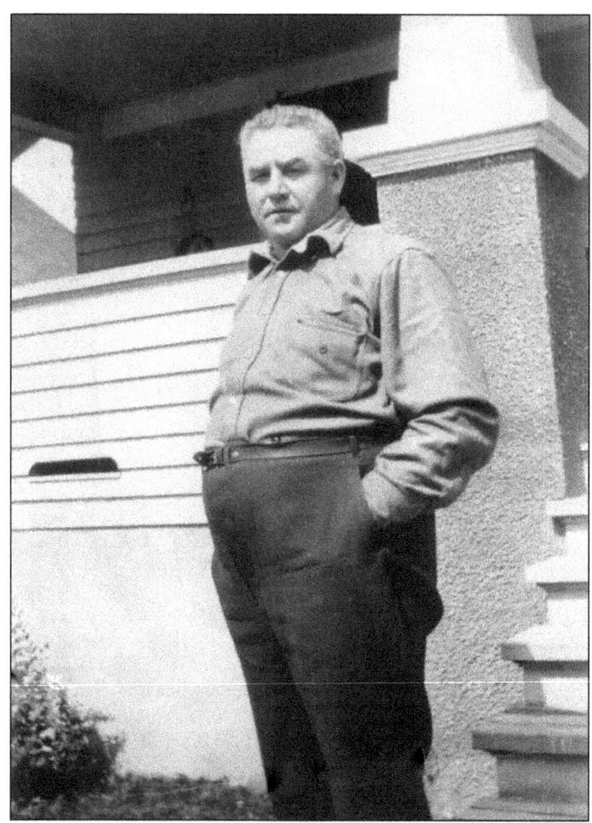

In earlier years, the crew and locals would sometimes pull pranks on passersby, "arresting" them on trumped-up charges in their makeshift "courtroom." Engineer John Meath played a fake judge named Grogan. The gag sometimes went on for a while before the not-too-happy victims caught on. Pranks were a common pastime in Wellington as there was not a lot to do there. At left is John Meath later in life. Below is rotary 800 with an unidentified group of people. (Left, courtesy of the Mrs. James Meath Collection, SHS, donated by Martin Burwash; below, courtesy of SHS.)

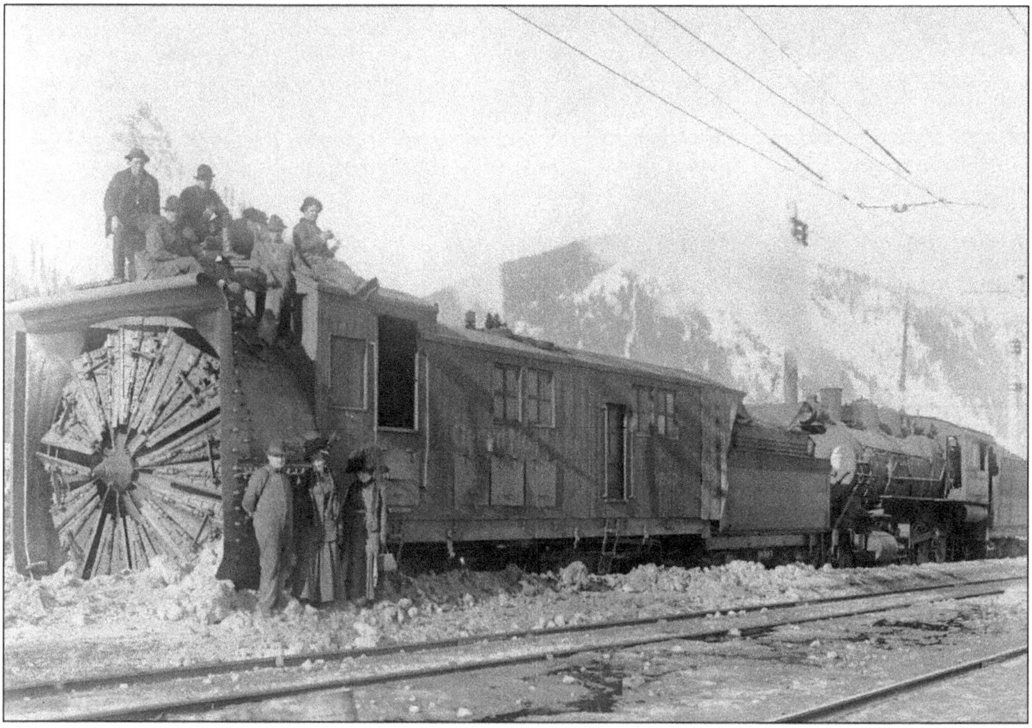

Two

The Progressive Era

The Progressive Era was a time of great change: socially, technologically, and morally. Fighting for rights and equality in everything was of great importance.

During the year 1910, women were struggling to win the right to vote. Recent advances included phonographs, light bulbs, typewriters, machine guns, skyscrapers, telegraphs, diesel fuel, the Brooklyn Bridge, the Eiffel Tower, microphones, and aspirin. In 1900, a train could carry passengers the same distance in six days that a covered wagon would cover in six months. Though the new automobiles traveled much faster than horses, only 8,000 cars and about 10 miles of paved roads existed in 1900 America.

The year 1910 was a time when man aspired to conquer Mother Nature with newly invented machinery, and the railroads were no exception. They pushed onward, digging through any mountain, laying track on any land, and plunging forward as fast as they could to get from coast to coast.

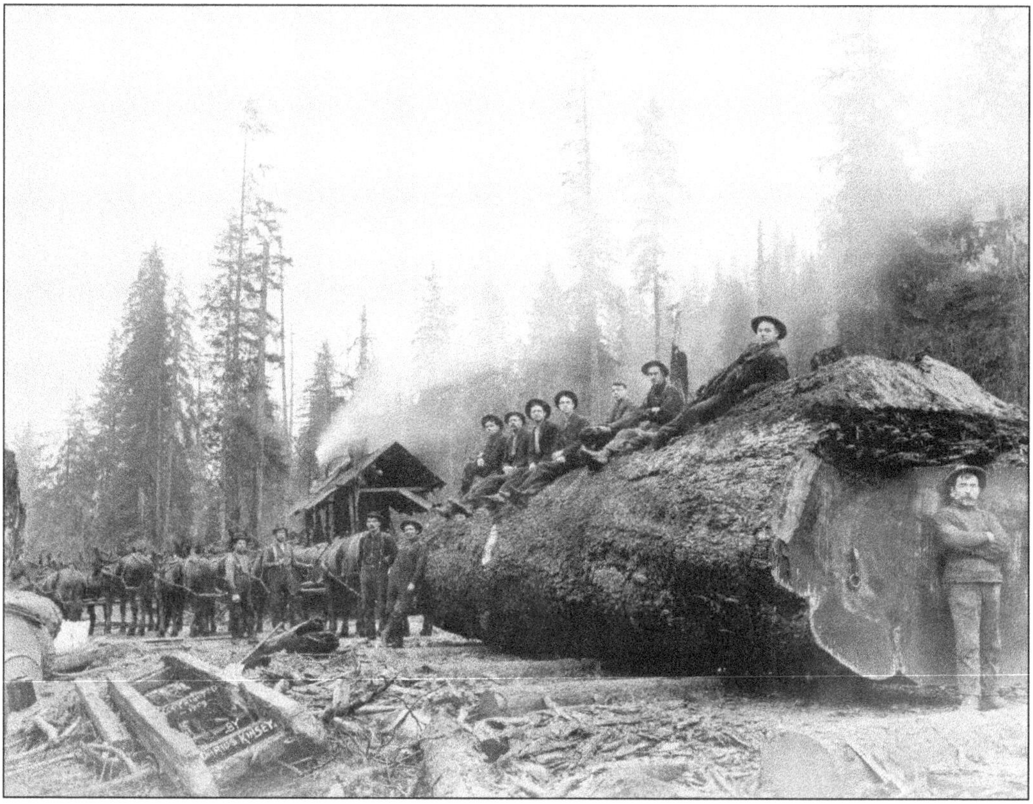

Horses are hauling a spruce measuring 30 feet in circumference in the Cascades in 1905. Life in the Cascades was extremely dangerous for both workers and locals. The weather could be brutal. (Courtesy of LOC.)

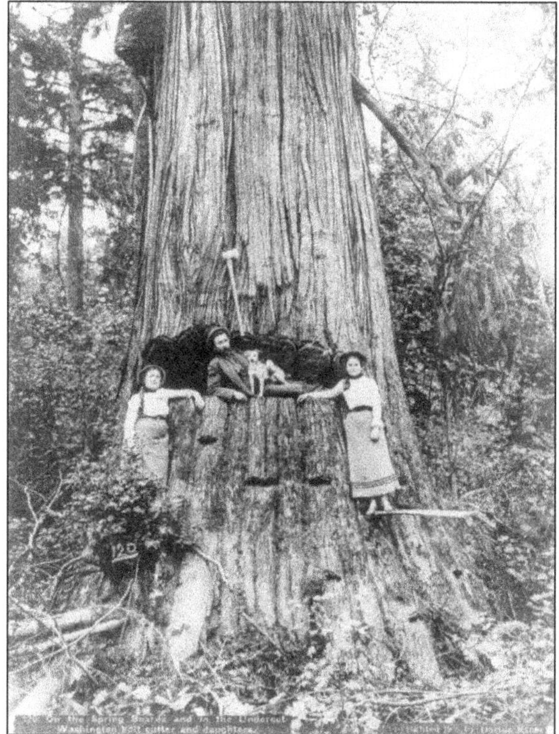

Two women, a man, and his dog are in the undercut of a huge tree in the Cascades in 1905. In the 1860s, the mills produced over 70 million board feet of lumber. Timber was a vital resource in the Pacific Northwest. (Courtesy of LOC.)

A man poses on two-wheeled bicycle-like roller skates. Other inventions from the era include neon lamps, the headset, teabags, cellophane, and instant coffee. For the better-off families, washing machines, telephones, refrigerators, and vacuum cleaners made life easier. (Courtesy of LOC.)

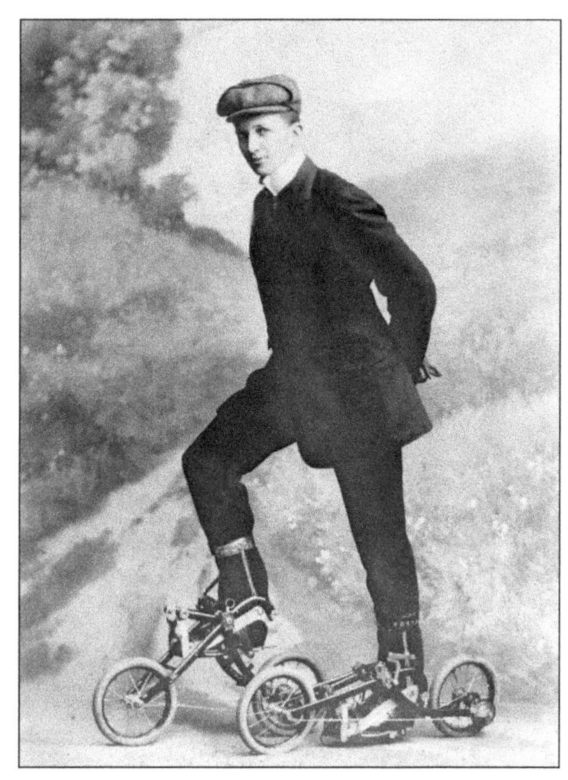

This couple enjoys a 1910 Ford Tourabout, which had two doors, a windshield, gas headlamps, a generator, a speedometer, and a convertible top with side curtains. Although almost 17,000 of these were produced in 1910, none probably ever drove on the muddy streets of Wellington. (Courtesy of LOC.)

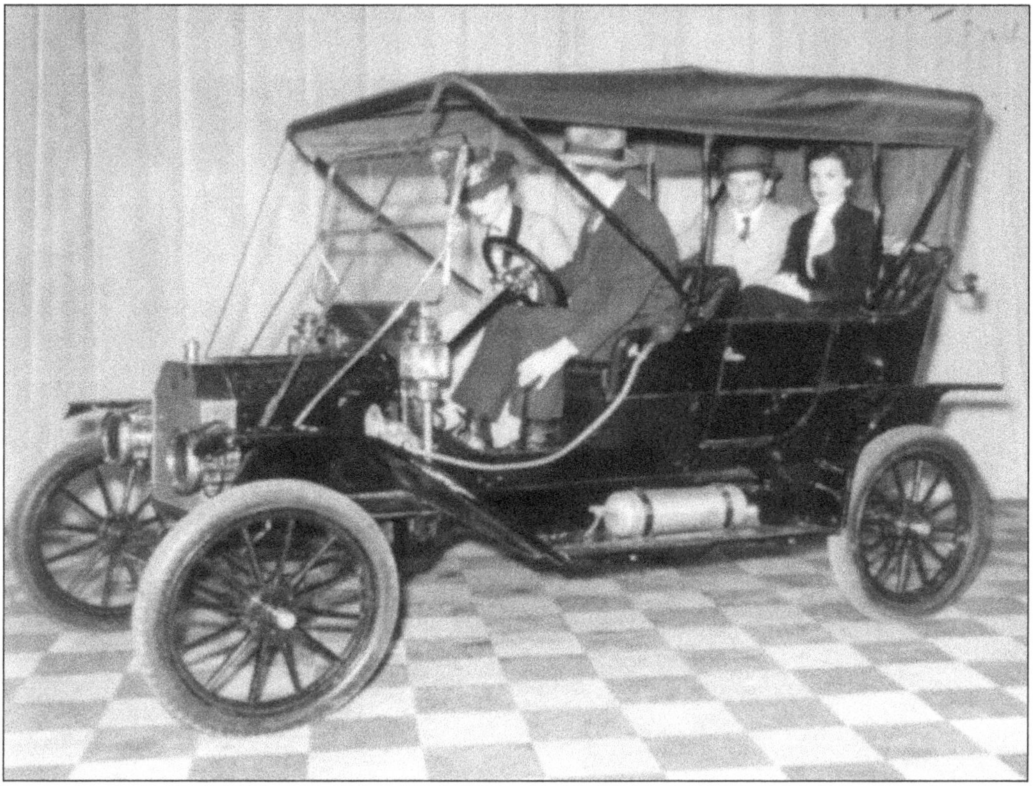

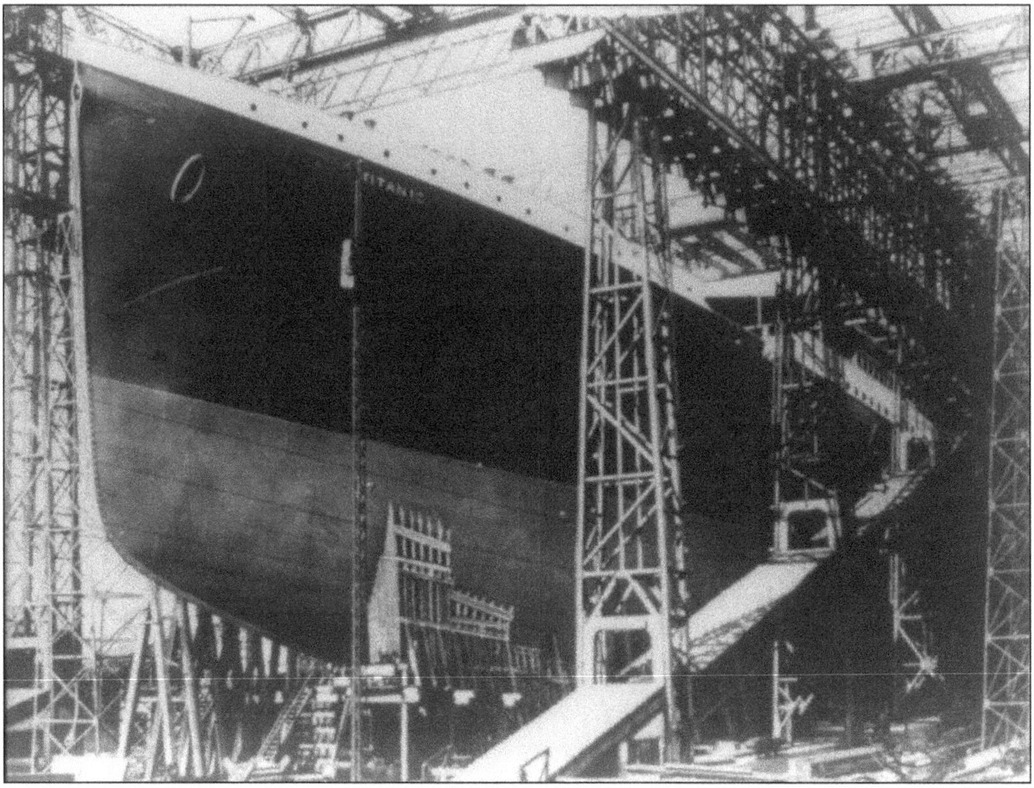

One of the most well-known achievements of this era was the building of the *Titanic*. Work began in 1909 and continued for two years. The steamship sank on April 15, 1912, in the North Atlantic during its maiden voyage. More than 1,500 lost their lives. During this time, men continually strained to conquer both sea and land by ship, train, and autos. (Courtesy of LOC.)

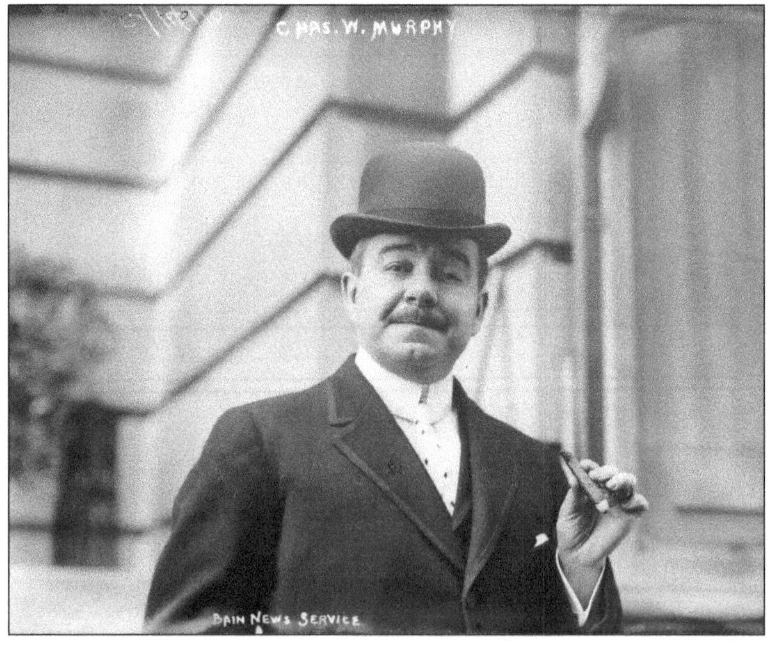

Cigarettes were not allowed in the state of Washington in 1910, but curiously, cigars were still legal and many people enjoyed them instead. Passenger Libby Latch wanted to smoke while her train was stranded in Wellington, but complained there was "nowhere on the trains to accommodate ladies!" (Courtesy of LOC.)

Three

The Obstacles and the Storm

The snow was relentless and even Wellington old-timers were in awe. As soon as a section of track was clear, another slide would come down, again burying the tracks deep under the dreaded "Cascade Cement."

Great Northern employees worked nonstop, desperate to get the trapped trains moving again. Snow shovelers by the dozens, if not hundreds, could not keep up with the snow and soon gave up; the labor-intensive and freezing task was hardly worth the 15¢ per hour they were earning. The trainmen fought to keep the rotaries moving, but were short on coal and clean water, so they resorted to dumping snow in the tanks, which clogged the injectors.

Each new slide had to be cleared by hand because the rotary could only penetrate snow that was free from any wood or other debris.

On Wednesday, February 23, the storm raged, and they were pelted with five feet of new snow.

O'Neill shut down the entire Cascade Division, something that had never been done before. He had run over 4,000 trains through the Cascades and never had his trains been stalled for more than 24 hours. His telegram read, "Will not run any trains until conditions change for the better."

On Saturday, February 26, O'Neill knew he had finally been beaten by the storm. The telegraph lines were all down. The rotaries were either broken or unable to move. The snow would not stop, even for a minute.

The storm had won the battle.

H.L. Wertz, a passenger from No. 25 who hiked out on Monday, said "I do not see how it could be possible for a man to do any more; a man can work all the time and do all that is in his power, and I could not see anything possible for them to do more than what was done."

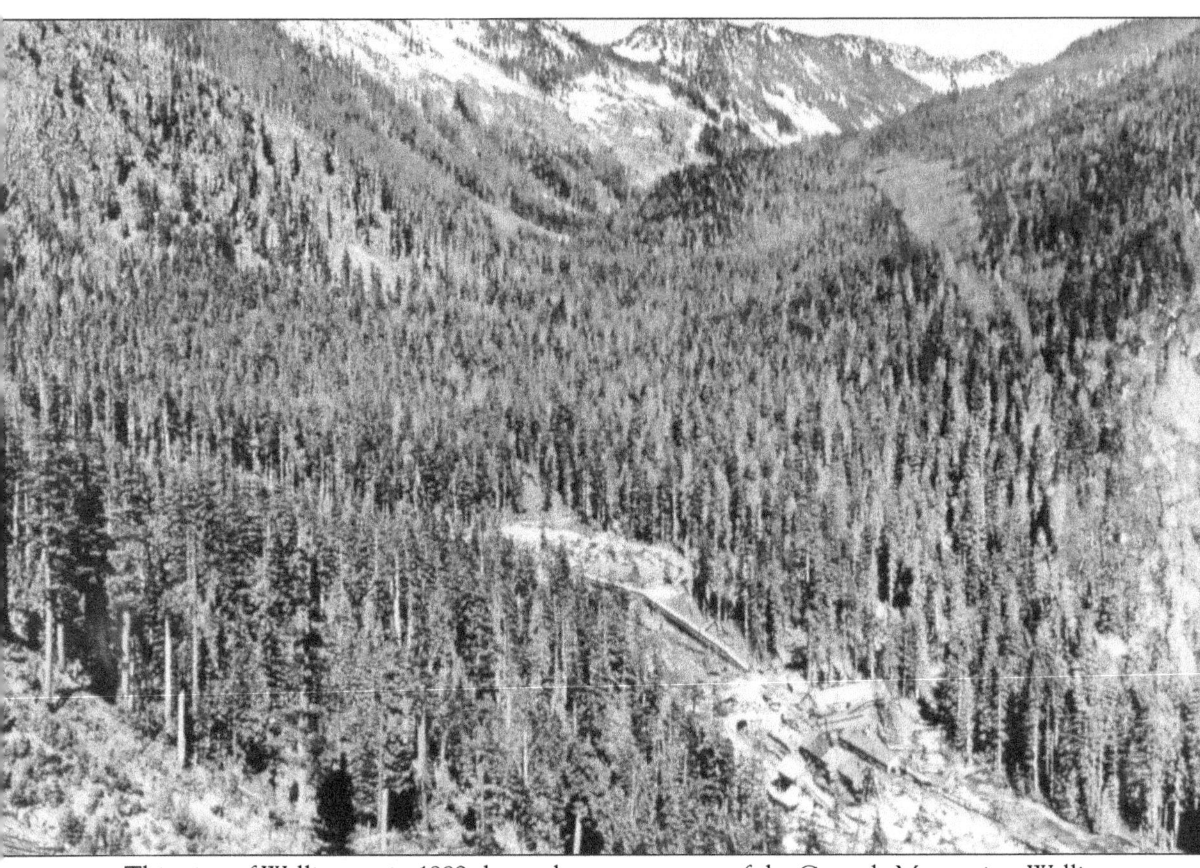

This view of Wellington in 1889 shows the vast expanse of the Cascade Mountains. Wellington consisted of only about 300 people and a dozen buildings in the late 1800s. In 1910, on February 23, the town was hit with five more feet of snow, and by Thursday, the snow gauge at Bailets Hotel marked 17 feet; it was considered the coldest winter in the area since 1887–1888. William and Susan Bailets owned the hotel and general store, along with the post office, tavern, and 10 cottages, and had lived in Wellington for 18 years when the disaster occurred. During the avalanche, the hotel barely escaped being pushed into the ravine, as the side of the slide came very close to the building. The building had tons of snow pressure on its back side, which worried the owners very much. (Courtesy of SHS.)

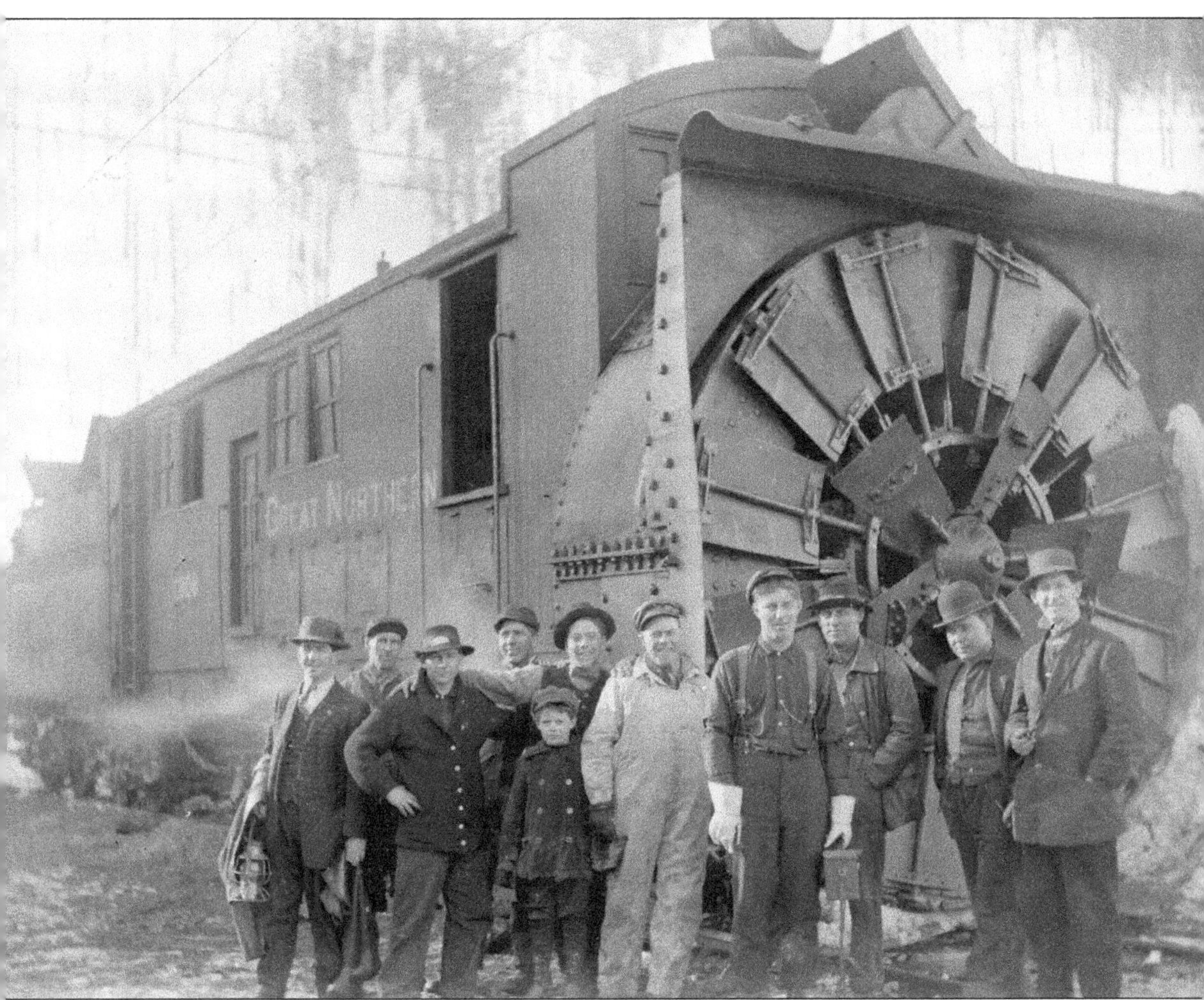

A GN crew poses in front of rotary snowplow X808, the fifth of the Cascade Division's rotaries. Under master mechanic J.J. Dowling's direction, X808 was kept busy clearing snow until the steam engine's injectors became clogged on February 28. The rotaries could only plow 13 feet of snow, so anything over that had to be dug out by hand. If there were any rocks or timber in the snow, this too had to be removed by hand as it could damage the rotary's blades. During the avalanche, Dowling was working at Scenic, which probably spared his life. He testified, "O'Neill came down from Wellington and I found out from him that the situation was very serious . . . then we discussed getting us some relief as we had been on duty something like 96 hours." (Photograph by Casper Hansen, courtesy of the Northwest Railway Museum, Oberg Collection.)

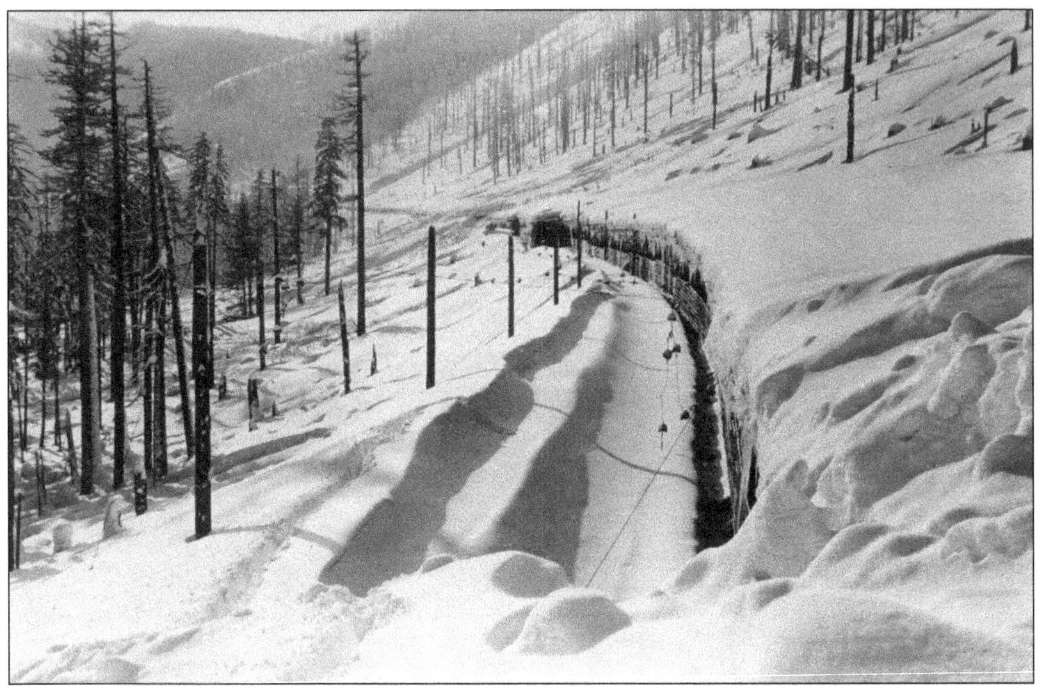

Locals had never seen a slide in the particular spot where the trains were parked. When William Bailets was questioned, he answered, "We had never had a slide there and I would have felt just as safe in one of them cars as I would be here . . . [at Bailets Hotel]. I have stood and wondered day after day how it could have occurred with the force that it came down with." On February 27, another slide came down at snowshed 2, and O'Neill testified that the slide was about 900 feet long and from 20 to 30 feet deep. This slide contained a great amount of green timber and took out the telegraph line and four poles. (Both, courtesy of LOC.)

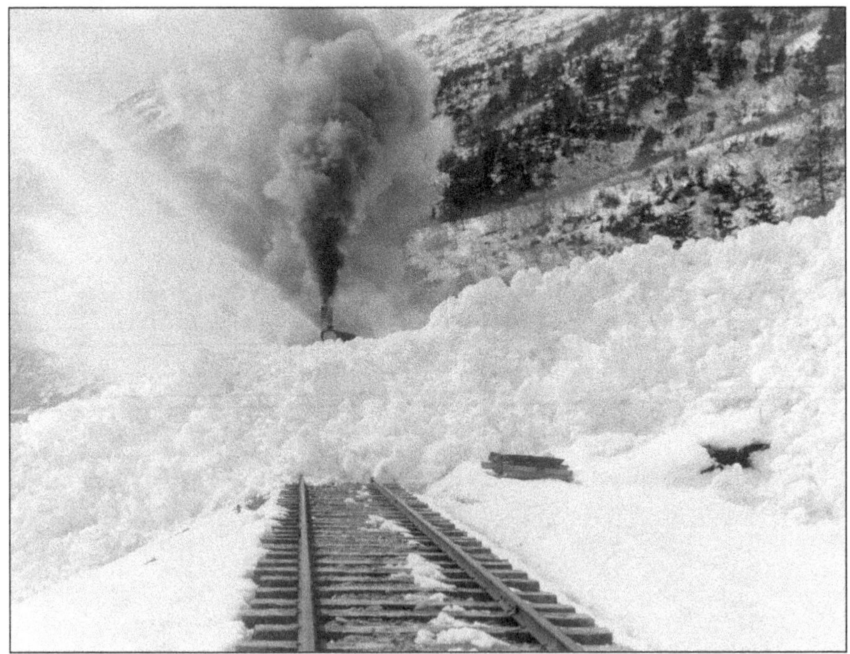

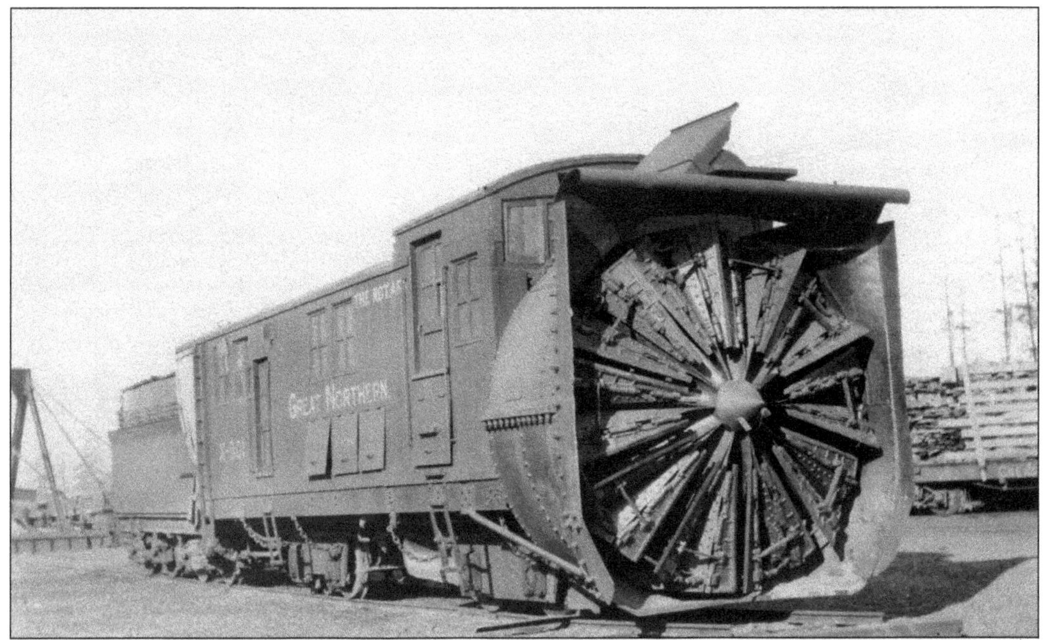

Rotary plows were vital in clearing the tracks of "Cascade Cement." The frustrated O'Neill stated, "How can I get two trains off the mountain when I can't even get the rotaries there?" But there was good news at 2:00 a.m. on Thursday, February 24. Purcell's rotary was finally back in service, and he and Blackburn hooked their rotaries together at Alvin and headed to Wellington, which took them five hours. (Courtesy of SHS.)

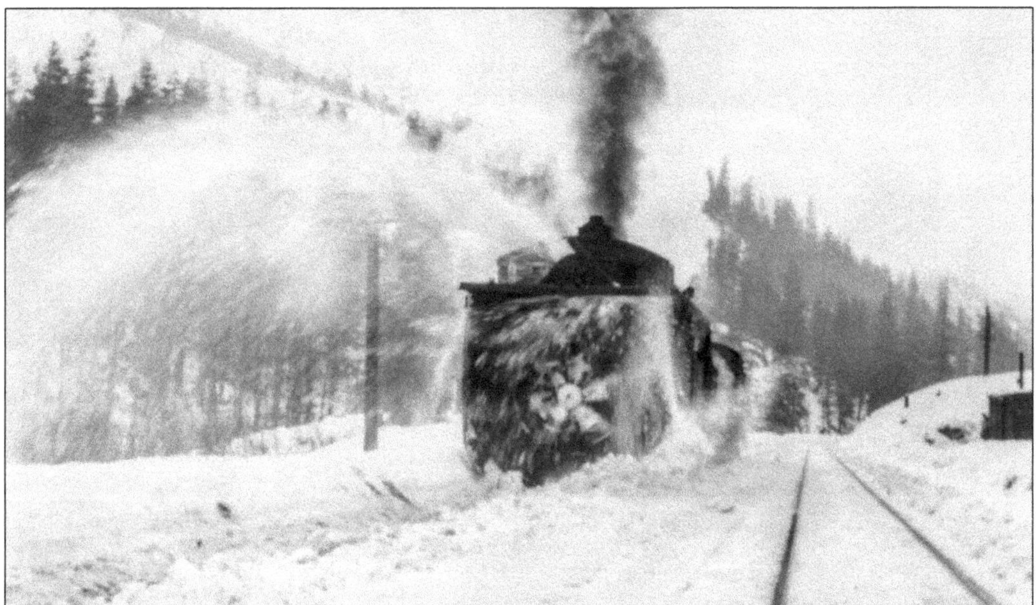

The crews running the rotaries worked tirelessly to clear the snow off the tracks. Before the Wellington incident, a rotary crew went missing at Windy Point with 20 men on board. O'Neill proclaimed at trial, "Sometimes you would jab the rotary into a slide and you would not get more than six or eight inches . . . sometimes you would not faze it at all." This image was published in the *Leavenworth Echo* on March 4, 1910. (Courtesy of SHS.)

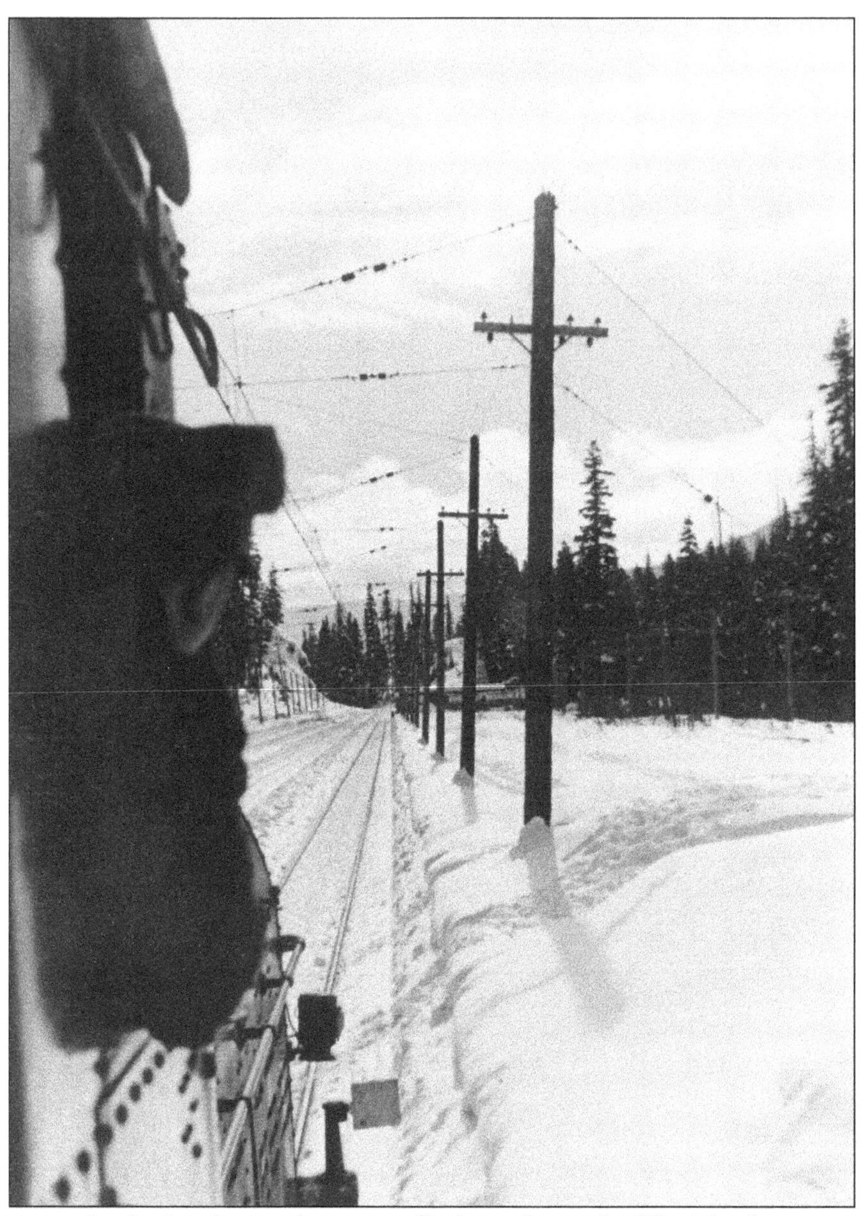

An engineer pokes his head out as his train rolls down the tracks. The Monday evening before the avalanche, 30 passengers left to hike to Scenic, but, quickly discouraged, returned to the safety of the trains. This was a bad move, as they were dead by morning. Passenger J.W. Merritt, an attorney from Spokane, remembered, "We were walking over the tops of the telegraph poles, probably 20 feet of snow there . . . and we did not know what minute the weight of ourselves was going to start a slide that would take us off the side of the mountain and bury the whole bunch of us." To get to Scenic, they had to slide down a steep slope risking death. Days before the avalanche, James O'Neill, Lewis Jesseph, John Merritt, George Loveberry, R. McKnight, Samuel Field, H.L. Wertz, Angus VanLarken, Guiseppe Dinatale, Edward Rea, John Rogers, E.A. Sperber, Joseph Pettit, Milton Horn, Edward Boles, and Frank Ritter all hiked down to Scenic, which saved their lives, except for Pettit, who returned to the trains to help the others. He perished in the tragedy. (Courtesy of Washington State Archives.)

Some women threatened to wear men's clothes so they could walk to Scenic. L.C. Jesseph, the 32-year-old Colville lawyer who hiked out on Sunday, said "I do not see how a woman could ever have gotten down 50 or 75 yards where we had to go; straight down almost . . . I know that I would not have taken any woman out over that trail." Pictured are rail passengers in the typical clothing of the time. (Both, courtesy of LOC.)

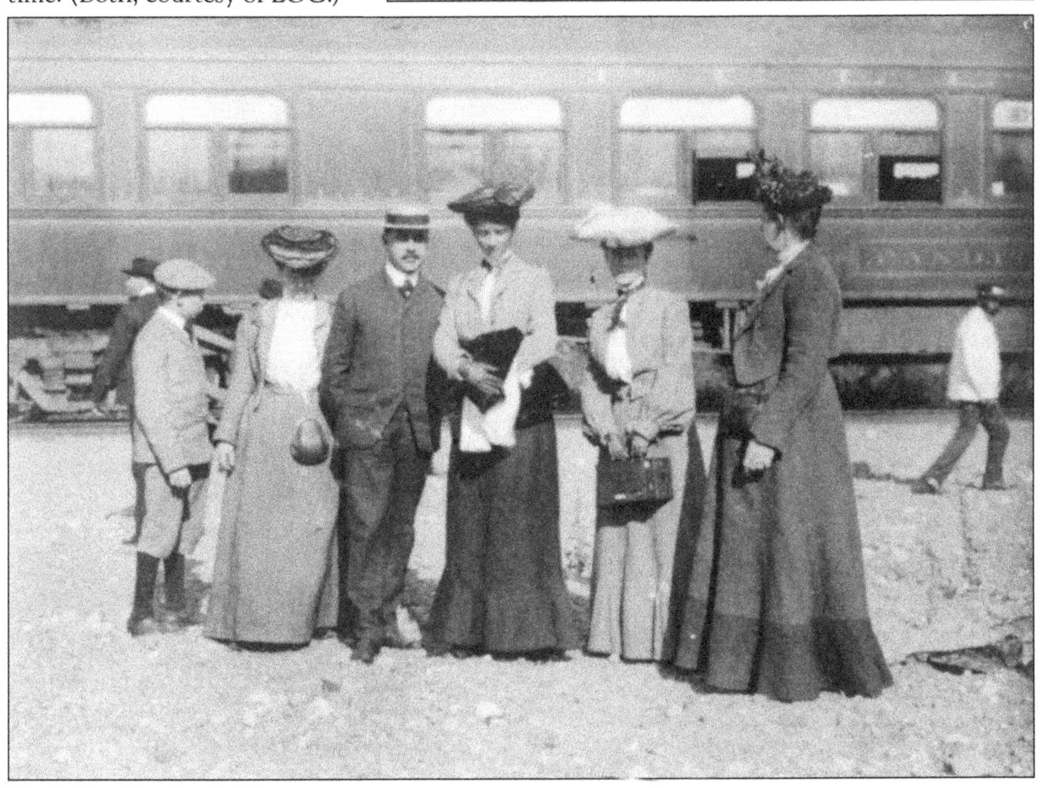

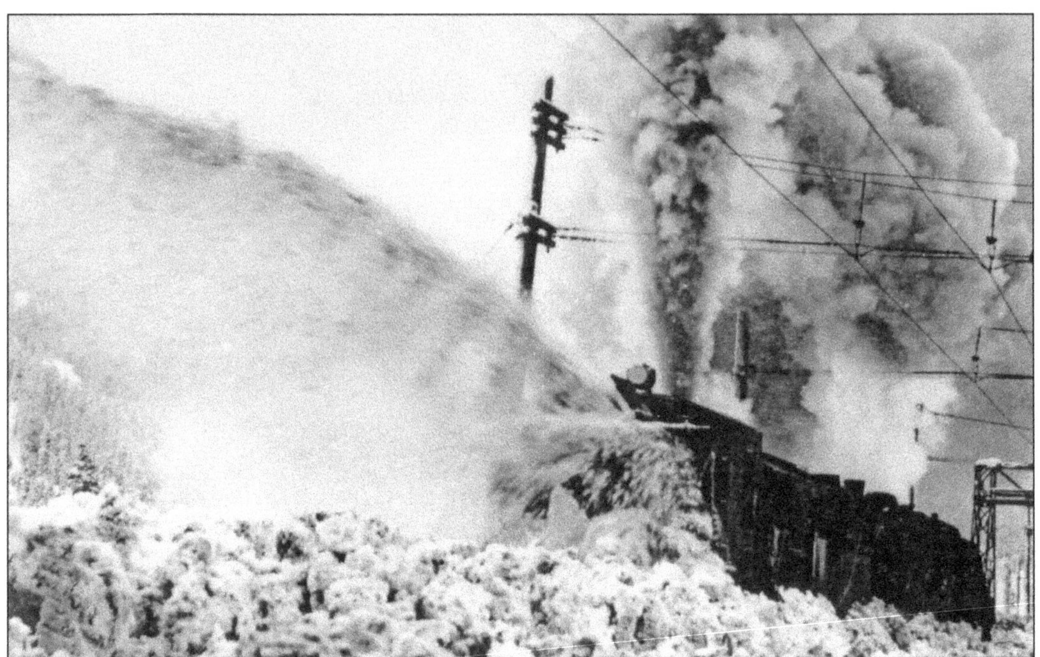

A rotary plow is busy clearing the tracks. James O'Neill said, "We started a rotary out of Wellington, and it was about 36 hours getting to Alvin, that is four miles, and it took them just as long to get back." (Courtesy of J.D. Wheeler Collection, SHS.)

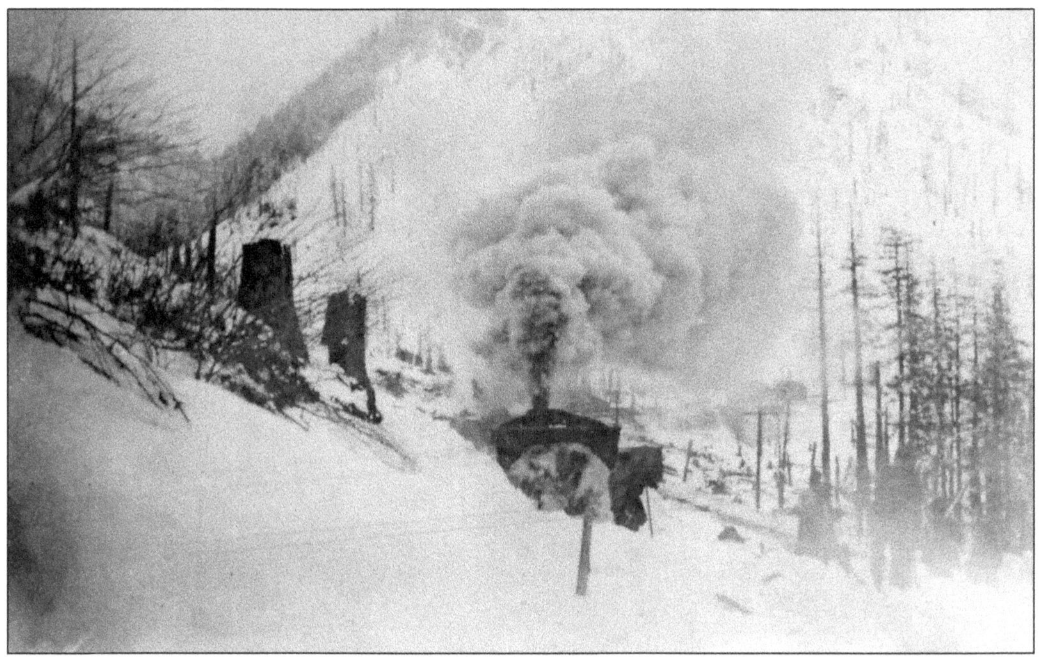

On Wednesday, February 23, five feet of snow fell and O'Neill faced a dilemma. He had three options: hold the No. 25 until No. 27 caught up with it at Leavenworth and then send them both up behind rotary X802 (although this option would put the trains behind schedule), send the No. 25 and hope for the best, or return east and use the Northern Pacific's route. O'Neill chose the first option. (Courtesy of SHS.)

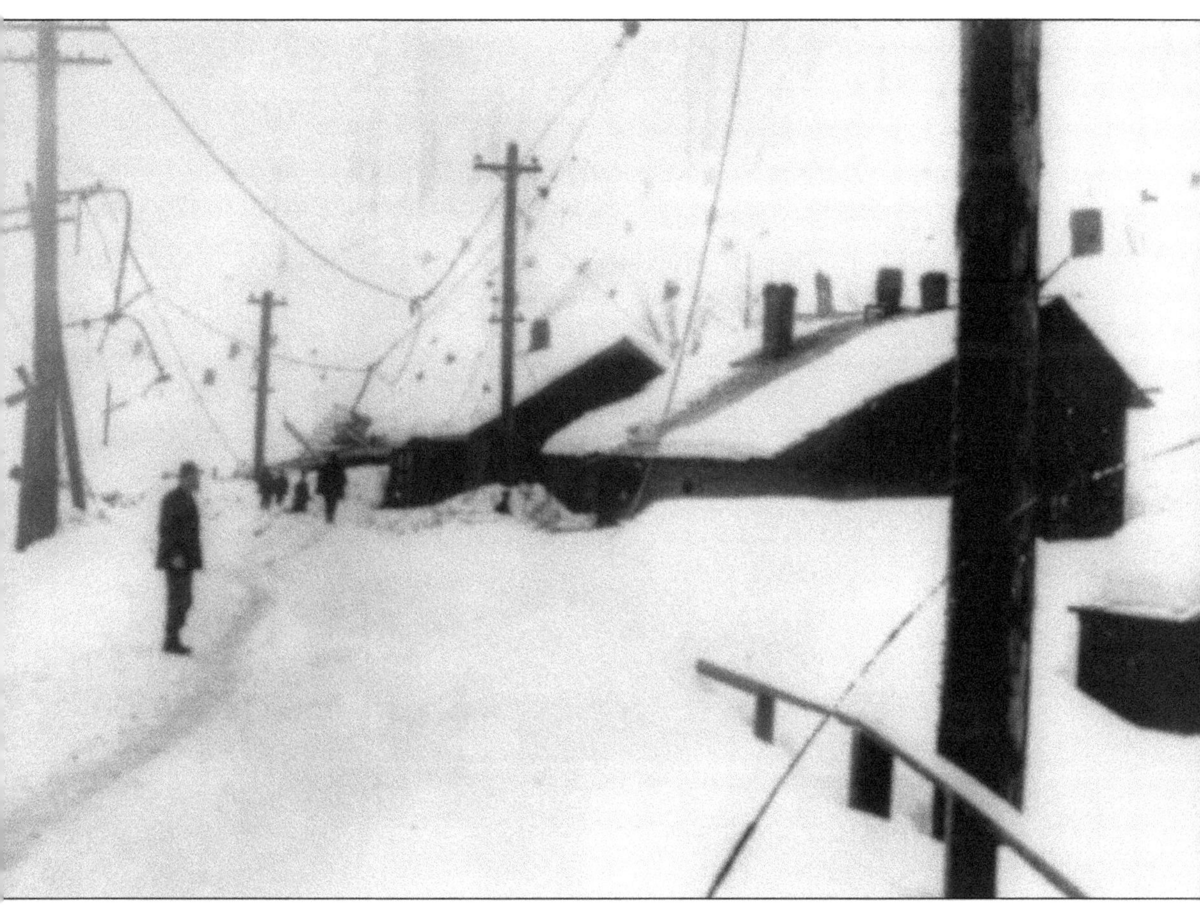

As the No. 25 pulled from the west portal, the passengers were shocked at what they witnessed. Alongside the tracks was the disabled X807 rotary and extra steam engine as well as three electric motors—all stuck in the snow. The fast mail finally pulled through the tunnel at 10:15 p.m. William Harrington, GN assistant trainmaster, also known as "the Snow King," said "I know it snowed 12 feet in 50 hours . . . at this time we had ten feet more snow than I ever saw before . . . 19 feet. That was on the snow gauge over at Cascade Tunnel." Harrington worked for the railroad for over 20 years and was injured in the avalanche but not killed. He was described as a very strong, hardworking man with a chest like a barrel. (Courtesy of SHS.)

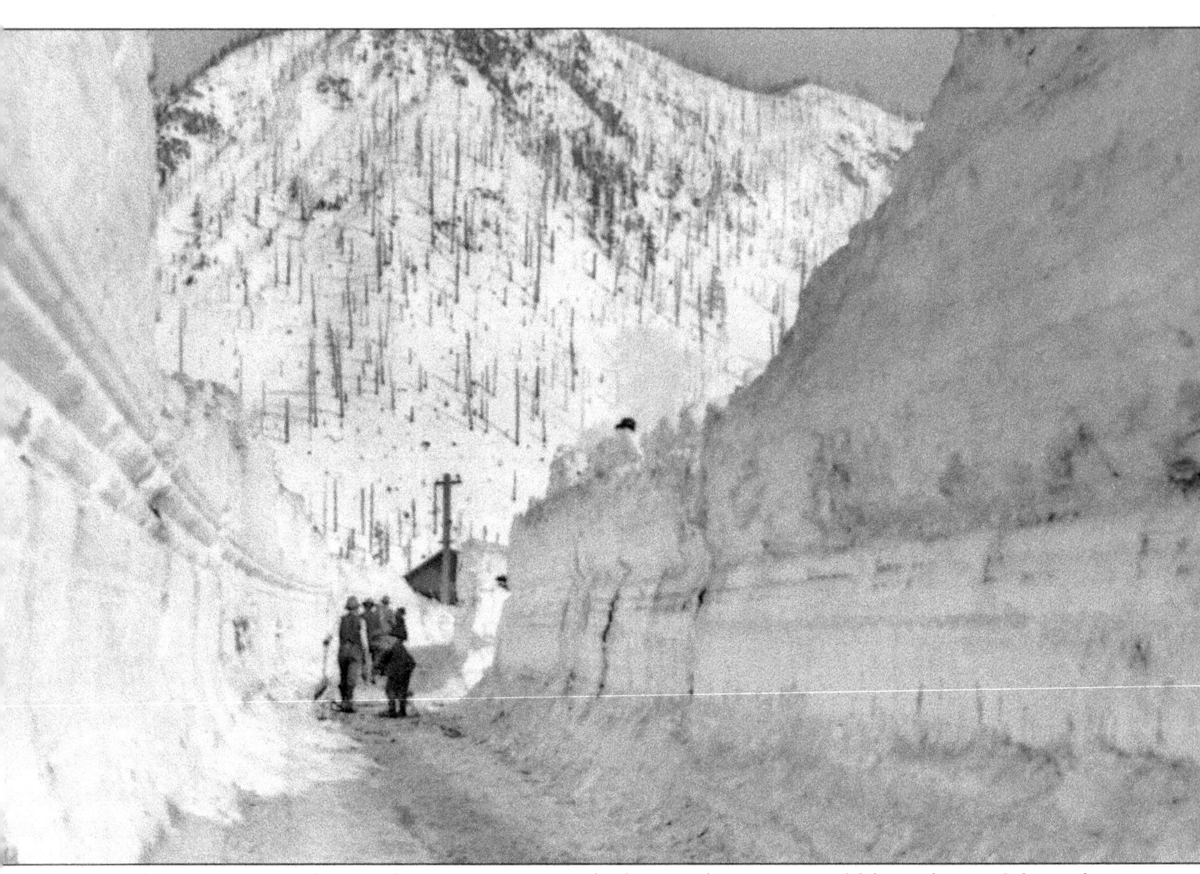

The extreme conditions the GN crew were dealing with were incredible and out of the ordinary, even in the Cascades. On February 24, the GN had already employed hundreds of men and was running multiple snowplows to try to clear the tracks. Snowshed 3.3 got hit that day with an avalanche that was 900 feet long and 25 feet deep. When some passengers chose to risk walking to Scenic, the snow was above the telegraph poles. When Merritt was asked about his hike later, he said, "To linger meant death. To proceed did not hold much more for us. When we came to the slope to Scenic, we settled back on our haunches and started to slide down 2,000 feet, we could not walk, only slide." This photograph was published in the March 3, 1910, issue of the *Wenatchee Daily World*. (Courtesy of Topping Collection 0024, SHS.)

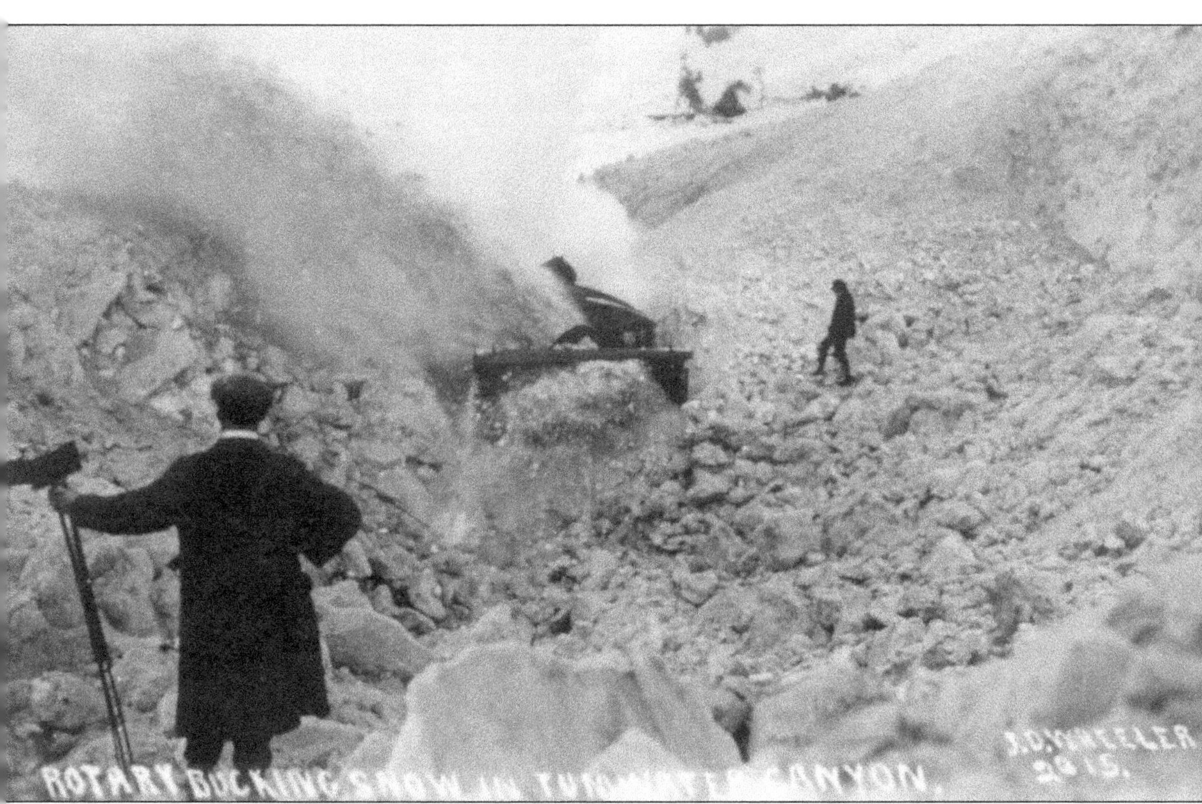

This image shows a rotary snowplow in action and a GN crew slowly bucking through another deep snow slide near Tumwater Canyon. The man to the left holding a camera in this J.D. Wheeler photograph may be Wheeler himself, who took the first known photographs of the disaster. On Thursday the 24th, just a few days before the fatal avalanche, Purcell encountered another slide at snowshed 3.3, and rotary X807 choked on a tree stump that broke its hoist. William Bailets, a Wellington proprietor, checked his written records and repeated to anyone who would listen that there had never been this much snow before. (Photograph by J.D. Wheeler, courtesy of Monroe Historical Society.)

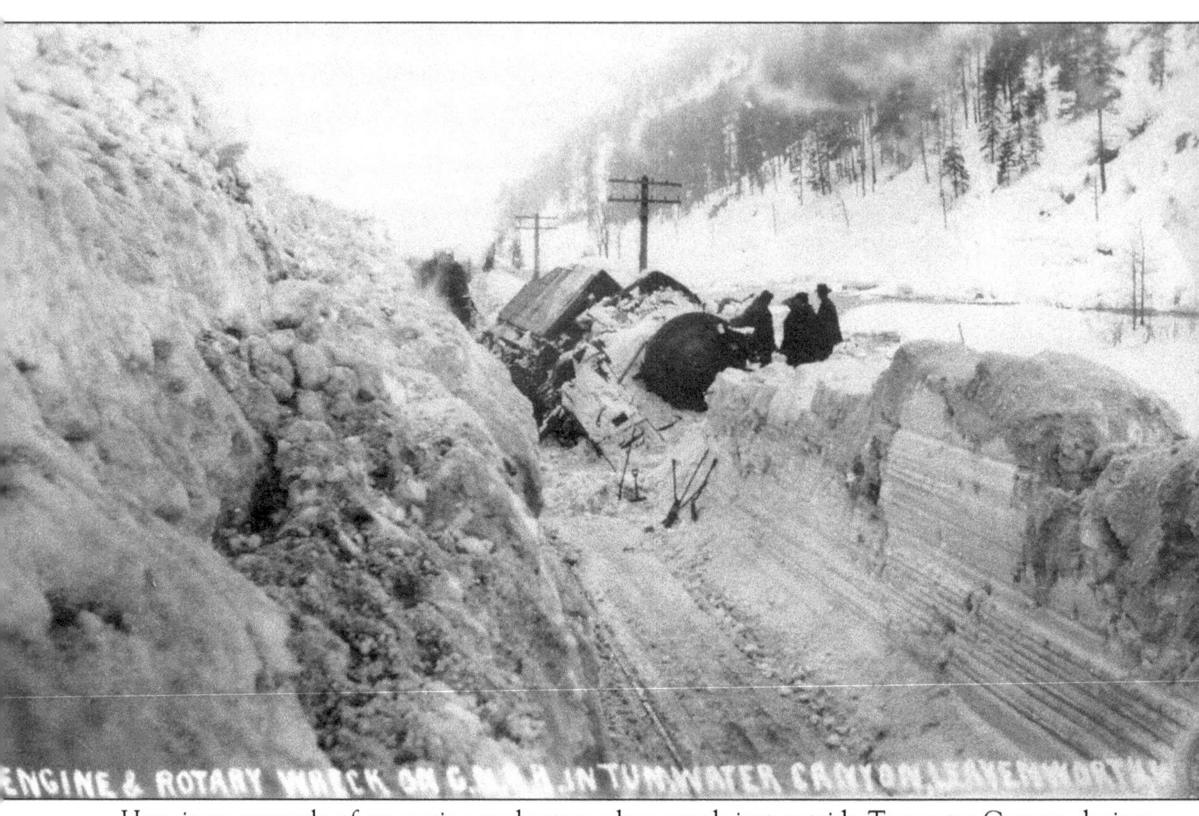

Here is an example of an engine and rotary plow wreck just outside Tumwater Canyon during another storm. The tracks were often a mess everywhere in the region, not just at Wellington. O'Neill had ordered multiple rotaries to plow nonstop to try to get the trapped trains moving again. That Wednesday morning, Purcell left Wellington and headed toward Skykomish, but was stalled 1.25 miles away by a 200-foot-long slide that took his crew four exhausting hours to clear. By this time, O'Neill and the rest of the railroad men had gone two days without sleep. The GN crew worked double shifts and went without food or water, living on cigars and prayers, hoping to stay one step ahead of the snow, which seemed impossible during this particular storm. (Photograph by J.D. Wheeler, courtesy of Monroe Historical Society.)

Four

The Little Towns near Wellington

Living in the Cascade Mountains was extremely difficult in the late 1800s, and the dangerous job of logging was a huge part of the economy. Life in the early 1900s was still difficult compared to today. Some people only washed their hair once a month, and a beaten egg mixed with water was used instead of shampoo. Diseases were common, as hygiene practices were often lacking. Most people did not even live to their mid-40s. Bathing was typically done once a week, and the schedule was usually youngest to oldest, reusing the same water, as the luxury of running water did not exist in most homes. While the Seattle Express No. 25 and the fast mail No. 27 trains were stranded at Wellington, it took the cooperation of the entire town to feed and care for the 100-plus extra people staying there.

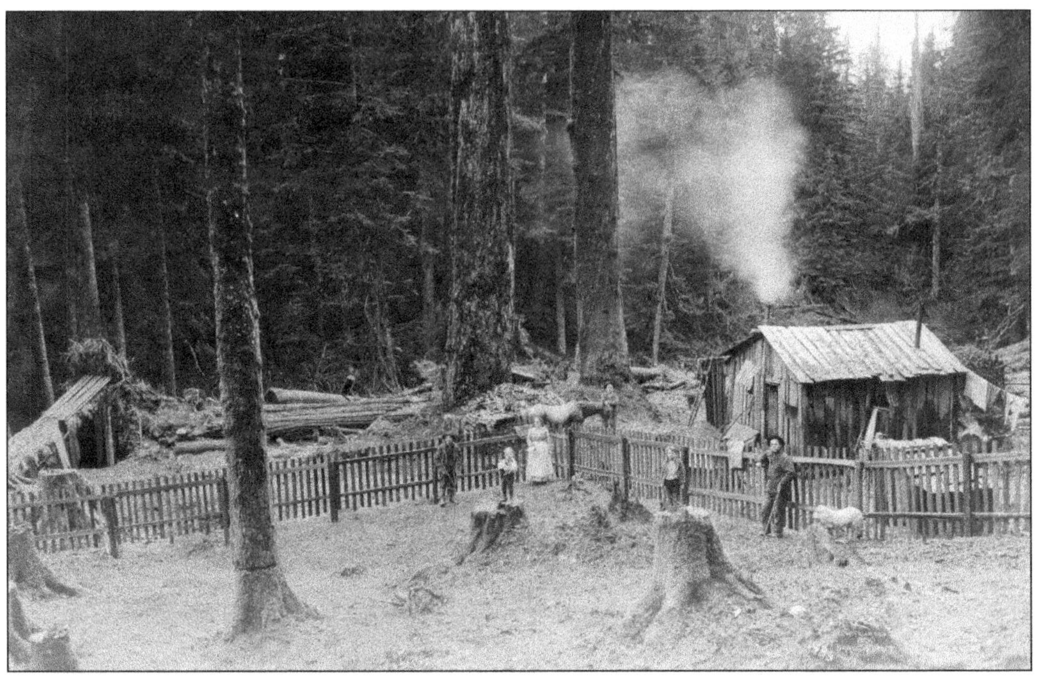

A family poses in front of their cabin while living in the remote and dangerous Cascade Mountains. Lumber operations were dangerous, and the men had only saws and a few other tools to work with. The logs would be pulled out by a team of oxen. (Courtesy of LOC.)

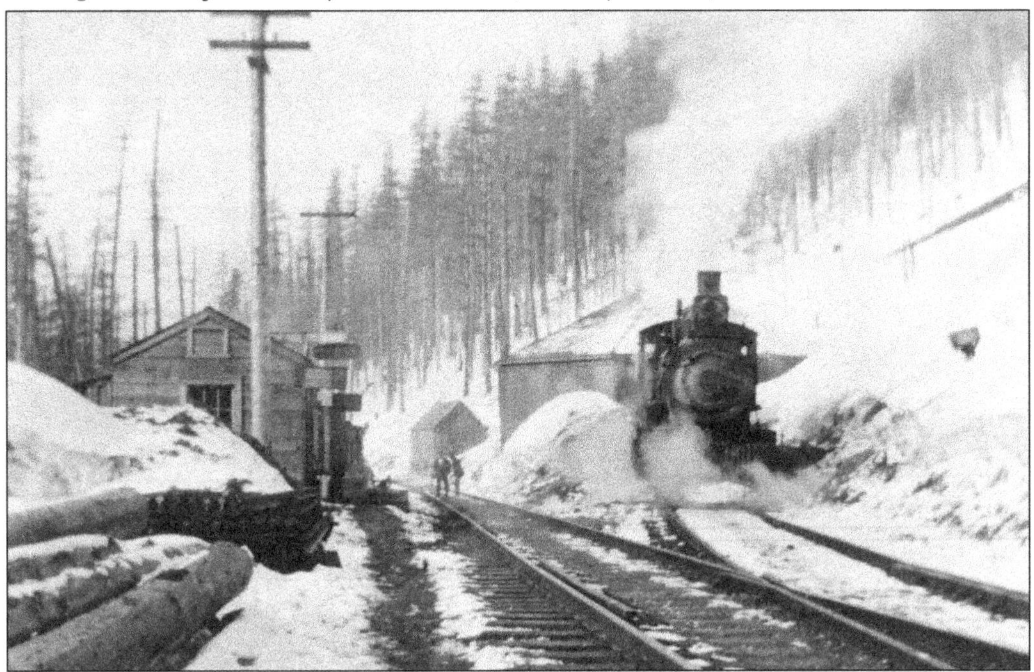

This is the view looking west from Wellington around 1898, with a train order board on the building. Train orders were delivered by hand if the train stopped, or placed trackside to be grabbed while the train continued past the station. With the latter, the paper order was placed in a train order hoop, either held by the operator or mounted trackside. (Courtesy of SHS.)

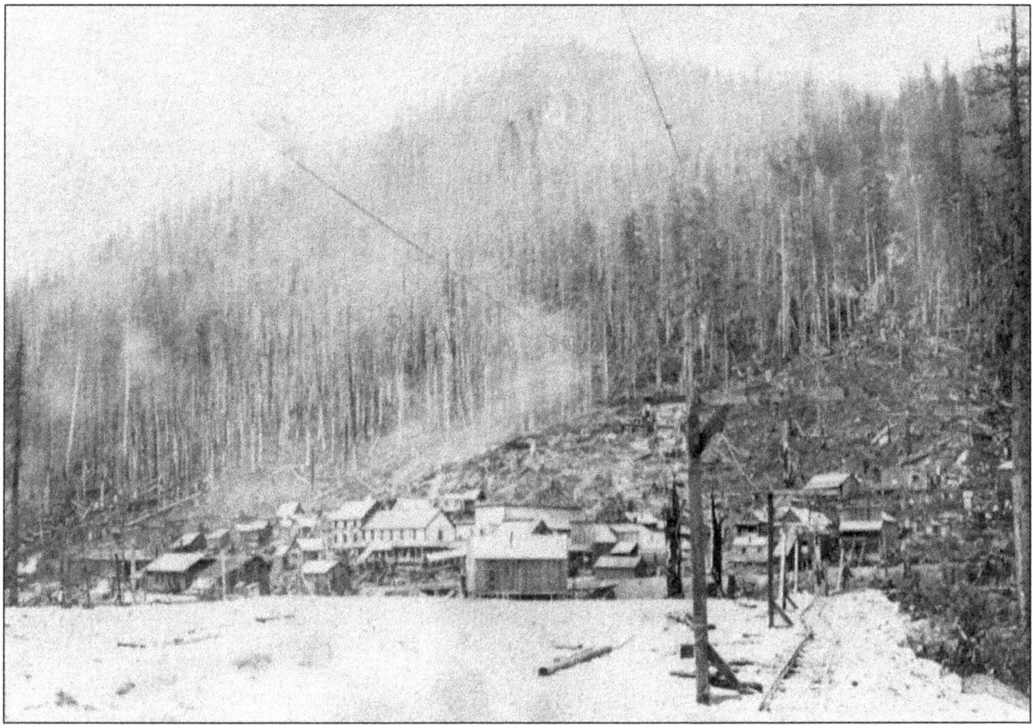

This c. 1898 image shows Wellington from the tracks. There were no streets, only wooden walkways. Wellington was built exclusively for the railway and consisted mostly of single, hardworking men. The Great Northern would frequently build a town for the purpose of the railroad, but the company also helped farmers and workers along the route with livestock and supplies. (Photograph by J.B. Woodard, courtesy of SHS.)

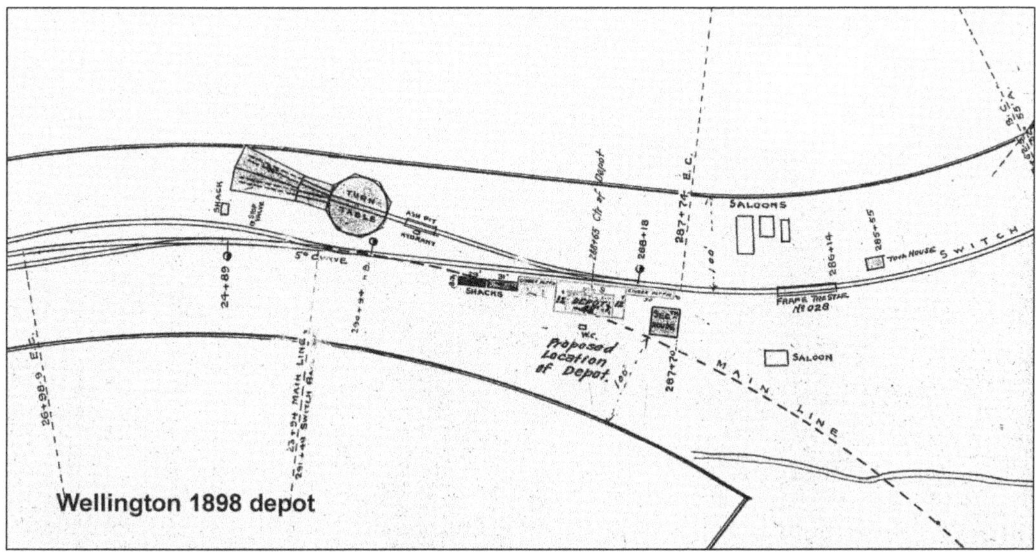

This map depicts Wellington in 1898. Marked along the main railway line are several shacks, a turntable, an ash pit and hydrant, the depot and section house, several saloons, a frame trestle, and a tool house. The town was started as a GN construction camp and was later founded in 1893. Some people called it the "end of the world" because it was so remote. (Courtesy of SHS.)

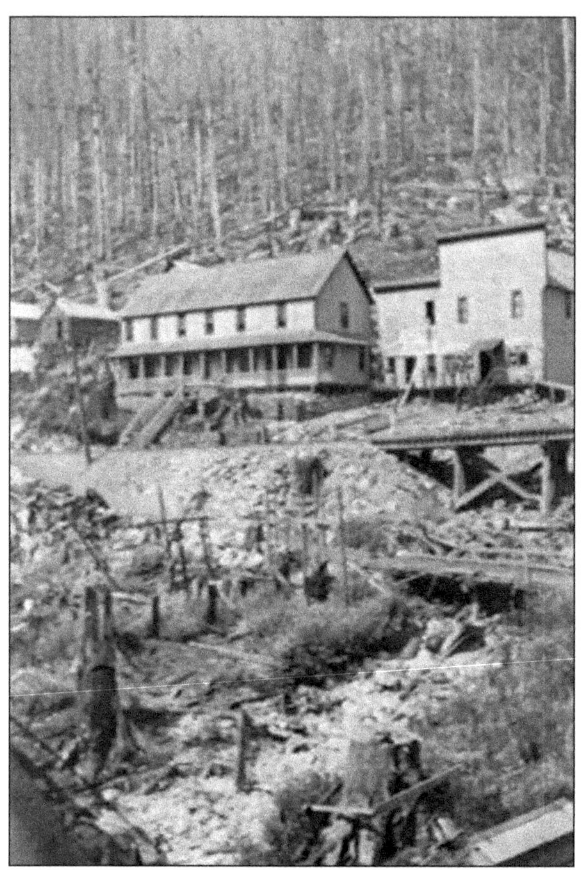

This photograph from August 1898 shows Bailets Hotel with a wraparound porch. The railroad tracks run right in front of the hotel and small cabins are to the left. The tavern, also run by William and Susan Bailets, is to the right of the hotel with the false front and a large sign that reads "Restaurant." (Courtesy of the J.D. Wheeler Collection, SHS.)

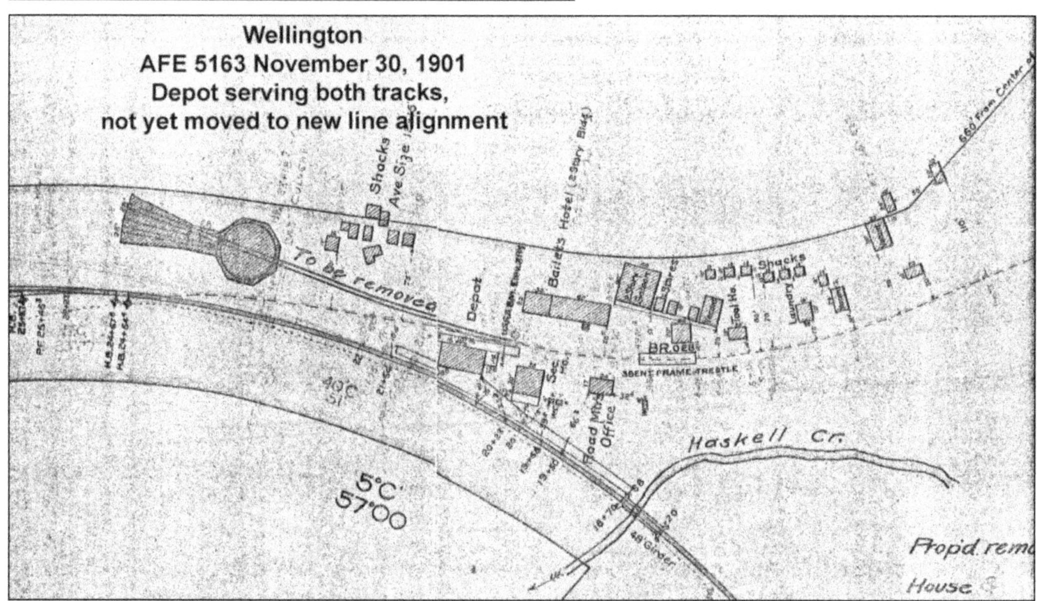

This 1901 illustration shows additional structures added to Wellington, including more shacks (average size noted as 12 by 15 feet), Bailets Hotel, a road office, a two-story school, stores, several buildings (some vacant), and a laundry room. (Courtesy of SHS.)

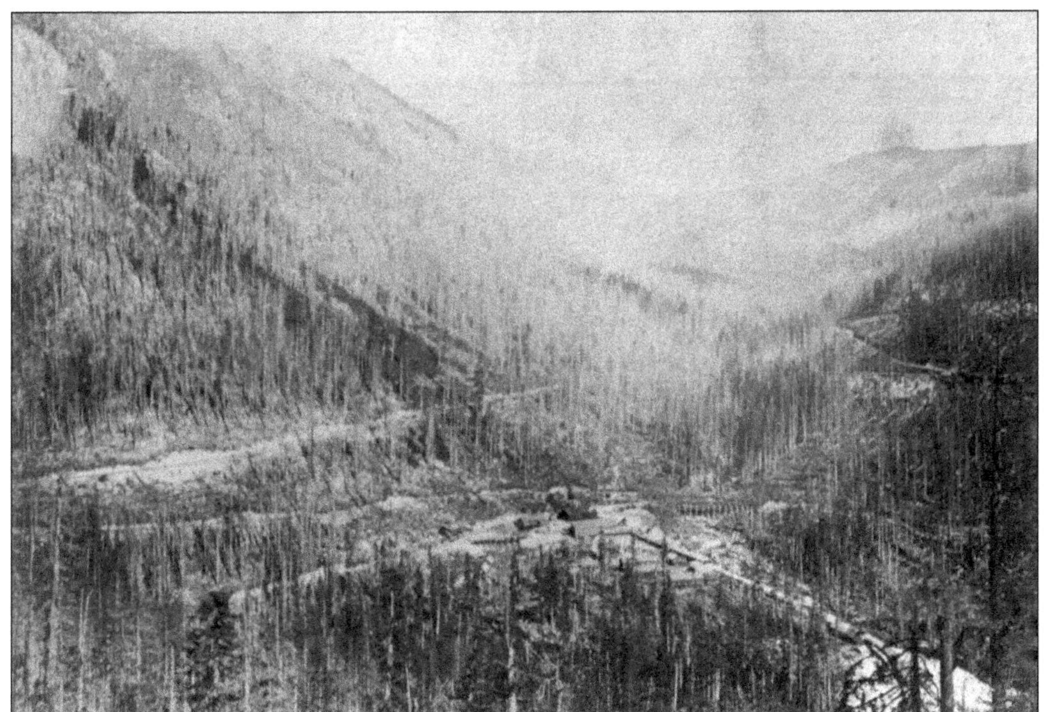

The switchbacks (sometimes called Death Mountain) are on the left, with a view of the old tunnel from the hill to the north of Wellington in this c. 1899 view looking toward Stevens Pass. The switchbacks consisted of eight tracks that zig-zagged on the mountainside—three on the east and five on the west—a total of 12 miles of grueling track. A special crew worked the switchbacks, as it was a very dangerous job. (Courtesy of the J.D. Wheeler Collection, SHS.)

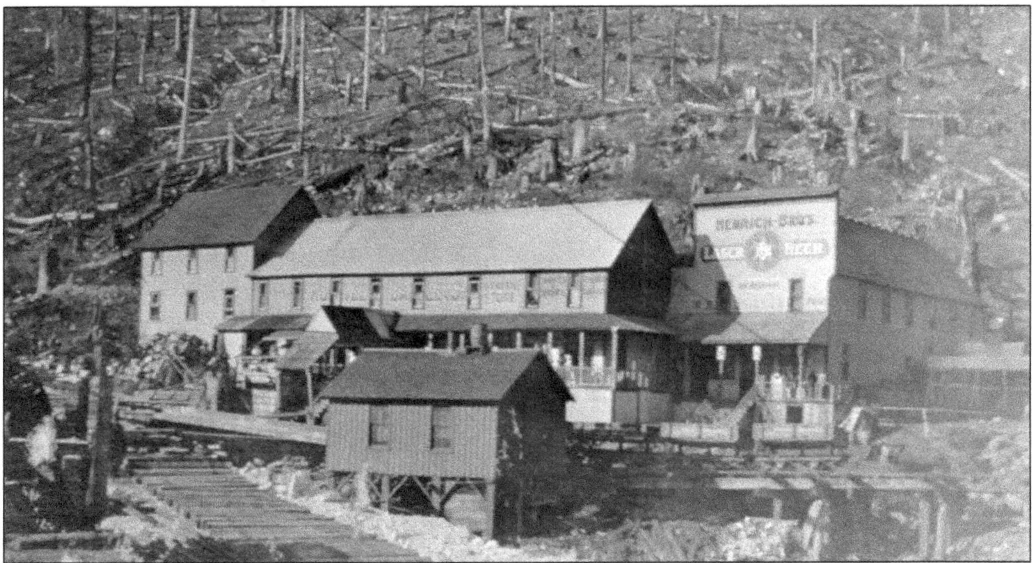

Burnt timber can be seen behind Bailets Hotel in this view from around 1900. Railroads passing through towns often caused fires due to the sparks shooting from the locomotives. Painted on the front of the hotel are "General Store," "Boots & Shoes," and "Cigars & Tobacco." The tavern next door prominently advertises Henrich Bros. Lager Beer "on draught." (Courtesy of SHS.)

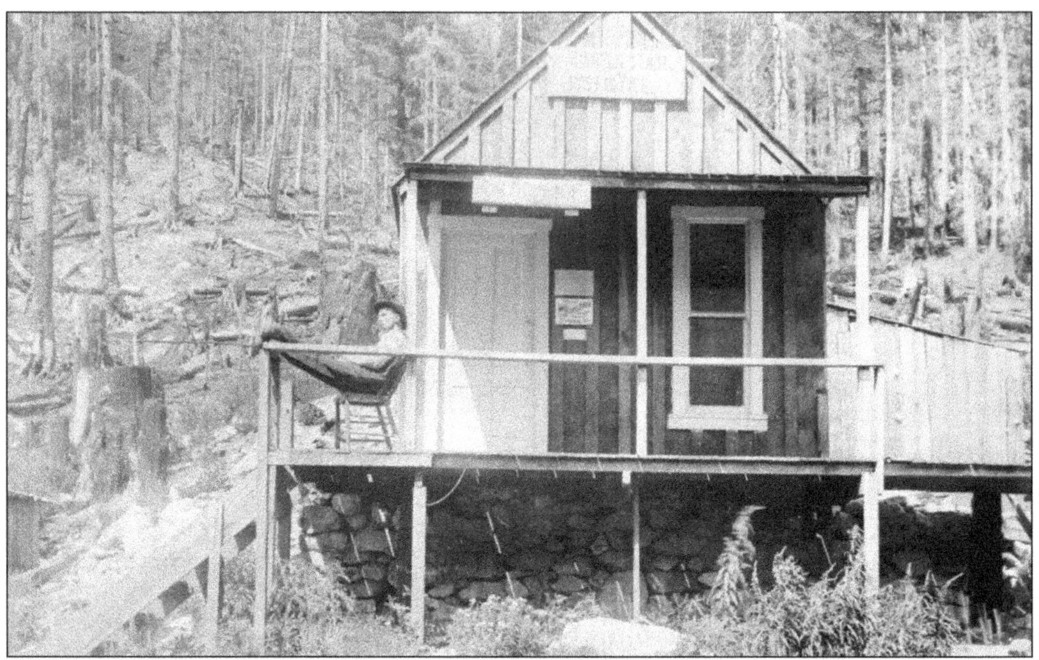

A man kicks his feet up and enjoys a corn cob pipe while manning the Pioneer Store & Post Office in 1895. The sign reads, "Dixie Queen Cut Plug Tobacco 2oz for 5¢." The Bailets owned the post office as well as the hotel, tavern, and 10 rental cottages. Wellington rested on a narrow ledge 2,900 feet above sea level approximately 300 feet wide. (Courtesy of SHS.)

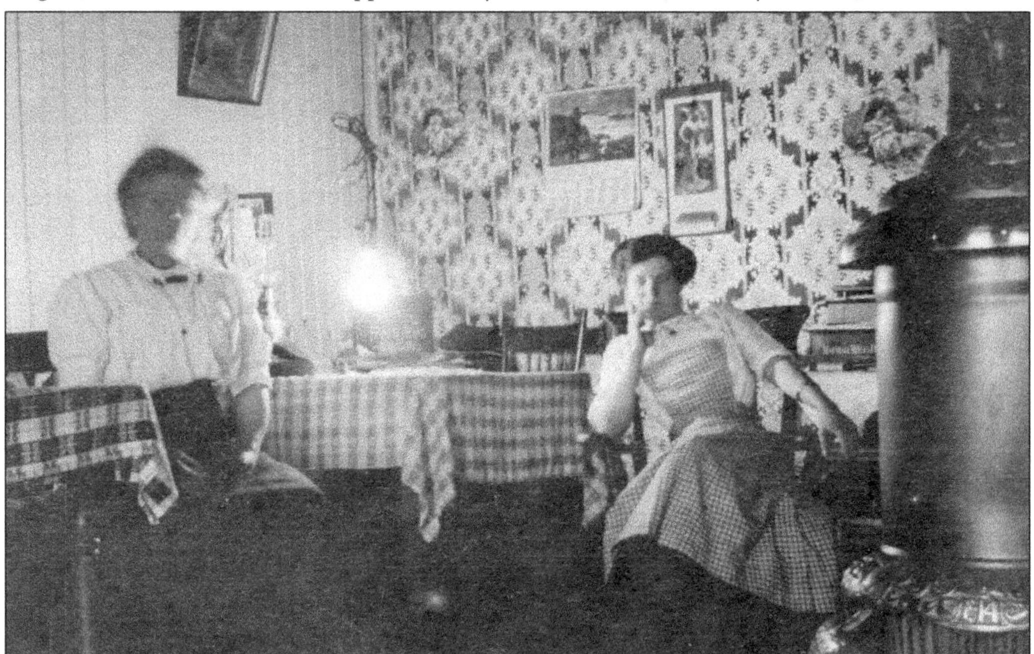

Pictured inside the Bailets Hotel are Rosy or Georgia (left) and Carol Thompson. The hotel had blue-and-white-checkered tablecloths, sticky sugar bowls, and taxidermy. The Bailets were married in 1876 and opened the hotel in the 1890s. Susan Bailets testified after the tragedy, "They all seemed to get a little nervous." (Courtesy of SHS.)

Two men pose for the camera in what might be the beanery built after the avalanche. Bailets said, "Five years ago we had about three feet of snow . . . and water came down through my building, it came in the back windows and I had two feet of water through my house and I had to shovel through that much mud." (Photograph by Casper Hansen, courtesy of the Northwest Railway Museum.)

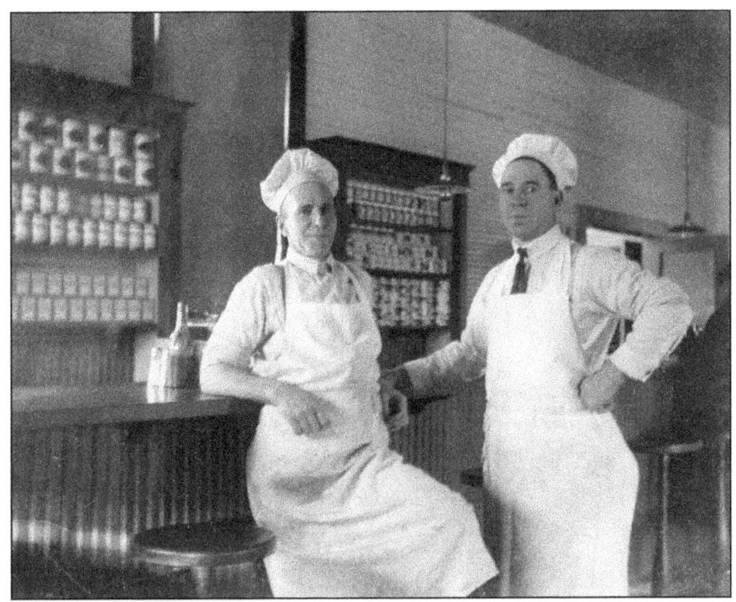

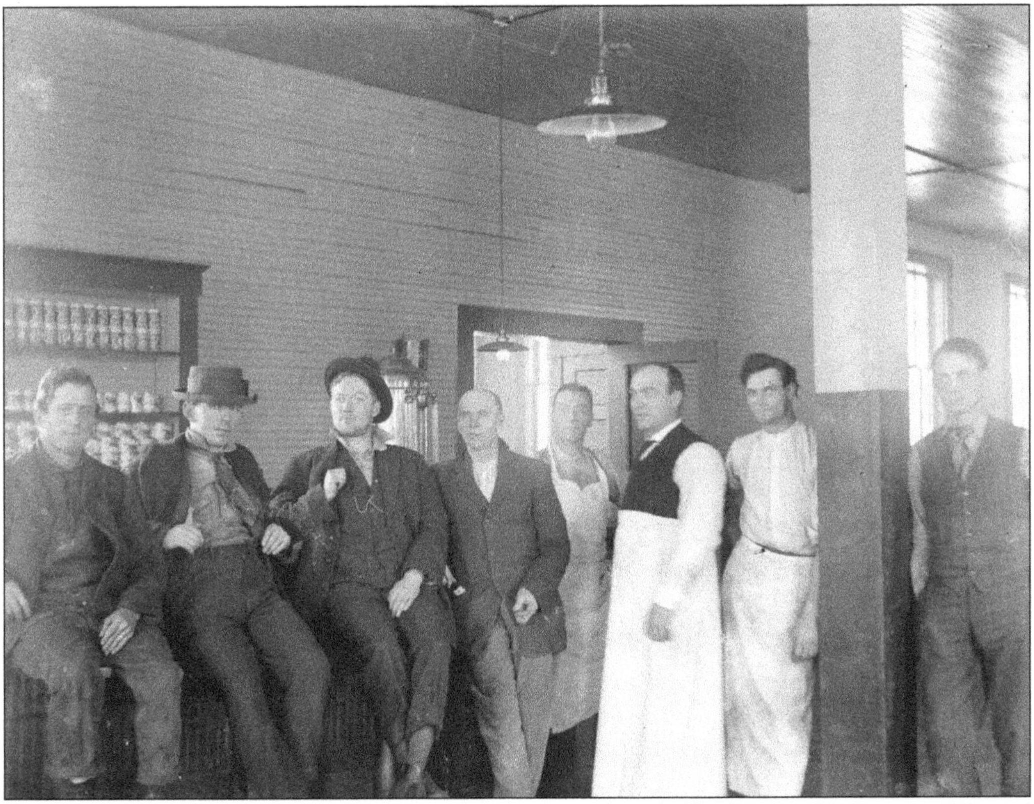

Patrons and staff members pose in front of a bar in an unidentified building in Wellington. Wentzel later recalled, "I was in Bailets Hotel when I heard the roar. I ran outside and saw the whole side of the mountain coming down, tearing up everything in its way. Trees, stumps and snow were rolling together in gigantic waves. . . . It was over in less time than it takes to speak a few words." (Photograph by Casper Hansen, courtesy of the Northwest Railway Museum.)

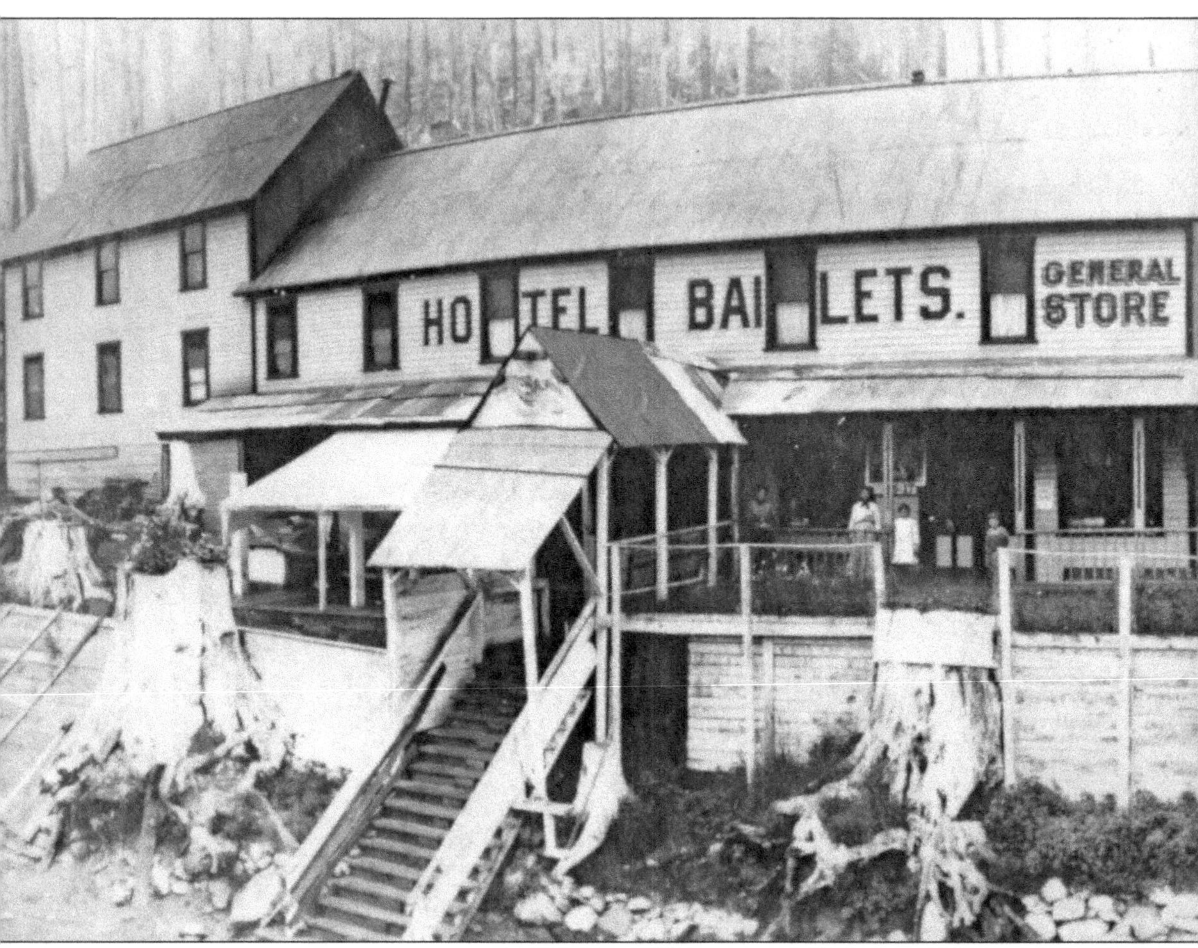

Several people pose on the porch of Bailets Hotel and the adjoining tavern, now advertising Tannhaeuser beer. The Claussen Brewing Association, which made Tannhaeuser, was established in 1901 by Hans Johanne Claussen, who came to Seattle in 1888. Passengers did not sleep at the hotel during the storm because most of the rooms had been compromised with either water or

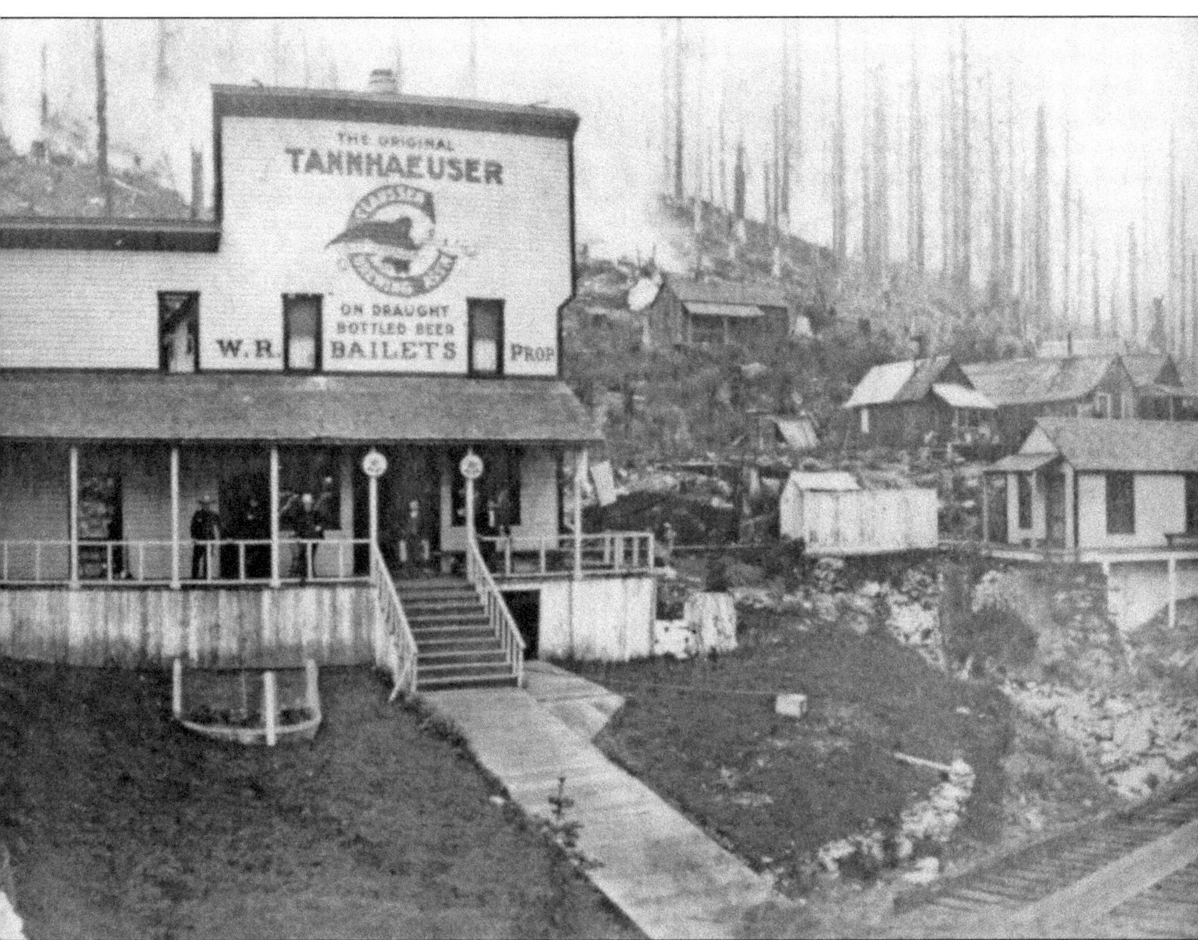

snow (or both) from the storm. When passengers asked William Bailets about renting the rooms, he offered that they could certainly rent them if they shoveled the snow out of them. (Courtesy of SHS.)

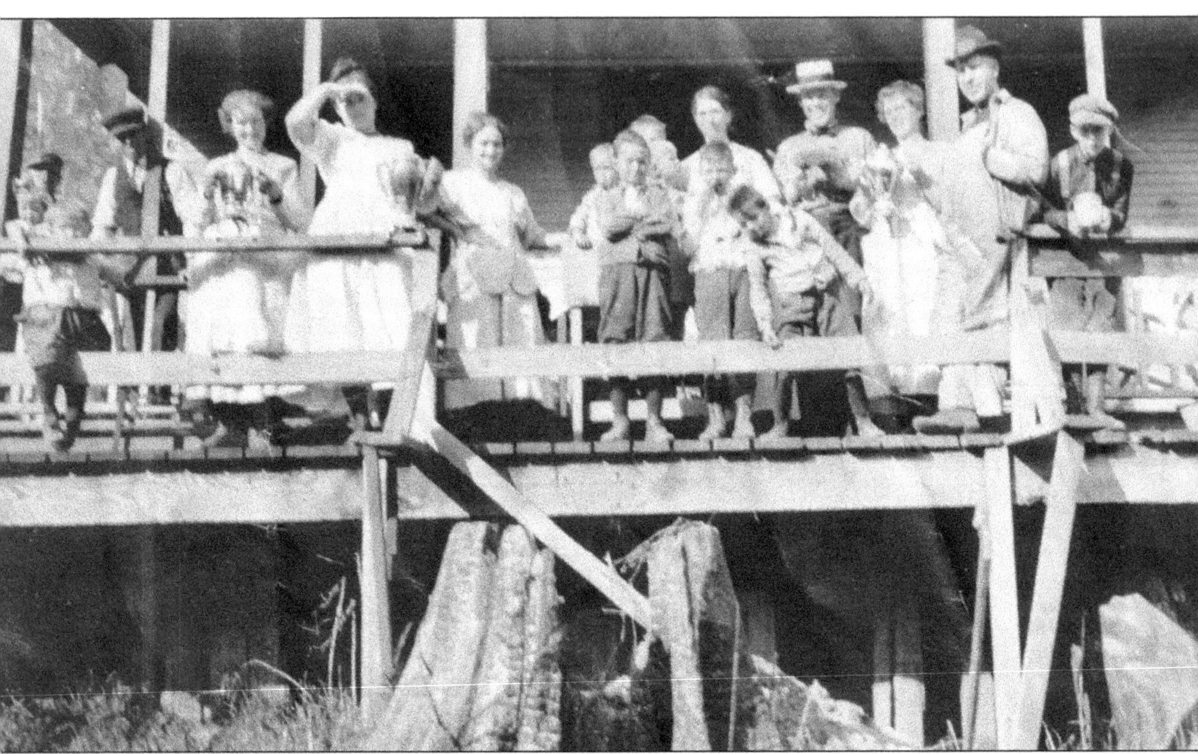

Wellington residents gather on a porch as several of the women proudly hold up trophies. The man fourth from right is holding up a plate and grinning, so possibly it was a pie contest. Wellington was created solely for the convenience of the GN and located at the west portal of the original Cascade Tunnel. There, trains would replenish their water and coal supplies. Men would grab a drink, play cards, have a meal, or stay the night at the hotel. At the time of the avalanche, the forest behind the hotel was meager, as it was not uncommon for the sparks from trains to create fires on the land near the tracks. The lack of trees on the slope above Wellington may have contributed to the force of the avalanche. (Courtesy of SHS.)

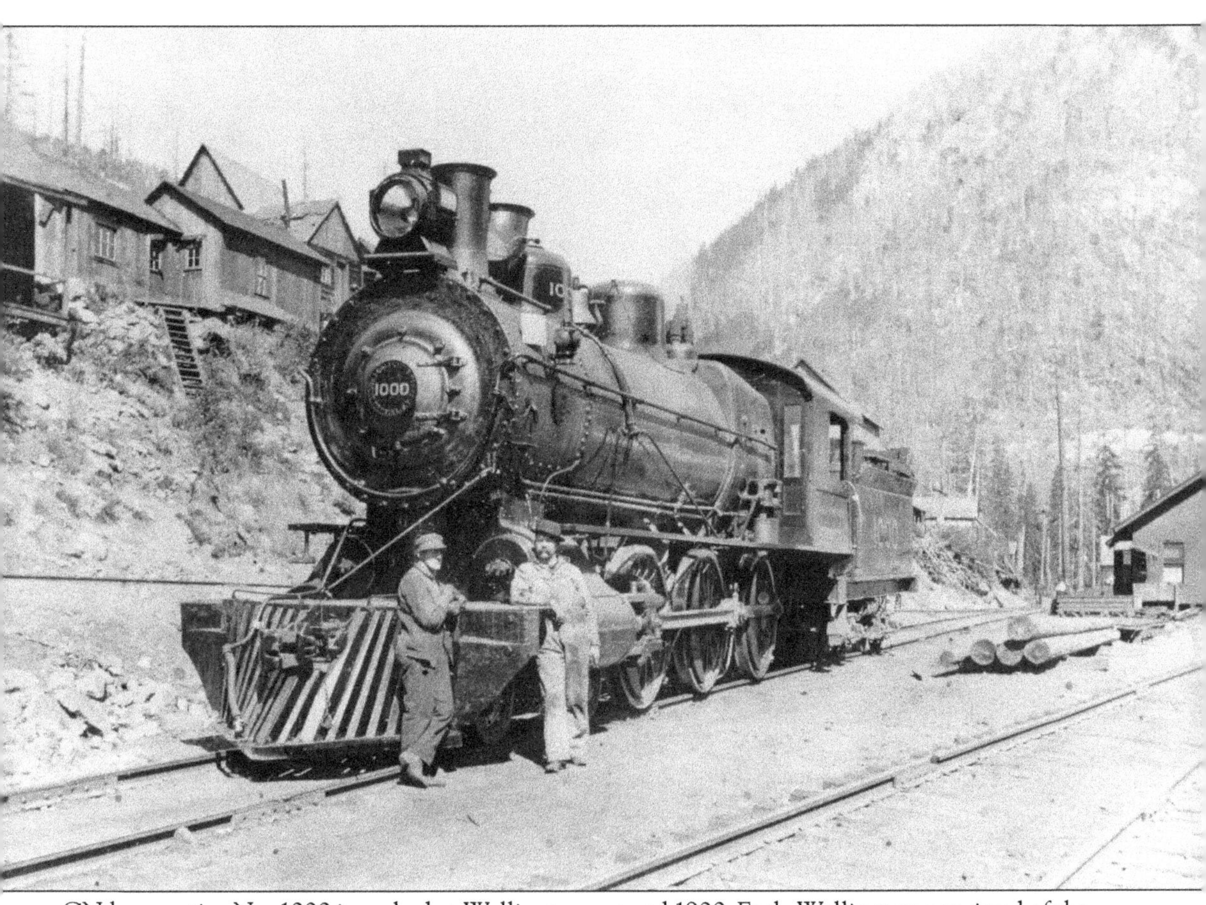

GN locomotive No. 1000 is parked at Wellington around 1900. Early Wellington consisted of the turntable, a power plant, a small hospital, Bailets Hotel and saloon, a post office, a grocery store, a few shacks, and the train depot. The three sets of tracks shown here are, from left to right, the runaway track, the switchback track (which the train is currently on), and the main line to the tunnel. The train depot is on the right, and the small buildings at upper left are cottages. There were three telegraphers working during 1910: William Flannery, Basil Sherlock, and W.V. Avery. Avery had only been at Wellington a couple days prior to the avalanche and was working the midnight to 8:00 a.m. shift. (Courtesy of the Dr. George Fischer Collection, SHS.)

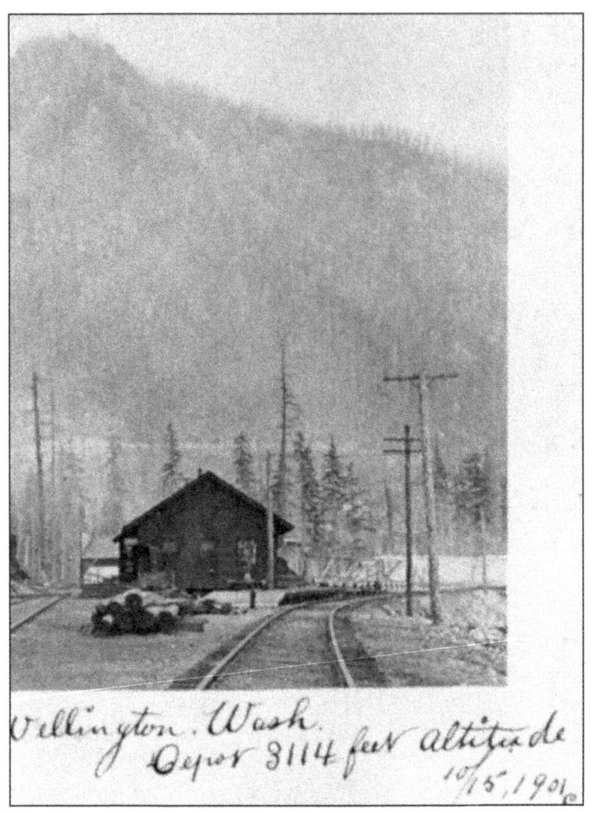

While constructing the original tunnel, Wellington catered to hundreds of workers. In an obvious exaggeration by GN officials, it was stated that there were 800 men working, 800 men sleeping, and 800 men standing at the bar. The GN depot is shown in this 1901 photograph inscribed "Wellington, Wash. Depot 3114 feet altitude 10/15/1901." (Courtesy of the Dr. George Fischer Collection, SHS.)

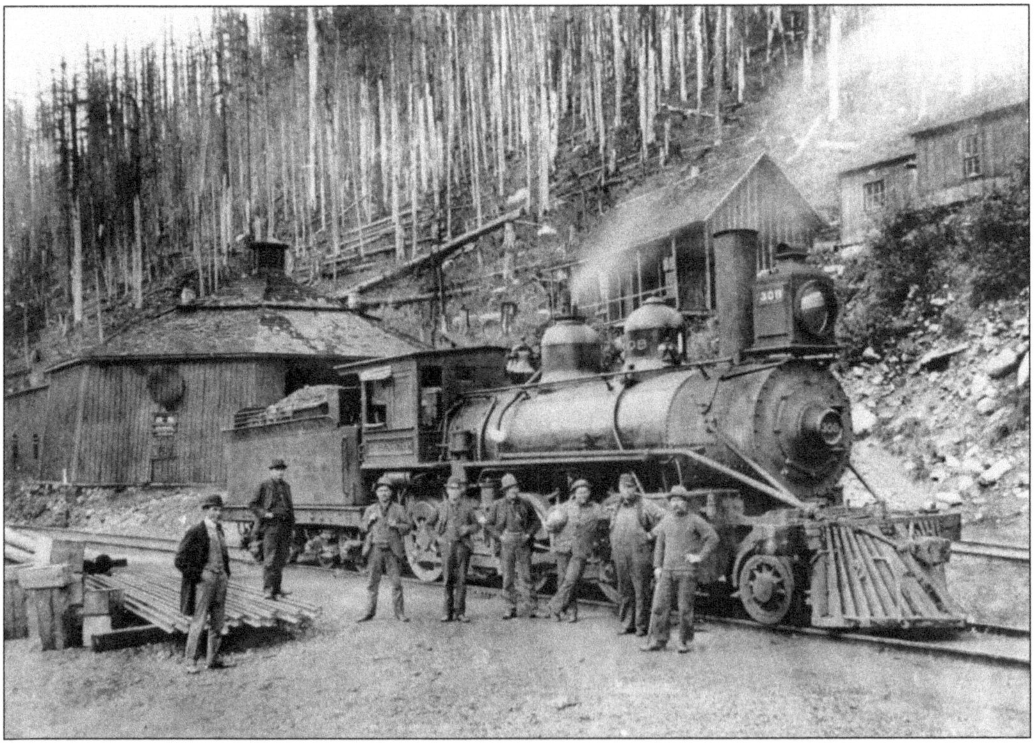

Eight men pose in front of locomotive No. 308 next to the covered turntable at Wellington. The turntable was removed in 1901, so this photograph was taken prior to that. The third man from the right proudly holds a large watermelon under his arm. Behind the train are several small shacks for the locals and workers. (Courtesy of SHS.)

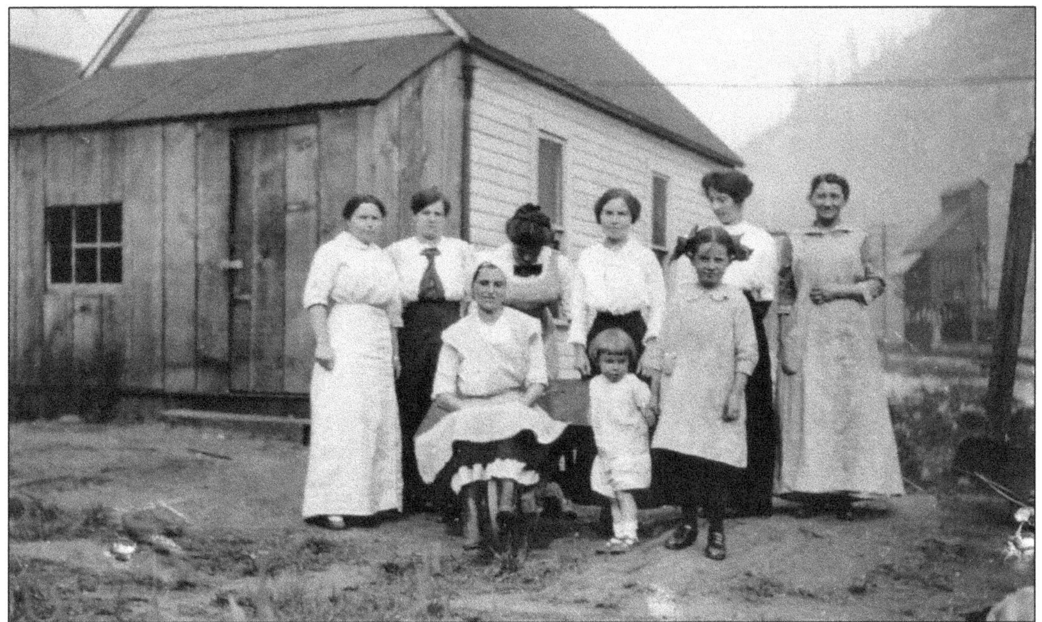

Wellington residents gather together for a photograph. In October 1910, engineer Duffy was doing a test run and lost the air in his brakes. Witnesses said he looked terrified as he sped past the horrified onlookers. Duffy waved his final goodbyes as the train moved at high speed down a steep grade. They found his body weeks later under the rubble of timber and train parts. (Courtesy of SHS.)

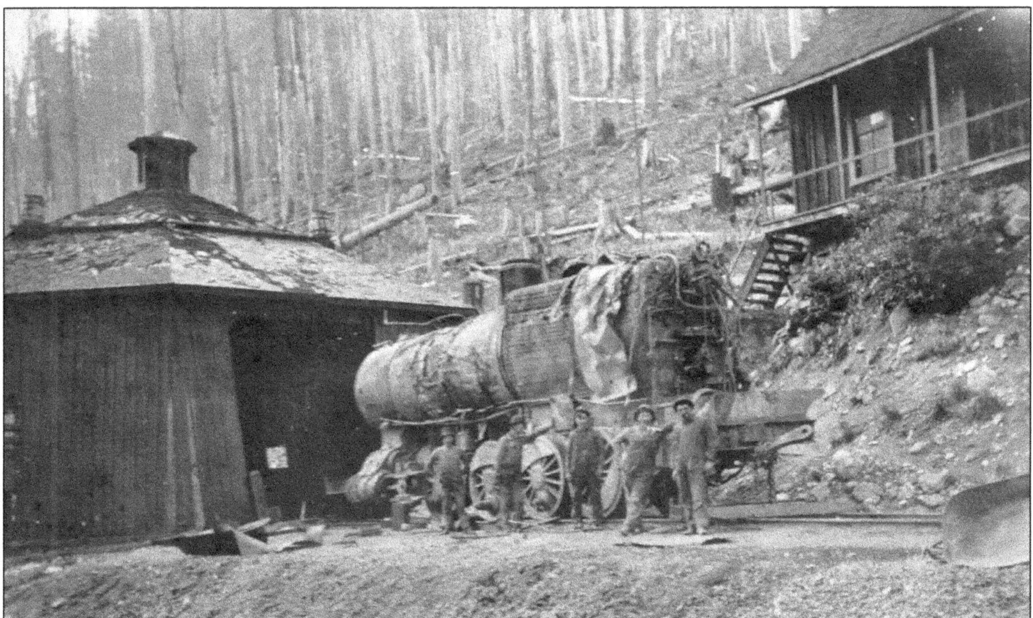

In 1902, a wrecked steam engine sits idle at the covered turntable at Wellington. Accidents were unfortunately common in the railroad industry. In Leavenworth in 1915, a slide hit a train and buried a section crew, killing four people. That same year in Alvin, a slide hit a train killing three people. In 1916, a slide in Corea hit a passenger train and killed eight people and injured twenty-two more. (Courtesy of SHS.)

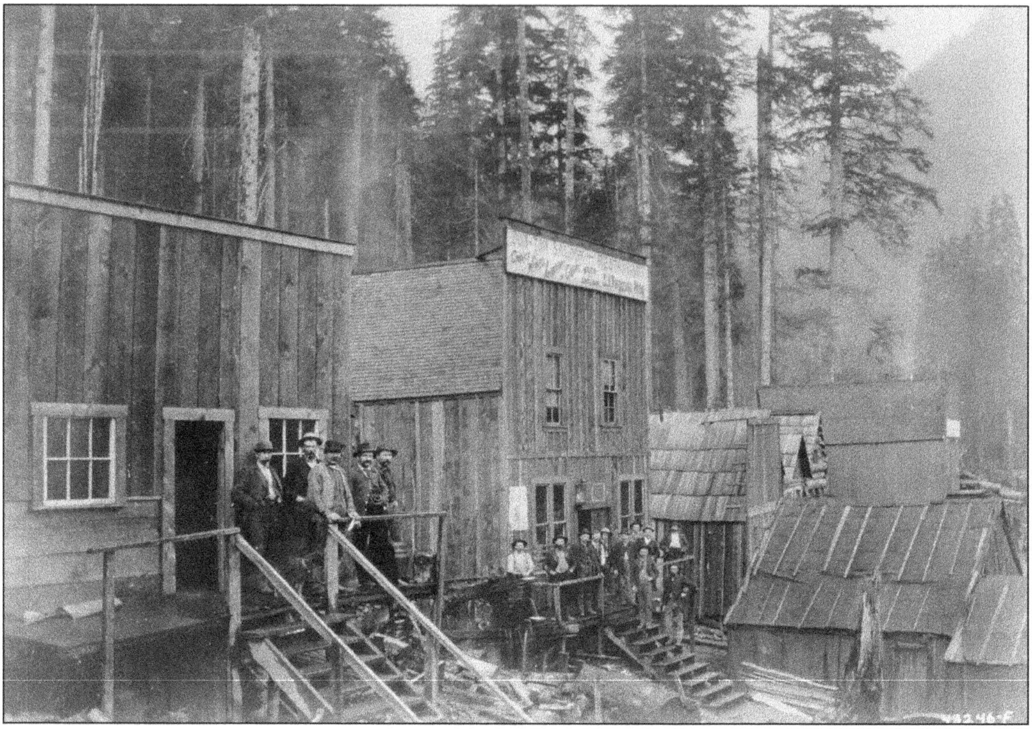

During railroad construction in the early 1890s, a group of men enjoy themselves at the Bon-Ton Saloon in Wellington, which boasts "Choice Wines, Liquors & Cigars," and beer on draught, with J.J. Ferguson as the proprietor. When the railroad men were not working, they enjoyed playing cards, smoking cigars, hunting, and fishing. (Courtesy of the Dr. George Fischer Collection, SHS.)

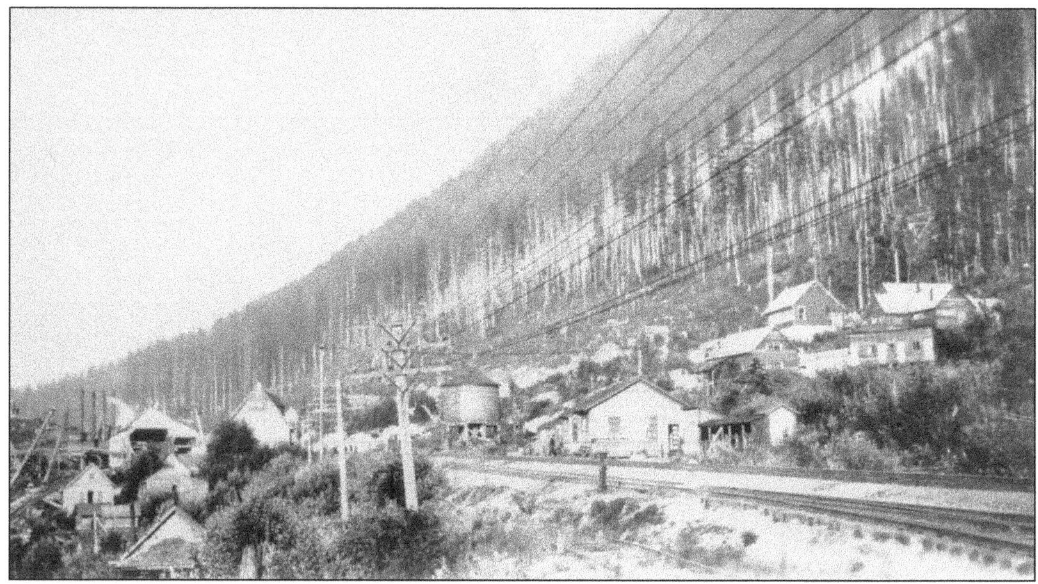

A GN train being pulled by two steam engines travels east through Alpine. Seen are houses where Alpine mill employees lived along Carroll Creek. Alpine was on the northern slope of Mt. Sawyer and was abandoned in 1929. It consisted of a mill, social hall, and a boardinghouse with offices and the post office. It was founded by Carl Lane Clemans. (Courtesy of SHS.)

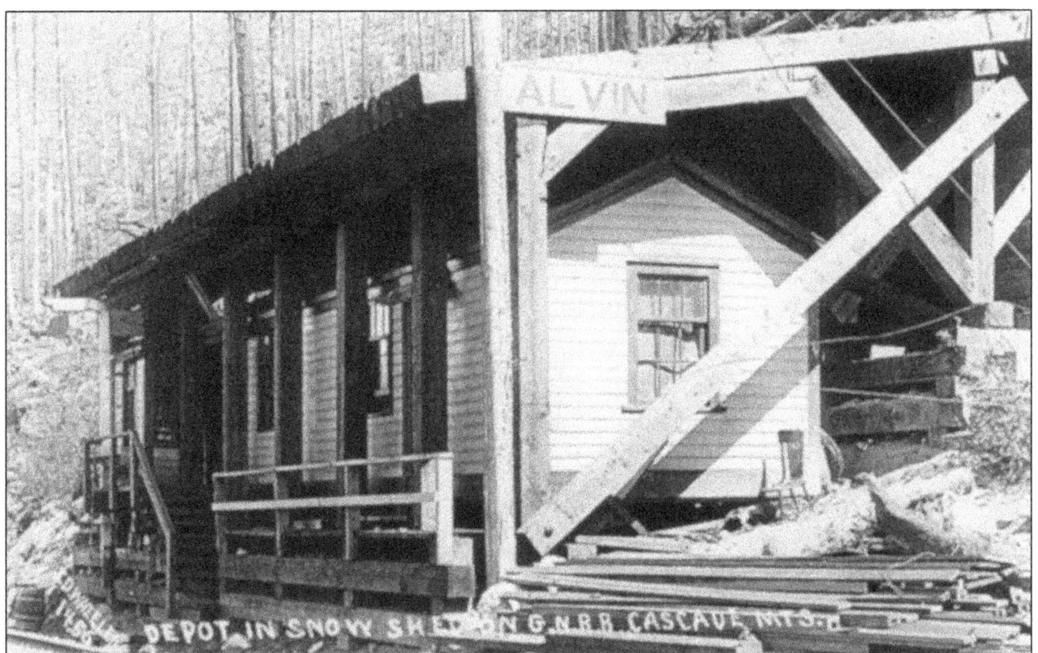

The telegraph lines were also down at Alvin on Monday, February 28. A few days earlier, rotary X801, with Blackburn in charge, came from Scenic and met the Purcell rotary at the Alvin station to be combined into a double rotary that headed back toward Wellington. The four-mile trip took an astonishing five hours due to the snow. Note that the depot is housed inside a snowshed. (Courtesy of SHS.)

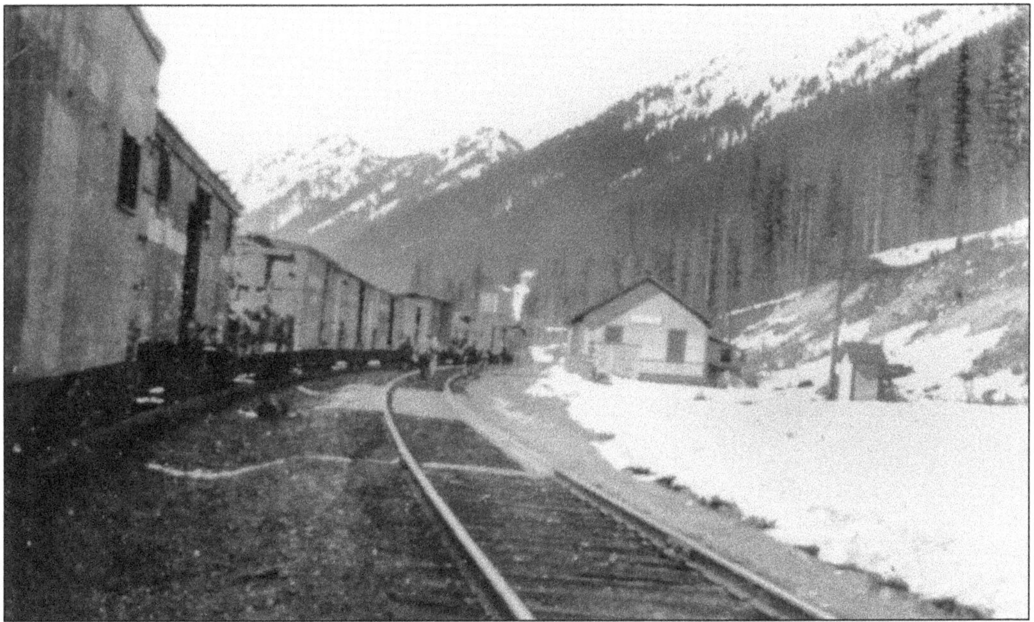

Days after the Wellington disaster, Berne encountered a slide that took four days to clear. Three Berne telegraphers were stranded without fresh food during the storm. Pictured is the Berne depot around 1923 with a supply car, outhouse, and water tank. Berne station is located at the east end of the new Cascade Tunnel and can still be accessed today. (Courtesy of the Howard Johnson family.)

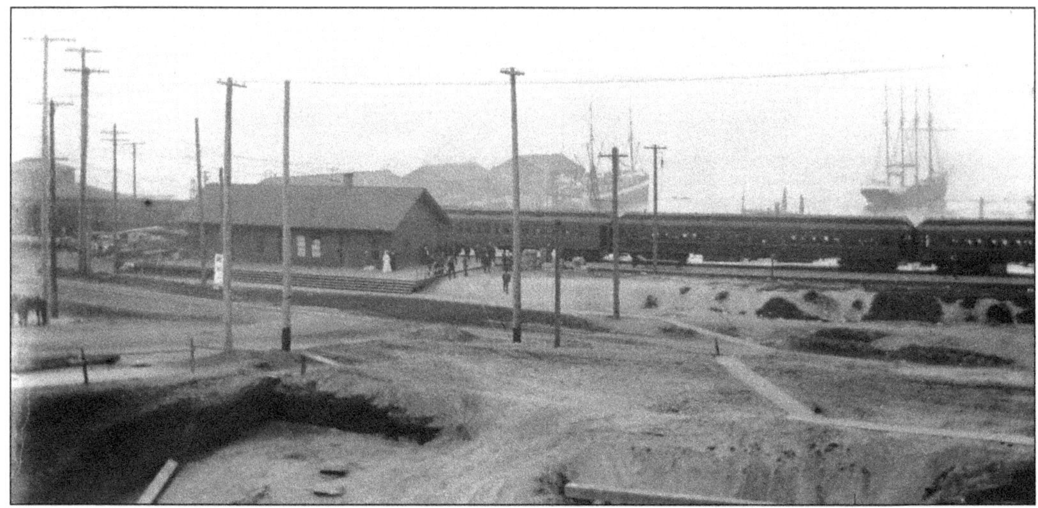

Everett has had several train stations over the years. Pictured is the GN Bond Street Station around 1910, with two beautiful ships in the background. This station was closed in 2002, and a new one was built costing $46.9 million. The population in Everett in 1910 was 24,814. In 2018, Everett is the seventh largest city in Washington, with a population of 110,079. (Courtesy of EPL.)

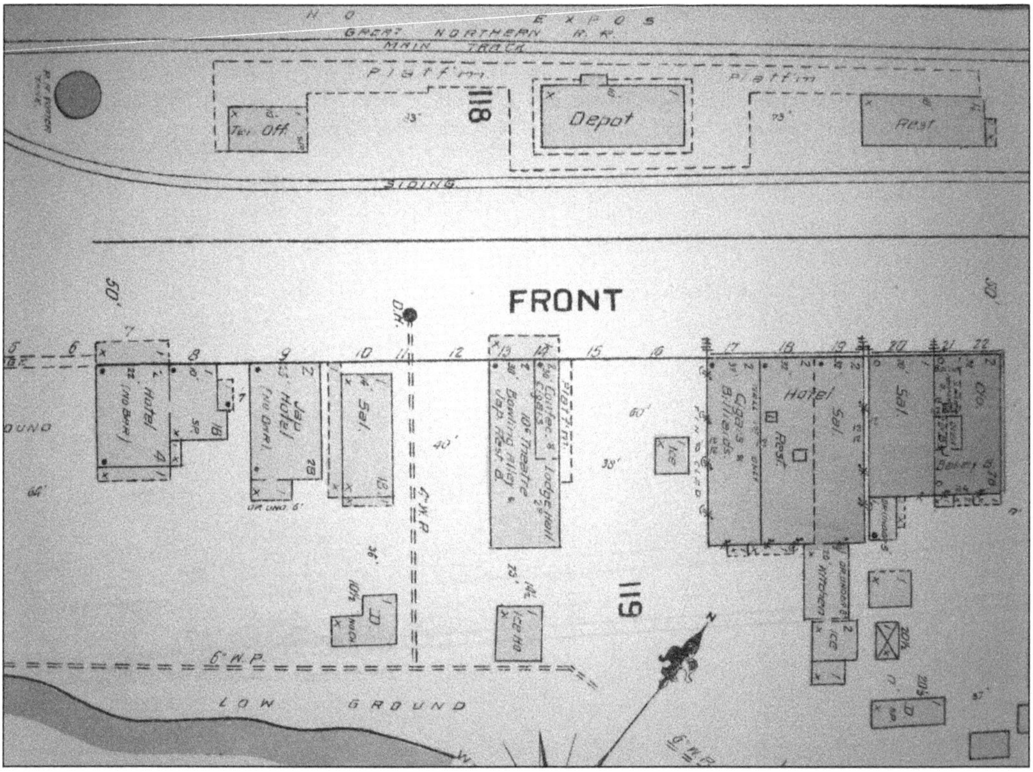

The GN made Leavenworth a division point in 1898. Here, GN crews changed shifts, gathered their supplies, and topped off fuel. Helper engines were added to trains for extra power to assist them through Cascades. The routine was to refuel at Leavenworth on the east side and at Skykomish on the west side of the mountains. This Sanborn insurance map shows the Leavenworth depot and nearby buildings in 1909. (Courtesy of LOC.)

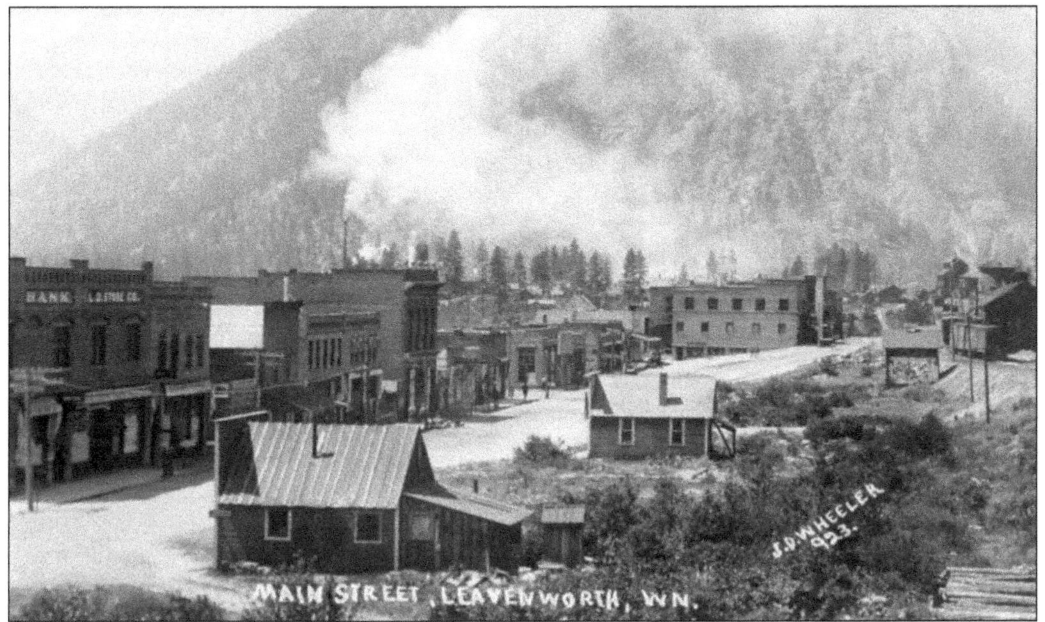

Seattle Express No. 25 arrived in Leavenworth on Wednesday, February 23, at 1:30 a.m. Conductor Joseph Pettit came aboard to begin his shift, and after surveying the harsh weather, knew it was going to be rough. Passenger Blanche Painter decided at the last minute to leave the train and stay in Leavenworth. Whether her choice was intuition or just a fluke, it saved her life. (Courtesy of SHS.)

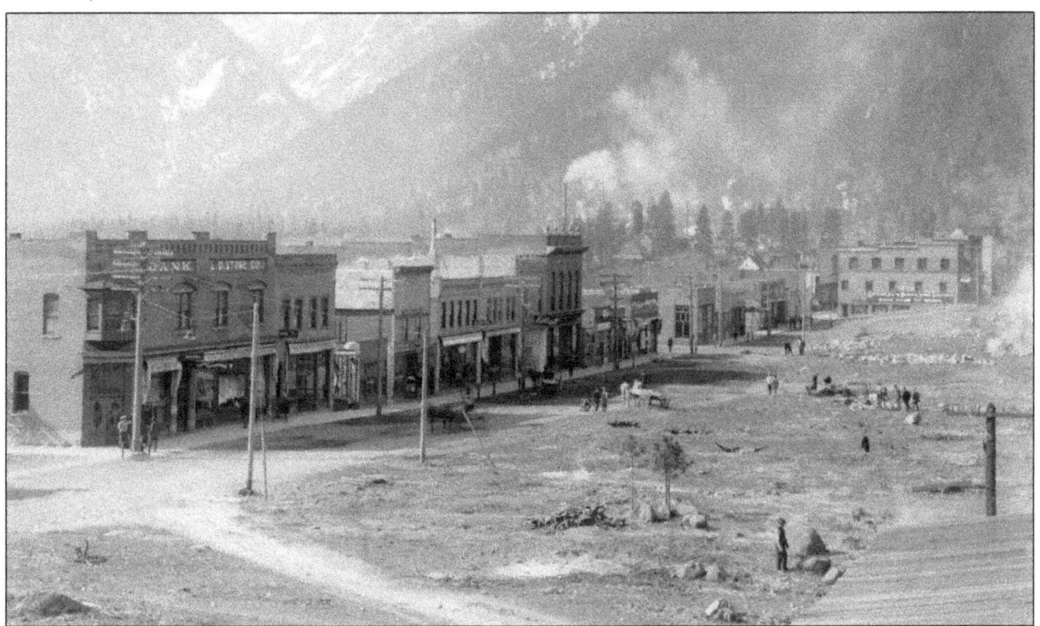

Early Leavenworth was originally called Icicle, and in the 1890s, the population was around 200. Some of the original pioneers were Doctor Hoxsey, George Briskey, J.E. Schubert, Frank Losekamp, Nick Kinscherf, Chas. Freytag, John Emig, Ezra Brusha, George Persinger, and of course, Captain Leavenworth. The original town was situated near the junction of the Icicle and Wenatchee Rivers, about one mile south of current day Leavenworth. (Courtesy of SHS.)

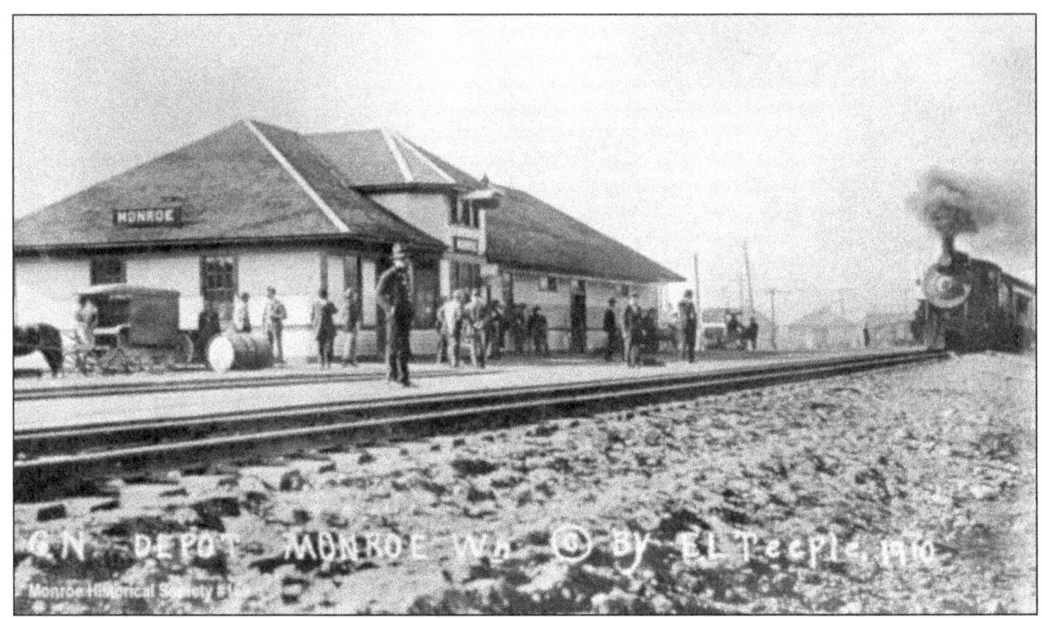

People gather at Monroe's second GN depot in 1910 near North Lewis Street. The Great Northern Railway began service through Monroe in the summer of 1893. The GN became Burlington Northern in 1970 after a merger with Northern Pacific. A GN superintendent said, "The Company does more business at Monroe than any other point on the line." In 1926, the Great Northern had multiple large greenhouses in Monroe, and 2,000 corsages were made and given to every woman boarding a train on Christmas. (Courtesy of E.L. Teeple, Monroe Historical Society.)

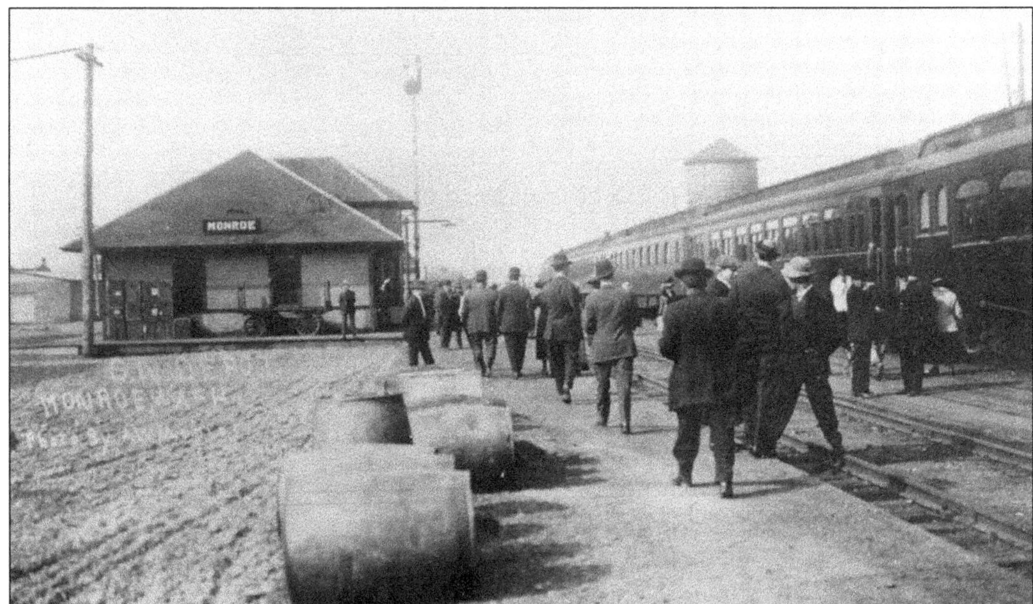

Here is the second Monroe depot sometime between 1916 and 1922. To the left, there was a spur track (known as the Ice Spur, constructed about 1916) that was still in place, which would have been at the very edge of the building. There is no sign of the spur in this photograph, which places it after 1916. The east end of the depot had a porte-cochere attached to it in about 1922, which is not in this picture either. (Courtesy of A.W. Monroe, Monroe Historical Society.)

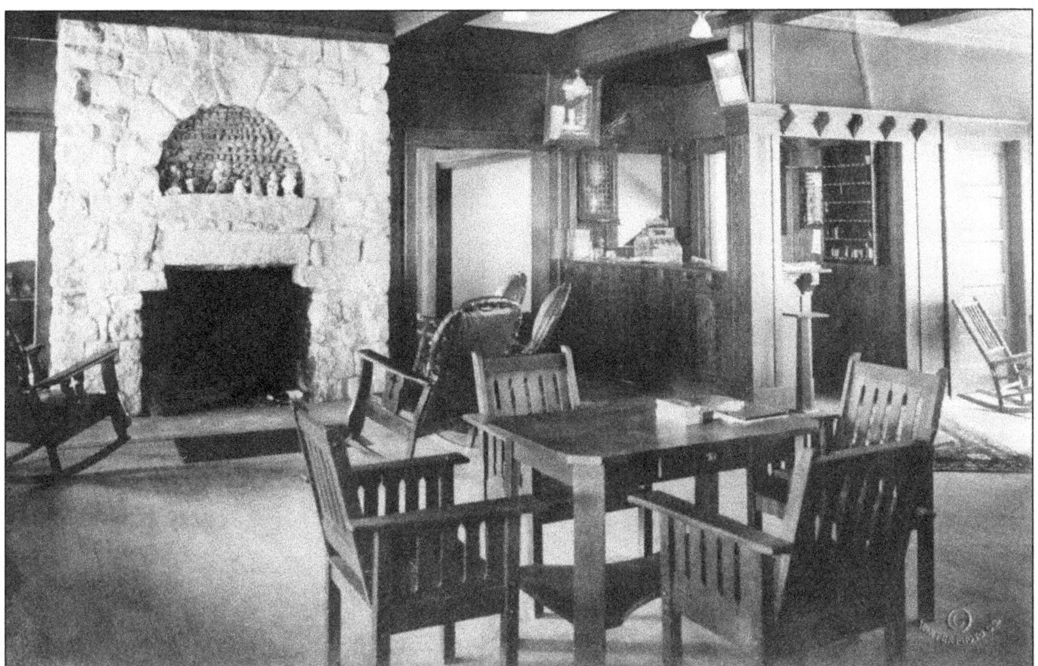

The photograph above of the lobby of the third Scenic Hot Springs Hotel features a stone fireplace and registration desk sometime after 1909. The exterior view of the hotel below shows guests enjoying the sun and grounds. The hot springs were originally found by John Stevens and C.F.B. Haskel in 1890 while surveying the area for the GN. In 1893, the first hotel was built; it was an impressive three stories and was named the Great Northern Hot Springs Hotel. In 1903, V. Prosser bought the hotel from George Murphy and enlarged it to accommodate 100 people, doubling the capacity. In 1908, the hotel burned down. Prosser rebuilt the hotel and quickly reopened it. It ran for 18 years until the GN slowly buried it as it built the rail line for the new Cascade Tunnel. Sadly, the hotel never was rebuilt or reopened. (Both, courtesy of Oregon Historical Society, Kiser Photo Company.)

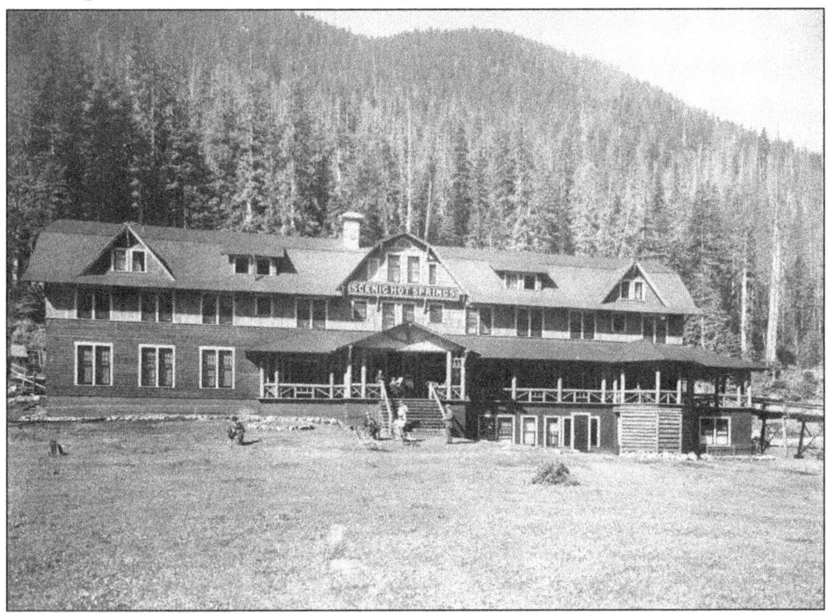

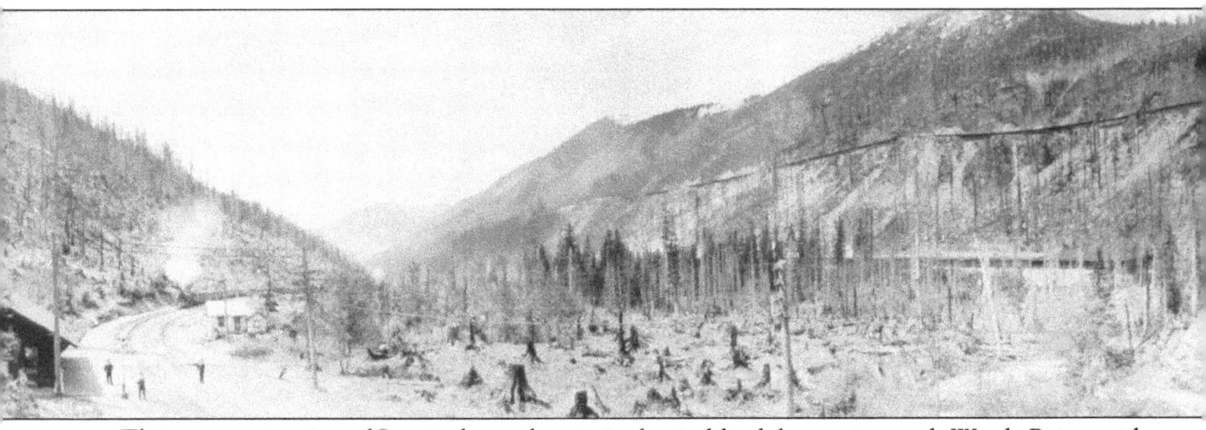

This panoramic view of Scenic shows the original switchback line as it rounds Windy Point, with long wood snowsheds in the center. Wellington is behind the water tower. These switchbacks were a part of the original plan for the GN route over Stevens Pass. In 1929, a new eight-mile tunnel

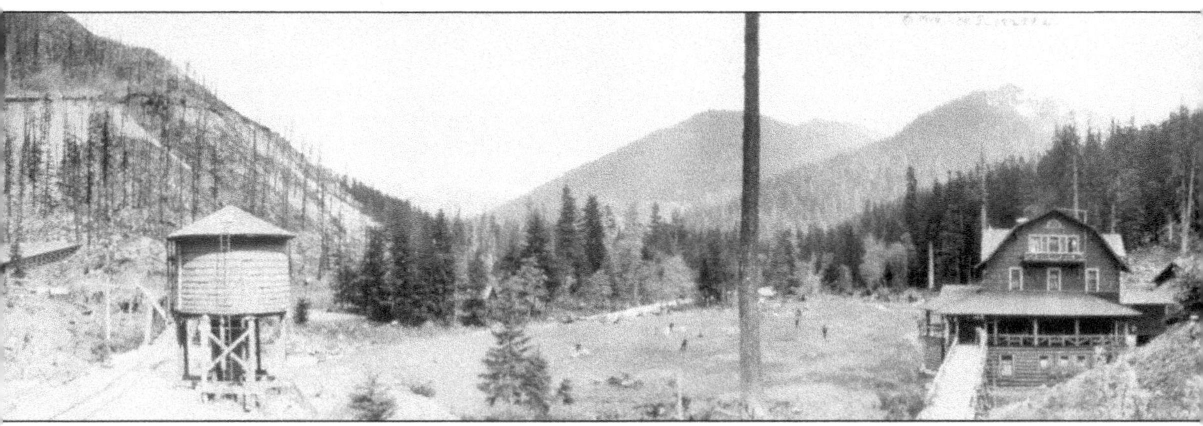

was completed with its west portal at Scenic, eliminating the need for the dangerous switchback route. The third version of the Scenic Hot Springs Hotel is on the right. (Courtesy of LOC.)

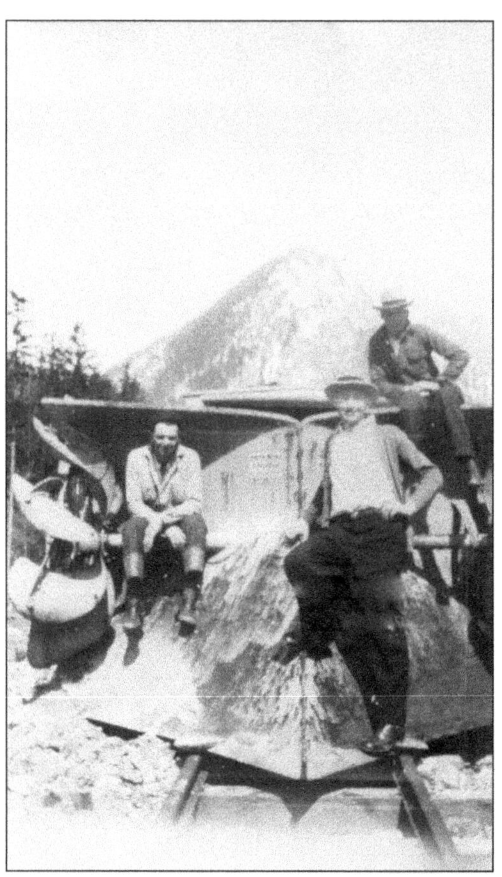

Three men are on a plow near Scenic. The old-style plows took up to eight steam engines to run. They would often become derailed while bucking a slide, leaving the crew to slowly dig it out. The new plow, invented in 1884, used two huge blades instead spinning in opposite directions. The first blade would cut the snow and the second would fling it out to the side. (Courtesy of WVM, 87-142-33.)

The first Scenic Hotel was called the Great Northern Hot Springs Hotel and opened in 1890. It was advertised, and believed by many, that the nearby hot springs had healing properties. During 1910, several anxious passengers risked their lives walking from the trains to Scenic, almost eight miles away. (Courtesy of SHS.)

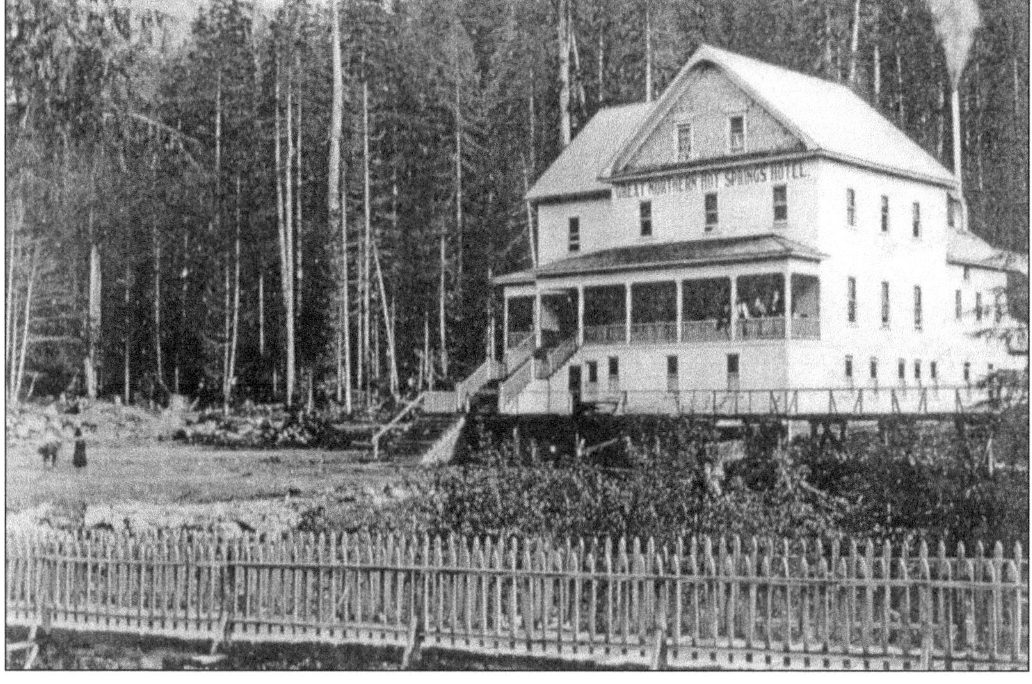

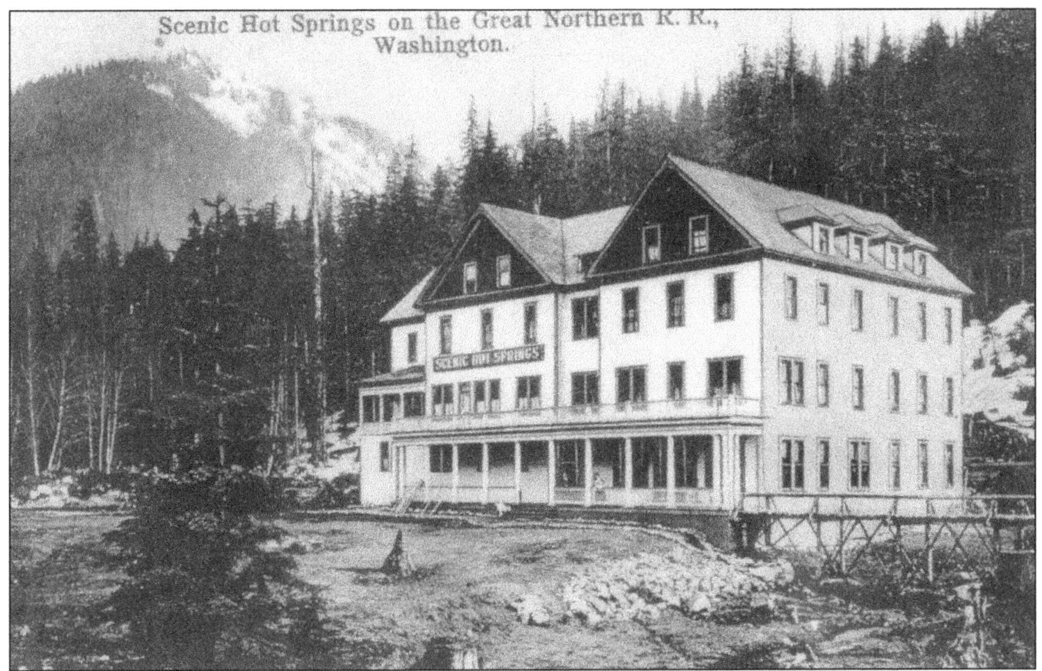

This postcard shows the second version of the expanded Scenic Hot Springs Hotel, with a woman and baby on the porch. This might be the J.V. Prosser family, who owned the hotel. Scenic was about 10 miles from Wellington. After the avalanche, Dowling and Mackey were put in charge of creating a relief team and soon headed back to Wellington, taking a nurse named Godby from Scenic with them. (Courtesy of SHS.)

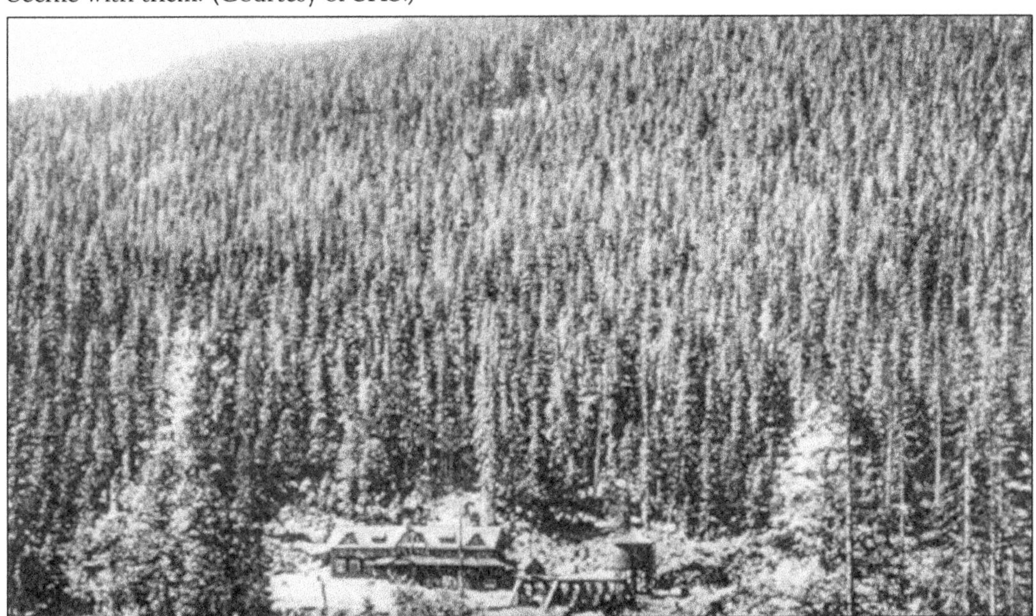

After a fire in 1908, the third Scenic Hotel was quickly rebuilt to serve people attending the Alaska Yukon Exposition in Seattle. It was frequently advertised that the water in the nearby springs could heal all sorts of ailments. The springs still exist today, but the land is privately owned and not open to the public. (Courtesy of SHS.)

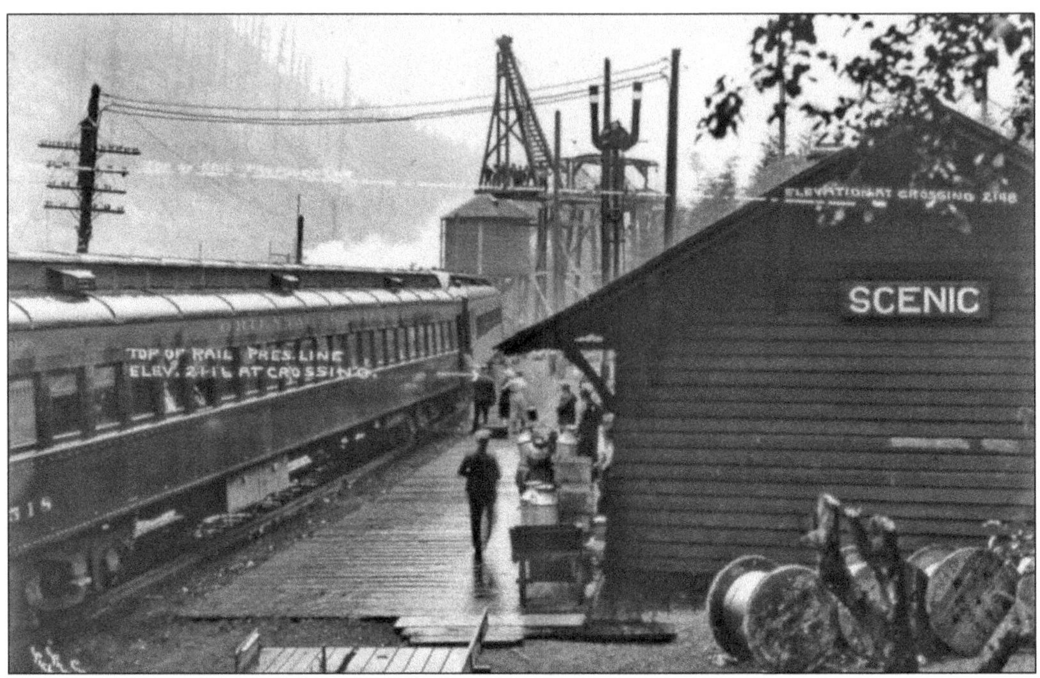

The Scenic train depot is seen here around 1928 during construction of the new eight-mile Cascade Tunnel. Scenic played an important role in the Wellington disaster. On Sunday, February 27, passengers wanted to risk hiking to Scenic, but locals discouraged this since it would include a very dangerous slide down a steep 1,000-foot slope. (Courtesy of SHS.)

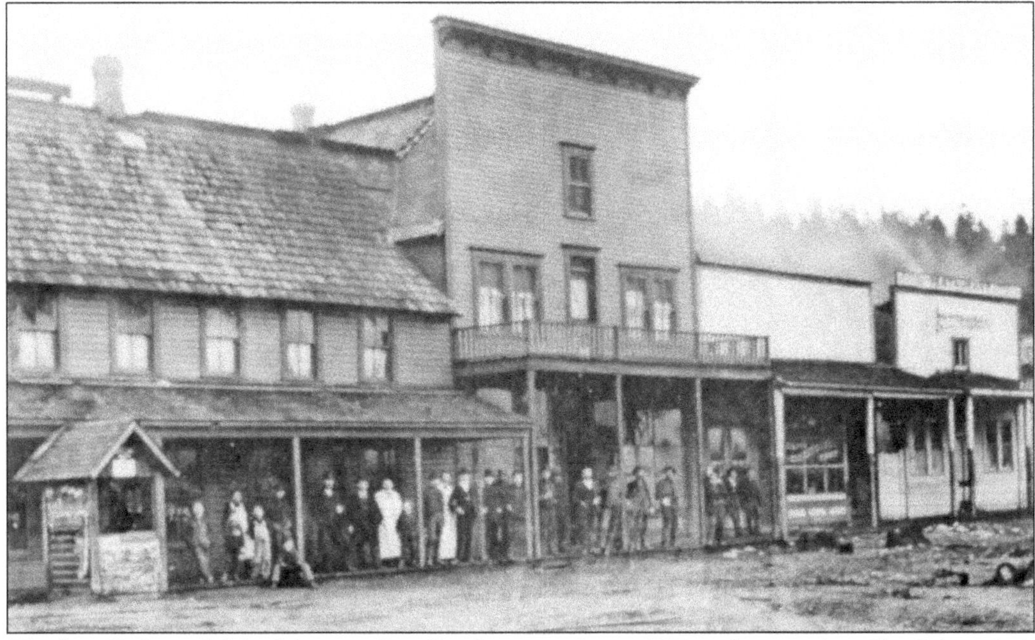

The first Skykomish Hotel (pictured) suffered a tragic fire in 1902 and was replaced by Schneider's Hotel, operated by H. Glass Sensiba, which was also destroyed in a fire in 1904. The current Skykomish Hotel was built by D.J. Manning in 1904 and cost $10,000. Skykomish was a regular stop for coal on the west side of the mountains. (Courtesy of SHS.)

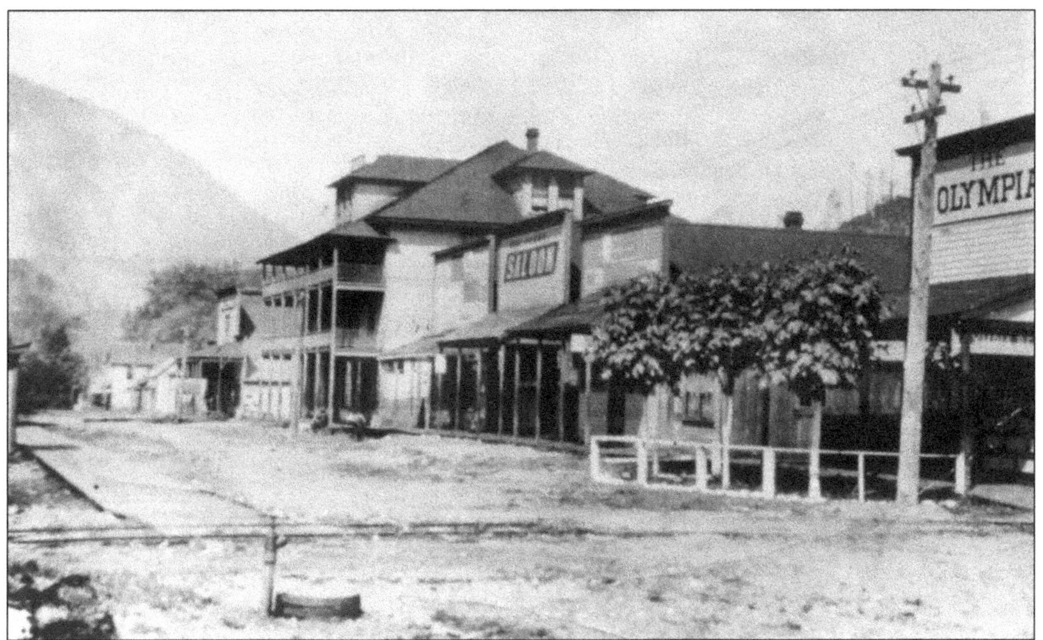

Pictured here around 1905, from left to right, are the Skykomish Hotel, Bill Richardson's Saloon, Mac's Cash Store, and the Olympia Tavern. (Courtesy of SHS.)

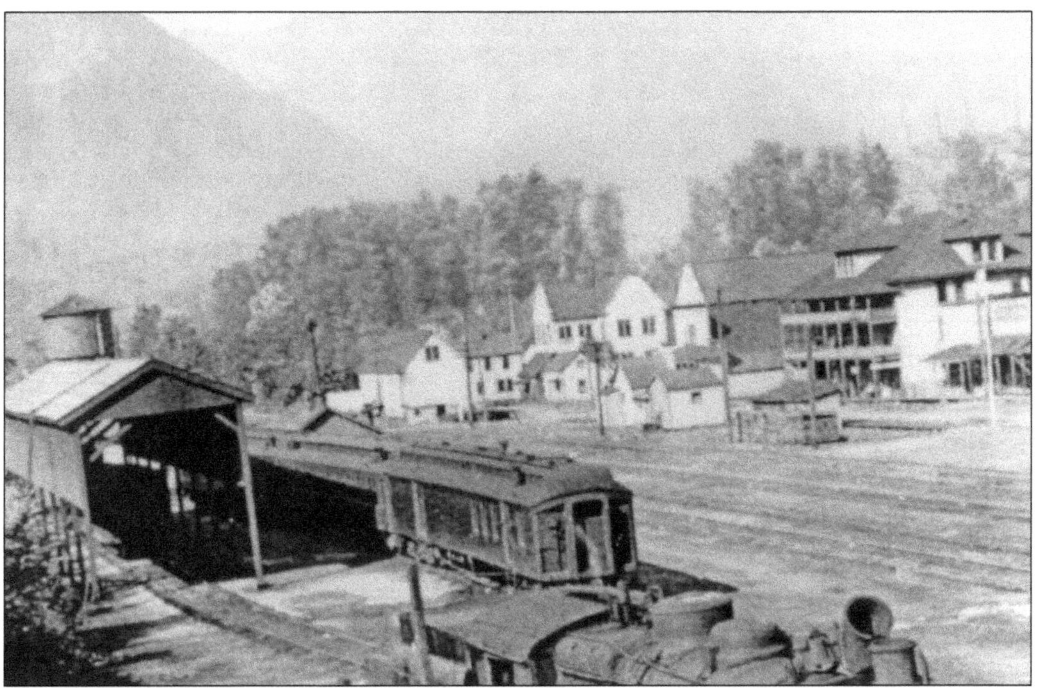

The GN depot (not pictured) in Skykomish was built in 1894 and was across from the Skykomish Hotel (pictured here with the three stories of porches). The depot was moved in 1922, then later moved back to its original location. The Olympia Tavern and pool hall was owned by a GN engineer named Patrick McEvoy in 1897 and was later renamed the Whistling Post. (Courtesy of SHS.)

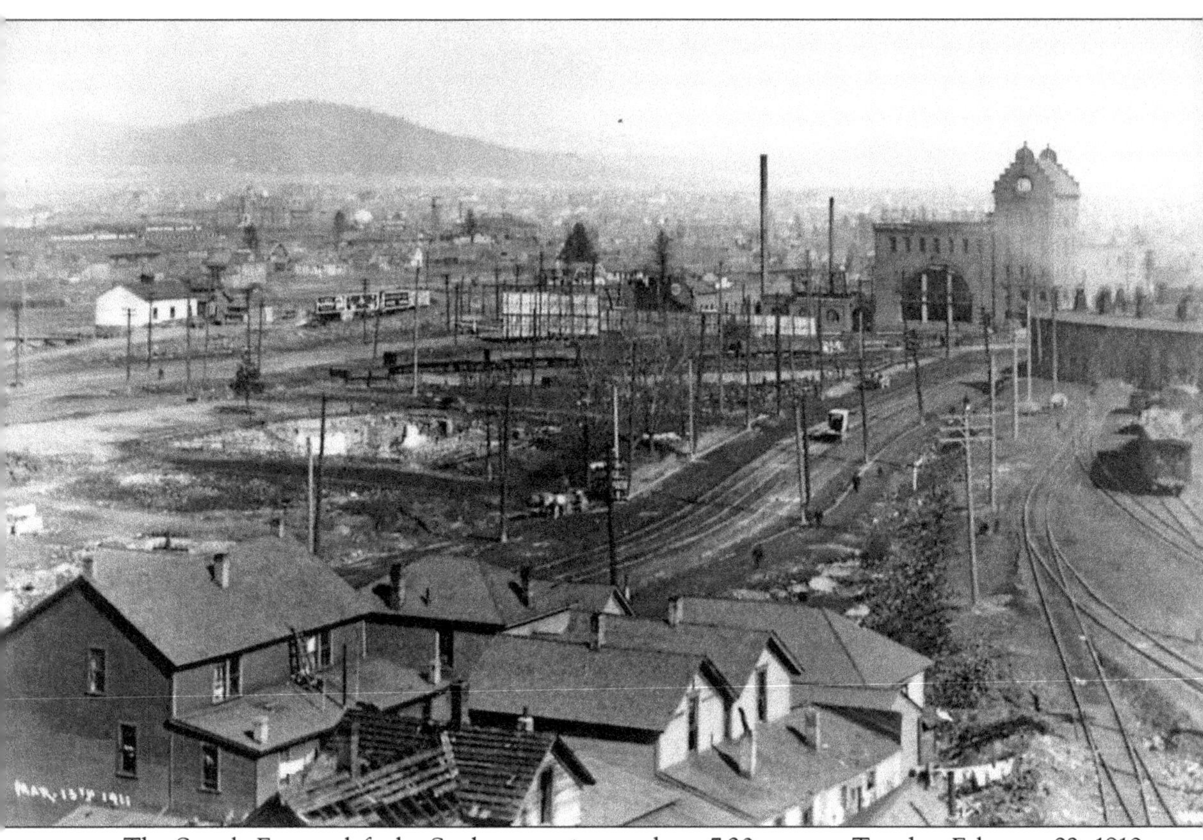

The Seattle Express left the Spokane station at about 7:30 p.m. on Tuesday, February 22, 1910. Spokane was quite large in 1910, with over 100,000 residents. Two competing attorneys boarded the train that night, Lewis Jesseph and John Merritt, both bound to appear at the same court case in Olympia later that week. Both men hiked out of Wellington the Sunday before the disaster, saving their lives. Pictured is a view of Spokane in 1900 looking southeast over downtown on the south side of the river. (Courtesy of Washington State Archives.)

Five

Great Northern Railway and James Hill

James Jerome Hill was considered one of the greatest railroad builders of all time. Unhampered by receiving only a limited education (he left school at age 15), Hill was a powerhouse throughout his career and a man to be contended with. He earned a reputation for being ruthless at times. In 1878, he and three partners saw opportunity in a bankrupt St. Paul & Pacific Railroad Company and, by 1893, began the legacy of the Great Northern Railway.

He used the construction of his railroad to influence many new settlers to come to various areas where his railroad was being built, thus improving many lives and planting new crops throughout the Pacific Northwest. He ran a demonstration crew that would teach locals new farming techniques.

The GN Pacific Extension in 1890–1893 included 800 miles of track, and the going rate was $200 per mile. Workers earned $2.25 per day to lay track. In 1889, Hill officially changed the name of the railroad to the Great Northern Railway. By 1901, his tracks finally ran from St. Paul to Seattle.

But possibly his greatest feat was tunneling through the mighty Cascade Mountains.

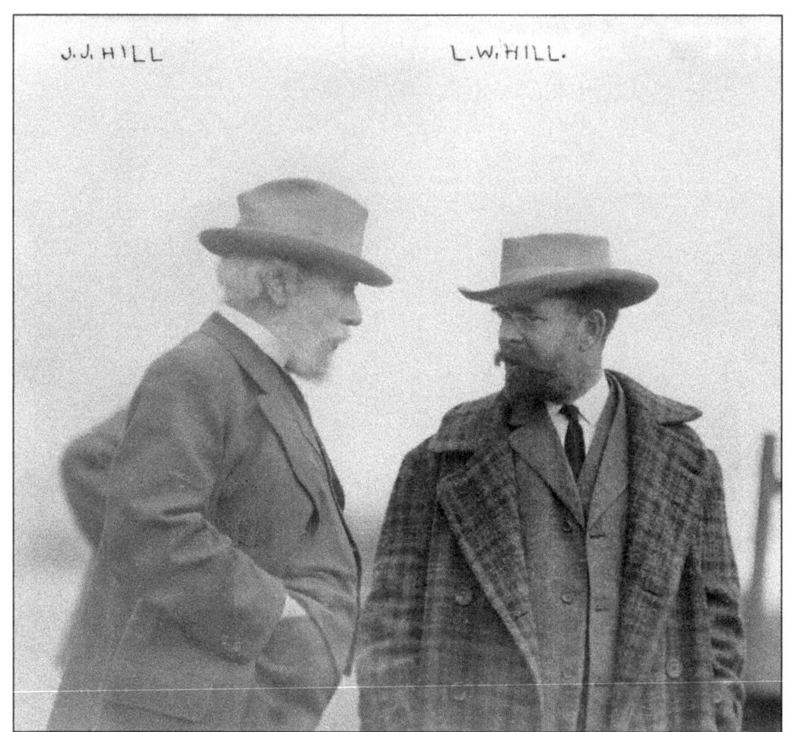

The tough-minded railroad executive James Hill (left) stands by his son Louis Hill probably discussing business. The original tunnel that James Hill and John Stevens envisioned began in 1897 and took three years to complete. (Courtesy of LOC.)

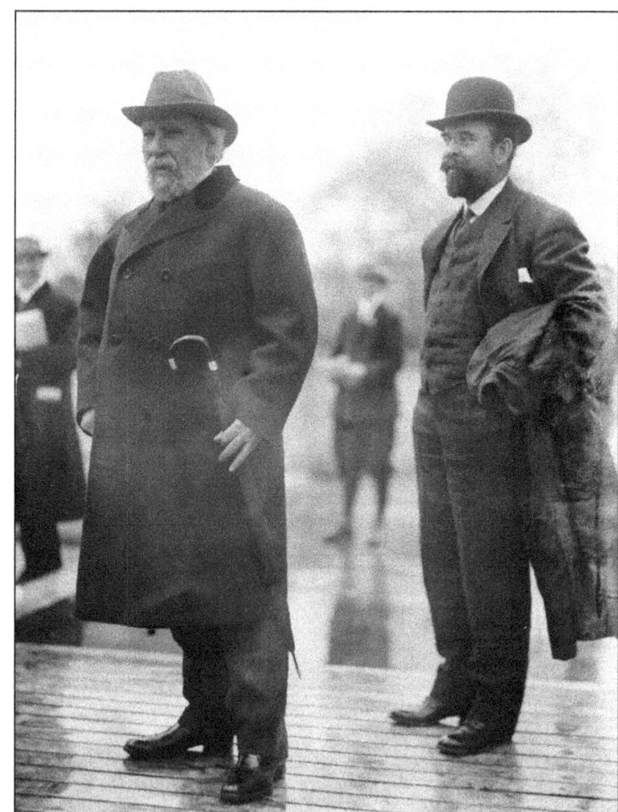

James Hill (left) stands with his son Louis on the sidewalk. James Hill was a visionary and very stern businessman. He took a liking to James O'Neill when he was young, as Hill was also a hard and determined worker. (Courtesy of LOC.)

James Hill was born in 1838 in Canada and later moved to St. Paul, Minnesota. He earned the nickname "Empire Builder." Between 1883 and 1889, he built railroads through Minnesota, Wisconsin, North Dakota, and Montana. When Hill spoke of building a transcontinental line, people laughed at him and said it could not be done without government funding; it became known as "Hill's Folly." (Courtesy of LOC.)

In his 70th year, James Hill (center) poses with four Great Northern Railway personnel in front of GN's first locomotive, the *William Crooks*, in 1908. Second from left is Albion B. Smith, who restored the locomotive after a fire in 1868. The locomotive was originally a wood burner and was later converted to burn coal. (Photograph by F.A. Hubold, courtesy of Wikimedia Commons.)

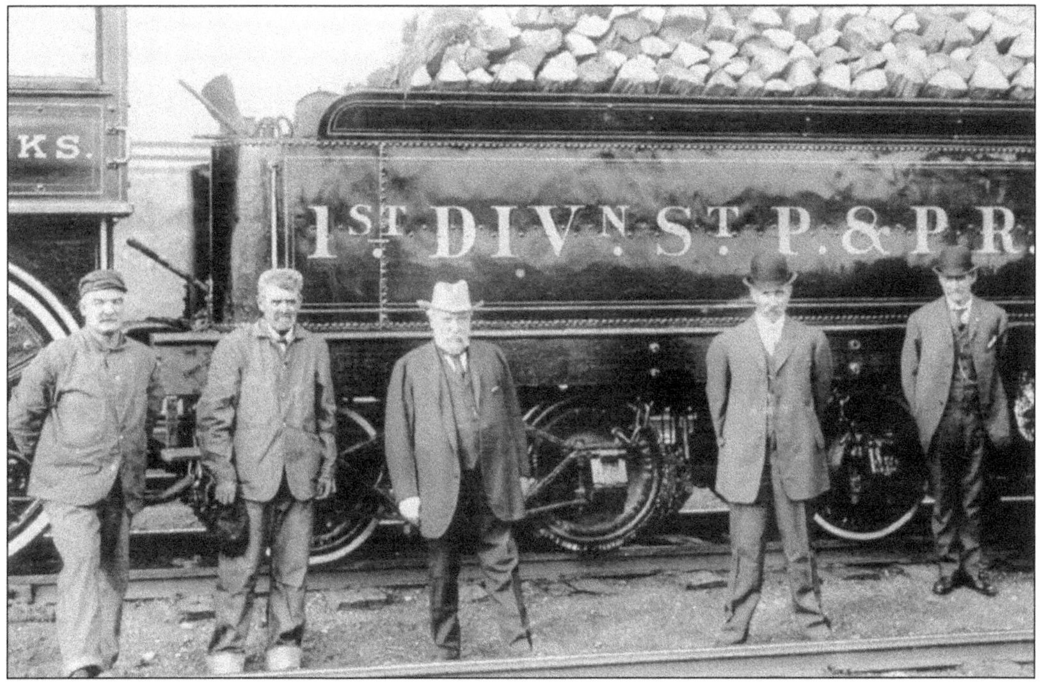

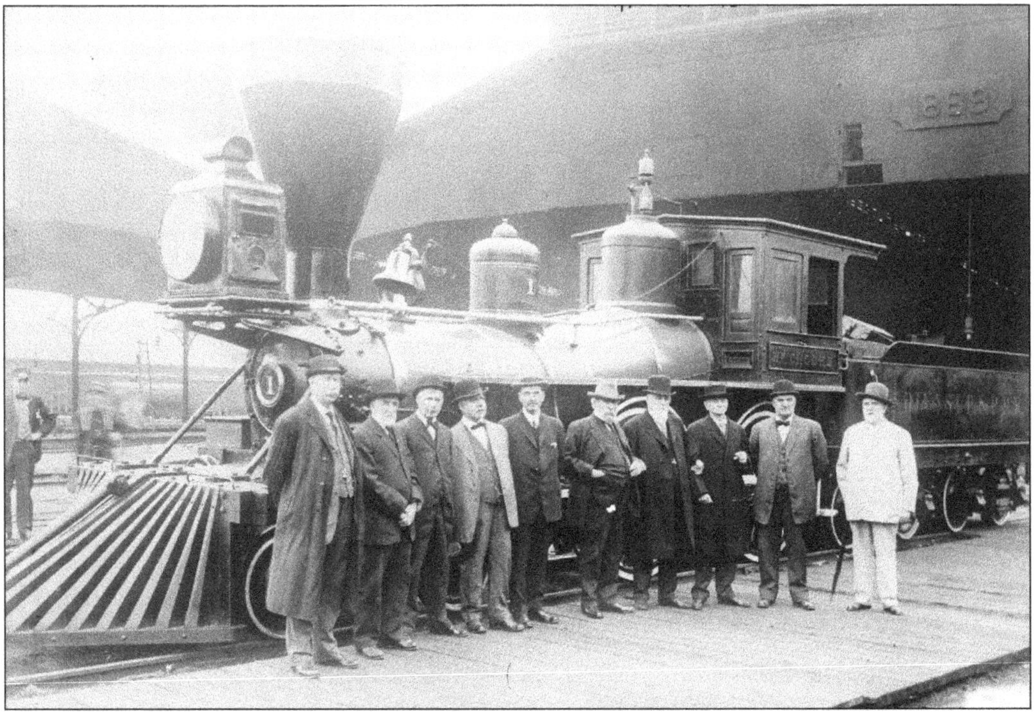

Here, 11 men stand in front of the *William Crooks*, the first locomotive to arrive in Minnesota, which was built in 1861. James Hill is at far right. Before his death in 1916, Hill was able to complete one of his most difficult challenges: the Cascade Tunnel. (Courtesy of LOC.)

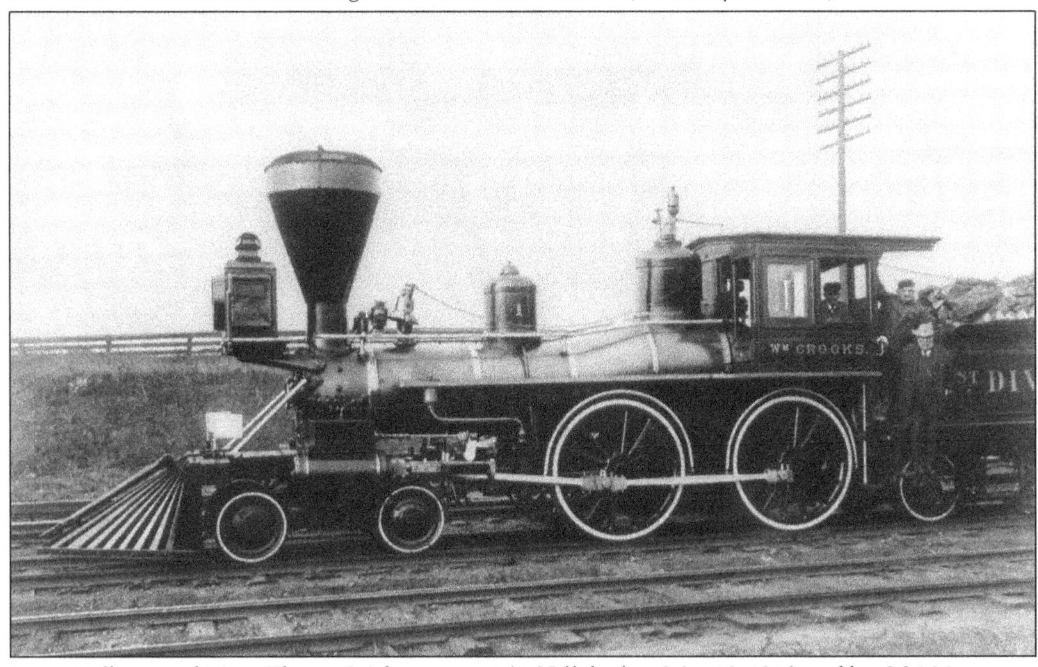

James Hill married Mary Theresa Mehegan in 1867. Hill died on May 29, 1916, and his 36,000-square-foot mansion is now a museum. The net worth of his company jumped from $728,000 in 1880 to $25 million in 1885. (Courtesy of LOC.)

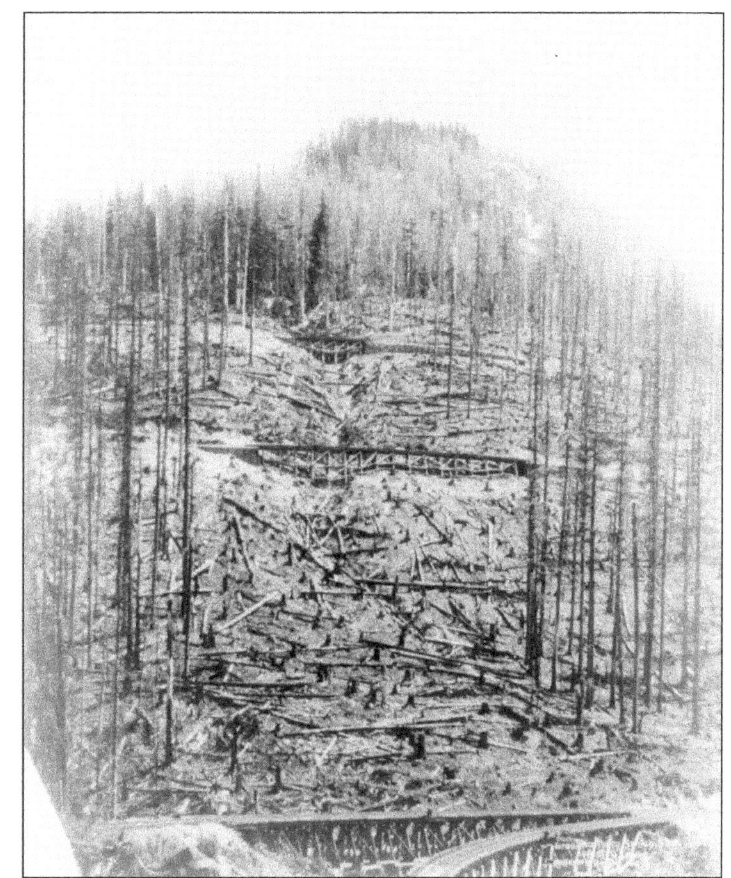

The switchbacks were considered both a marvel and a nightmare and were called Death Mountain due to their dangerous operations. To move a 110-ton locomotive from one end to the other required 3,000 pounds of coal. The grueling 12 miles took anywhere from 75 minutes to 36 hours and required a specially trained crew. The trains had to reverse direction several times, moving over the summit, then climb up steep three to four percent grades through sharp 12-degree curves to an altitude of over 4,000 feet. (Both, courtesy of LOC.)

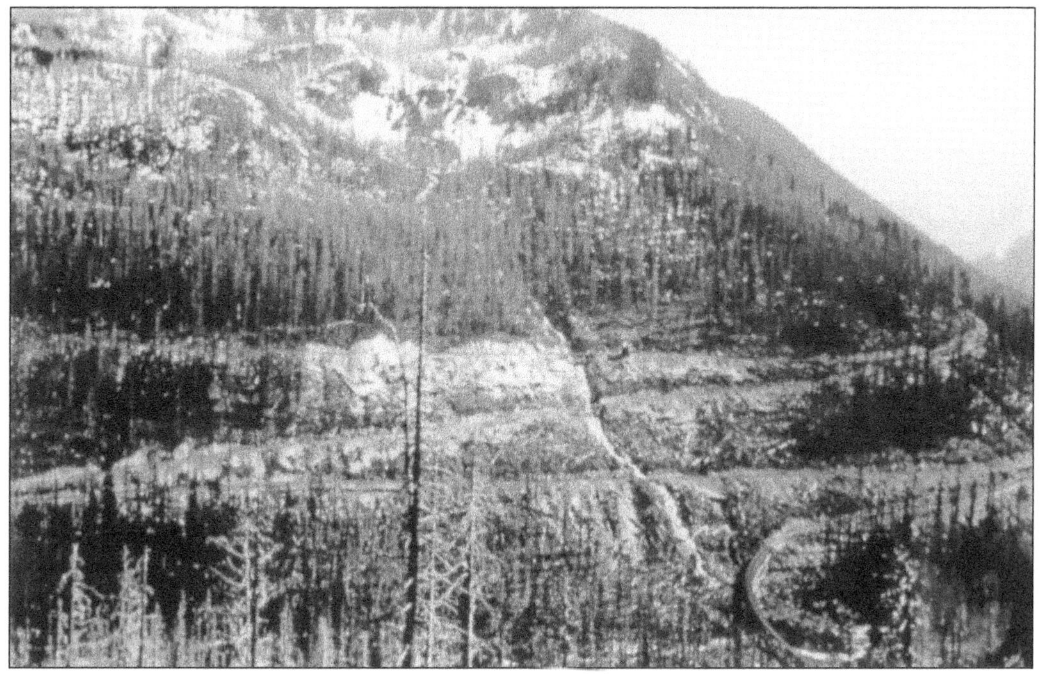

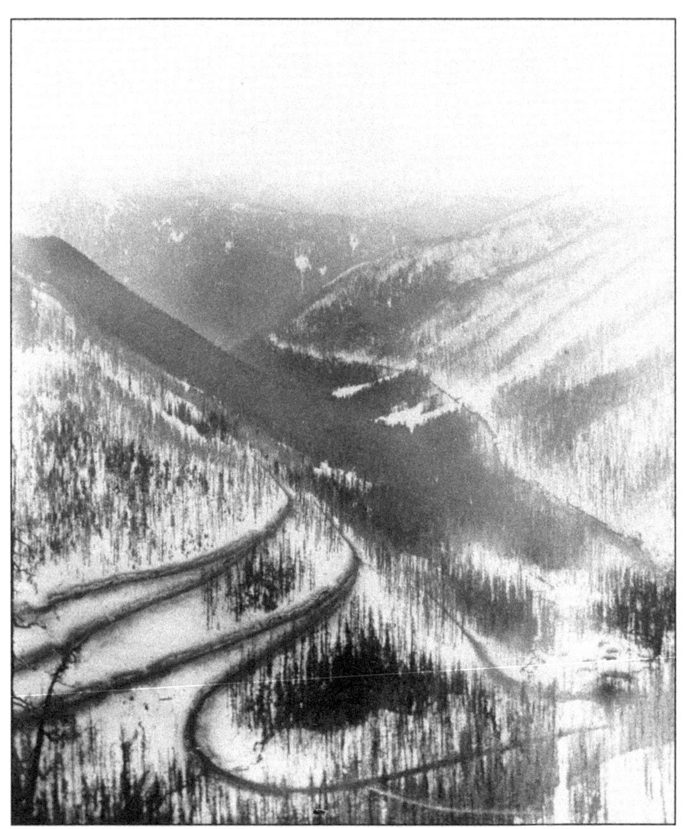

The treacherous switchbacks can be seen clearly here. With the construction of the Cascade Tunnel, these switchbacks were eliminated; a welcome relief to GN crew members. (Courtesy of SHS.)

An Oriental Limited train heads out of the east portal of the Cascade Tunnel in 1923. The Oriental Limited ran from Chicago to Seattle in 70 hours. The Chicago, Burlington & Quincy Railroad controlled the train from Chicago to St. Paul, and the GN controlled it from St. Paul to Seattle. (Courtesy of the Howard Johnson family.)

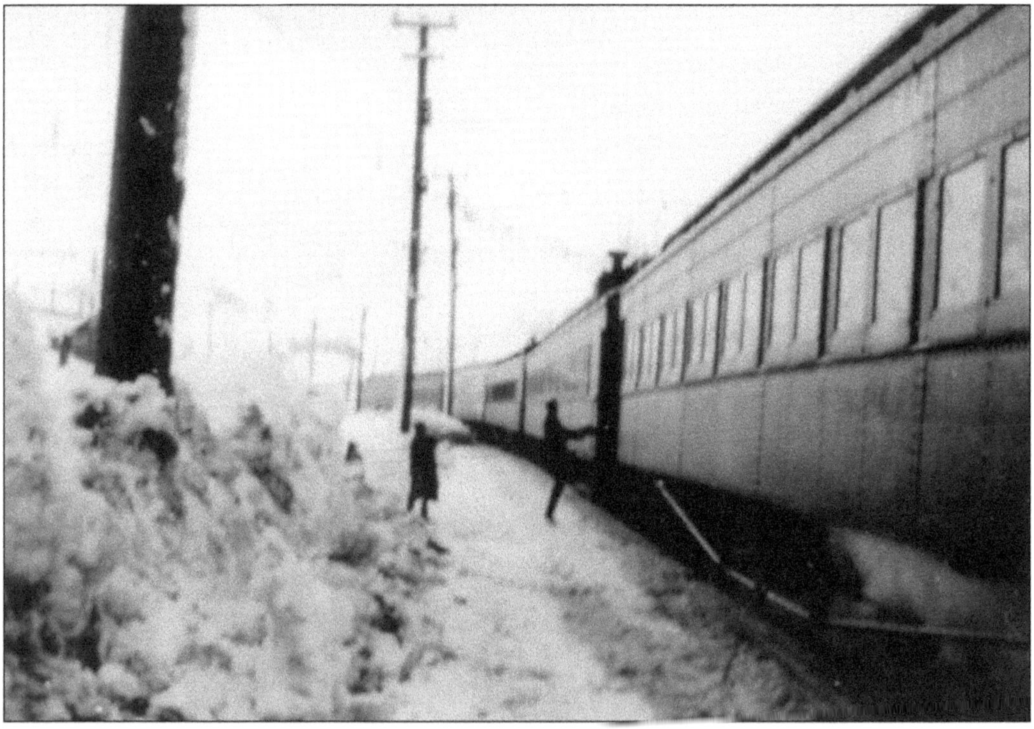

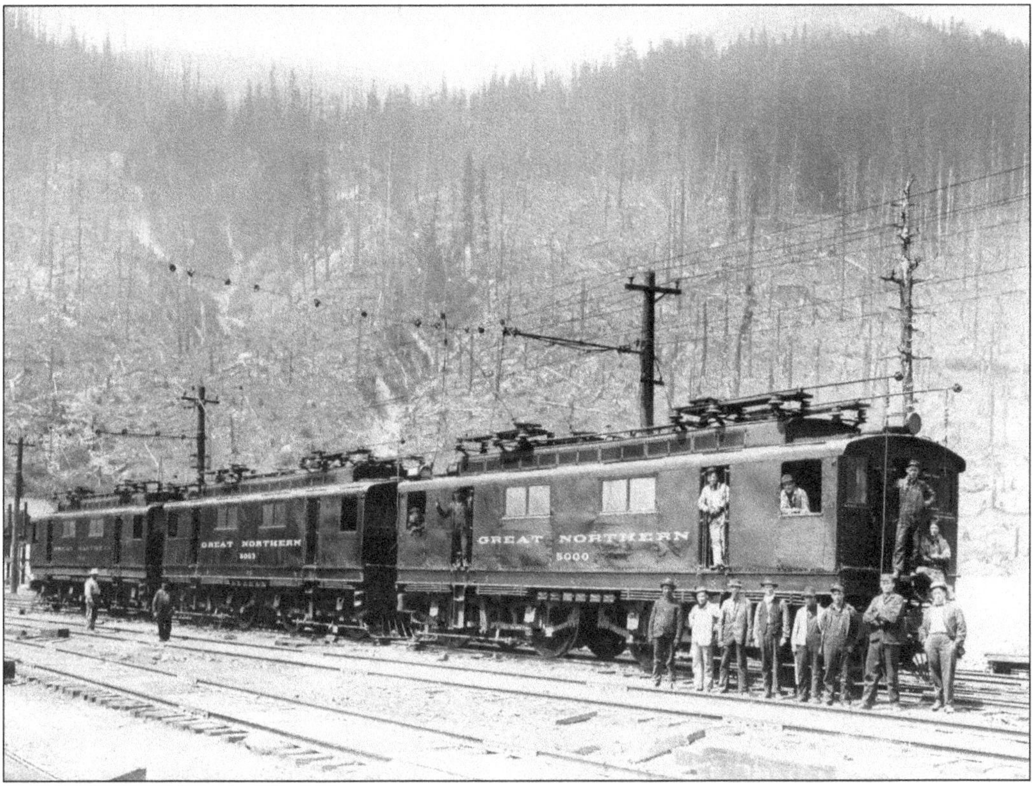

A crew is pictured with their parked train at Wellington. There were two brakemen per train, who had to crawl on top of the moving train to apply and release each handbrake. The brakemen who died at Wellington were William Bovee, William Dorety, Anthony Dougherty, Archie Dupy, Milton Hicks, Charles Jennison, John Kelly, William Kenzal, Archibald McDonald, William Raycroft, Andrew Stohmier, and Julian Wells. (Courtesy of Coughlin Collection, SHS.)

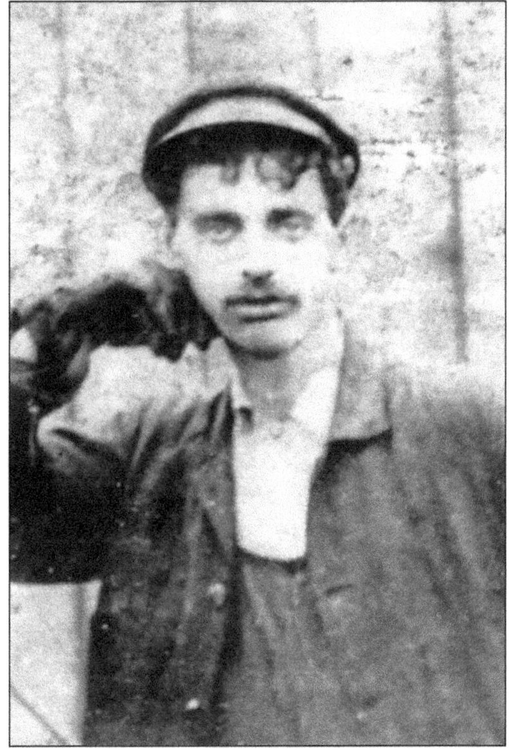

Sydney Herbert Jones was a fireman who began working for the railway just a few months before the avalanche took his life. He left behind three small children and a wife, Hester Dor. The job of a railroad fireman was to prepare the locomotives, shovel coal into the furnace, and tend to the boiler on an old-fashioned steam locomotive. They were also called stokers or boilermen. Sydney Jones, pictured here the year before the avalanche while working for the GN, was also a British soldier in the Boer War. (Courtesy of Bob Walters.)

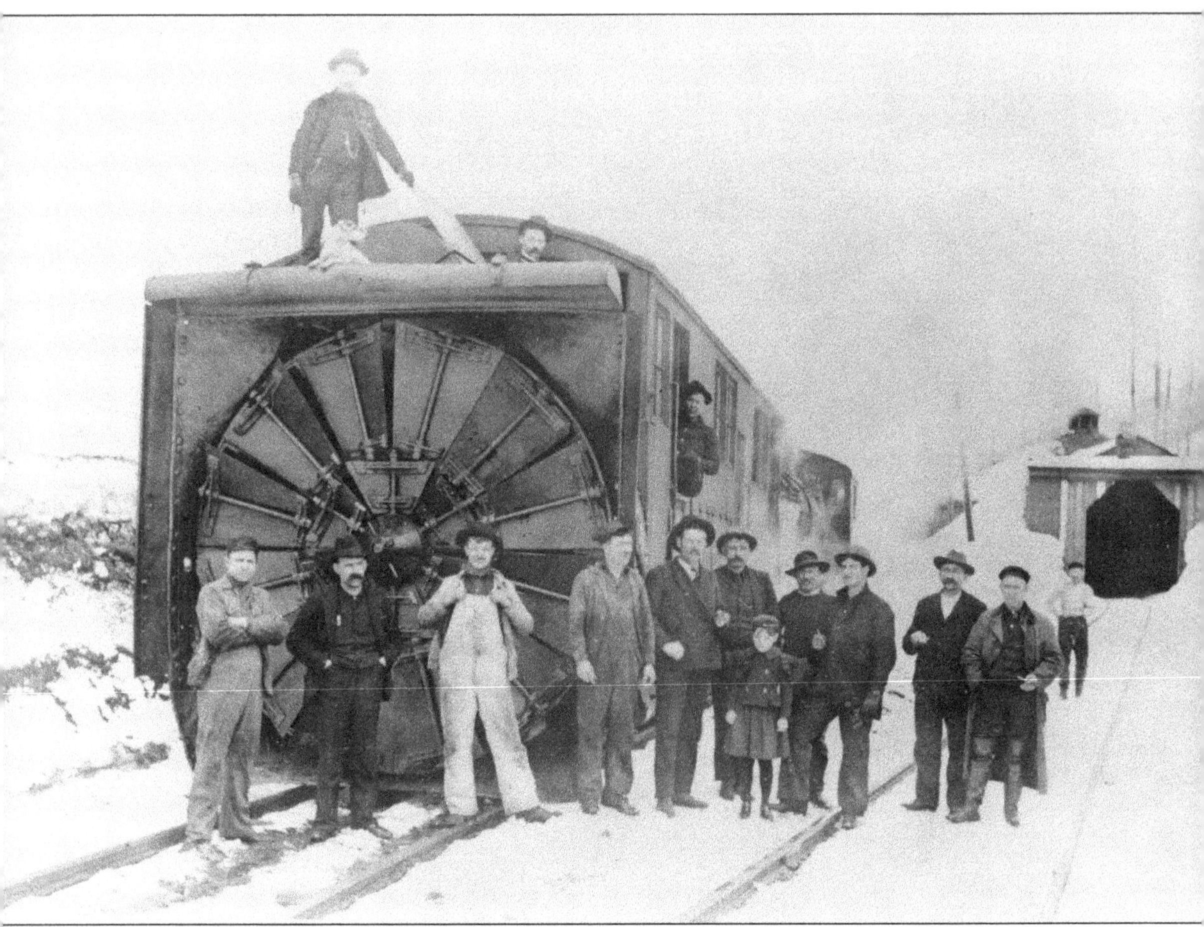

Pictured is a rotary snowplow with a coaling shed in the background and 14 men, a little girl, and a Jack Russell terrier on top. A rotary went missing at Windy Point, three miles west of Wellington, and many feared the entire crew of 20 was lost under a slide. No reports came from the crew for three days, and newspapers claimed they were never found. The GN rotary conductors who lost their lives at Wellington were Alex Campbell, Steven Lindsay, and John Parzybok. The GN firemen's role was to shovel the coal in and keep the trains running. Those who died at Wellington were Earl Bennington, Earl Fisher, G.R. Jenks, Sydney Jones, Harry Partridge, L. Ross, and G.R. Yerks. An engineer is in charge of actually running the train, and the ones who died were J.O. Carroll, Benjamin Jarnagan, Francis Martin, and T.L. Osborne. (Courtesy of the Dr. George Fisher Collection, SHS.)

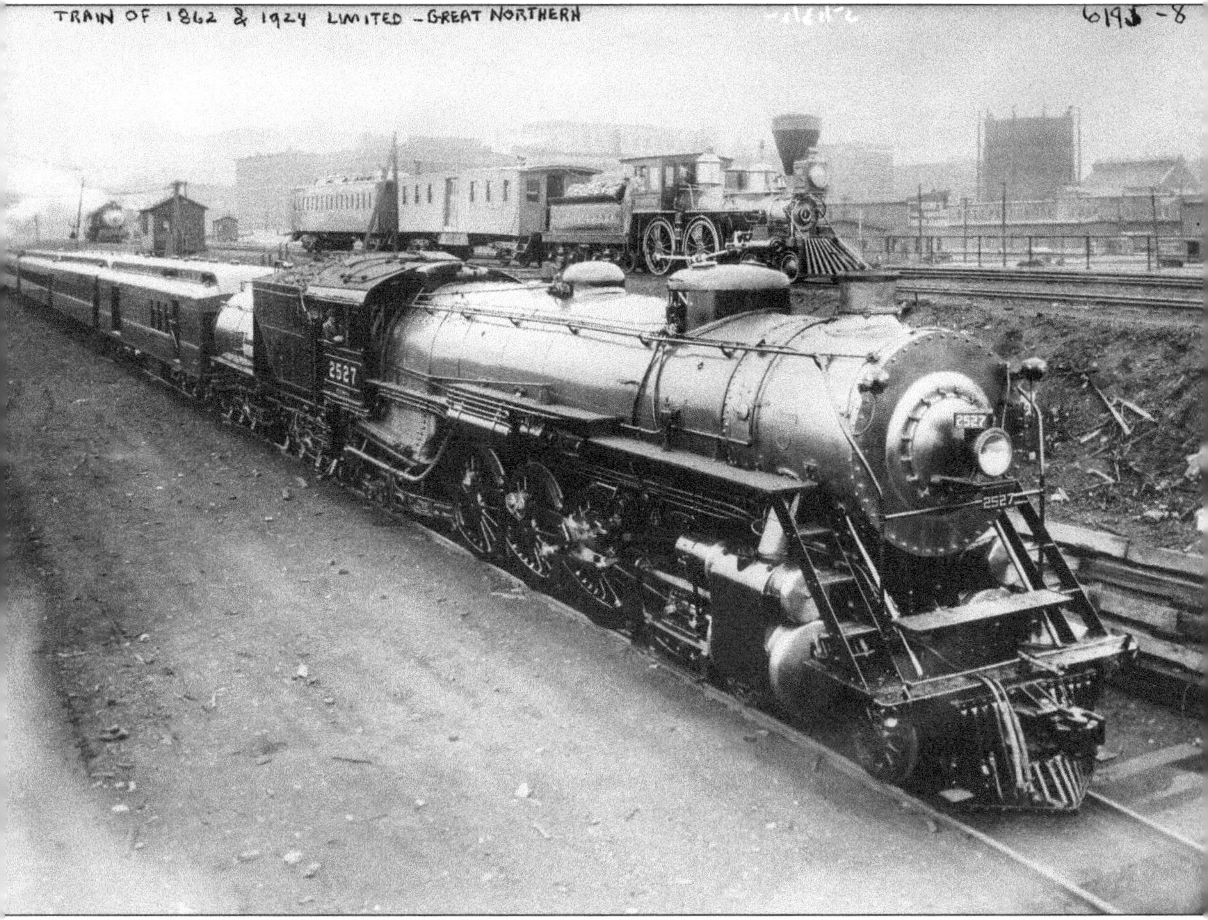

The *William Crooks* and Limited No. 2527 are both pictured in an unidentified city. The *Crooks* was a 4-4-0 steam locomotive that was the first locomotive to operate in Minnesota. It also was a wood burner and held only two cords of wood. If all of it was used before the train could reach more, the crew would pull up and use wooden fences. Luckily, the locomotive was later converted into a coal burner. (Courtesy of LOC.)

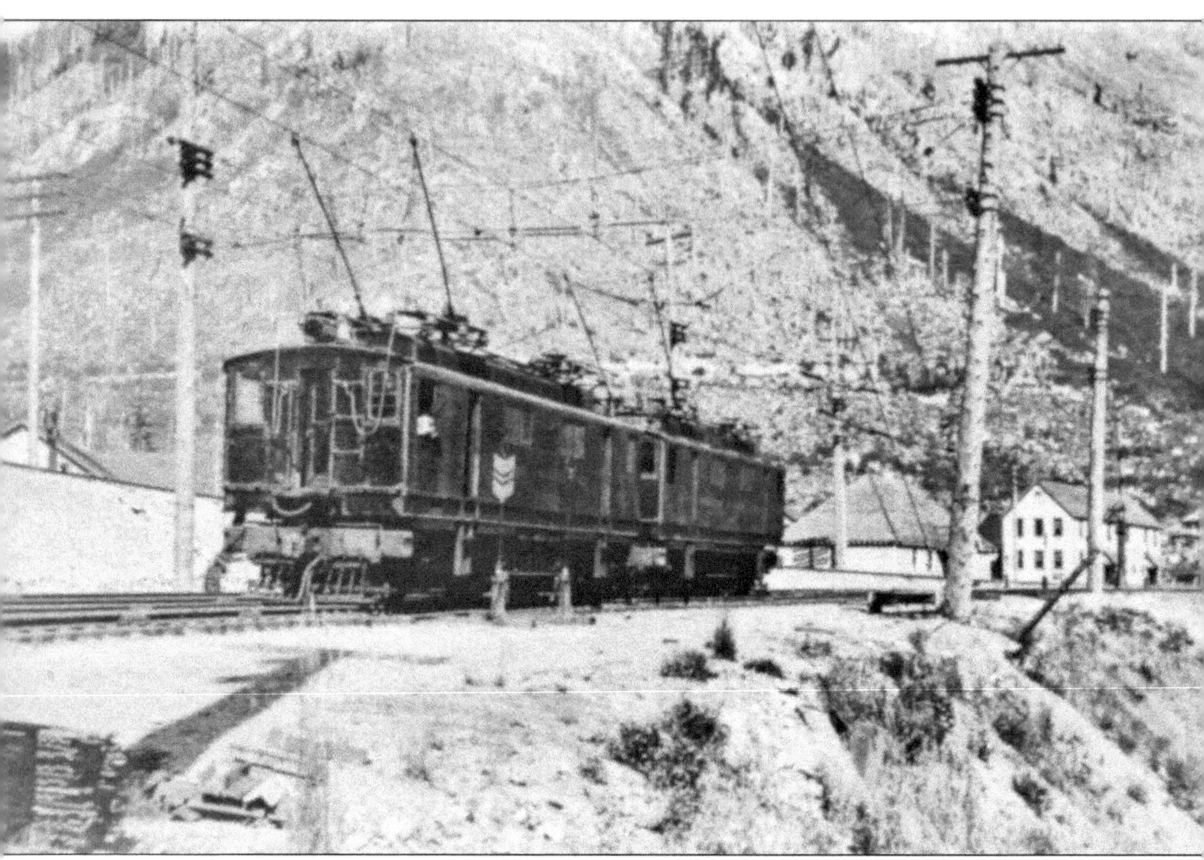

This electric locomotive is parked near the actual slide site at Wellington. The buildings to the right are the new beanery (the original one was destroyed before the big avalanche, killing the two cooks), and the larger building is another bunkhouse. The building above the bunkhouse is the end of the Bailets Hotel. The GN had 24 electric locomotives, four specifically for the Cascade Tunnel. They had a 6,600-volt three-phase AC system with two overhead wires (as seen here) that used the rails as conductors. This type of system was in operation between the western side of Wellington/Tye and the Cascade Tunnel Station just beyond the eastern portal. In the 1950s, electrification was abandoned because the new diesels could operate in the tunnel. The old tunnel was used for storage for many years, and doors were added to the openings. The new Cascade Tunnel is still in use today. (Courtesy of SHS.)

Six

The Passengers and Crew Members

Some historians suggest that prioritizing the fast mail over the passenger trains had something to do with which trains were parked on which tracks, but in the end, the avalanche had no mercy. It did not really matter where the trains were parked, as the slide was so massive, it swept them both off the tracks.

It was true that the fast mail contracts were a huge part of the Great Northern's income, and the mail trains being on time was non-negotiable. The fast mail trains earned $171 per mile for the first 5,000 pounds of mail, and each additional 2,000 pounds (up to 48,000 pounds) earned an extra $19.24 per mile.

In 1909, the average weight of the mail out of Spokane was 40,000 pounds per day. Great Northern's reputation was to get the mail from New York to Seattle in three days and from St. Paul to Seattle in just 47.5 hours. If the fast mail train was not there on time, the GN was fined substantially.

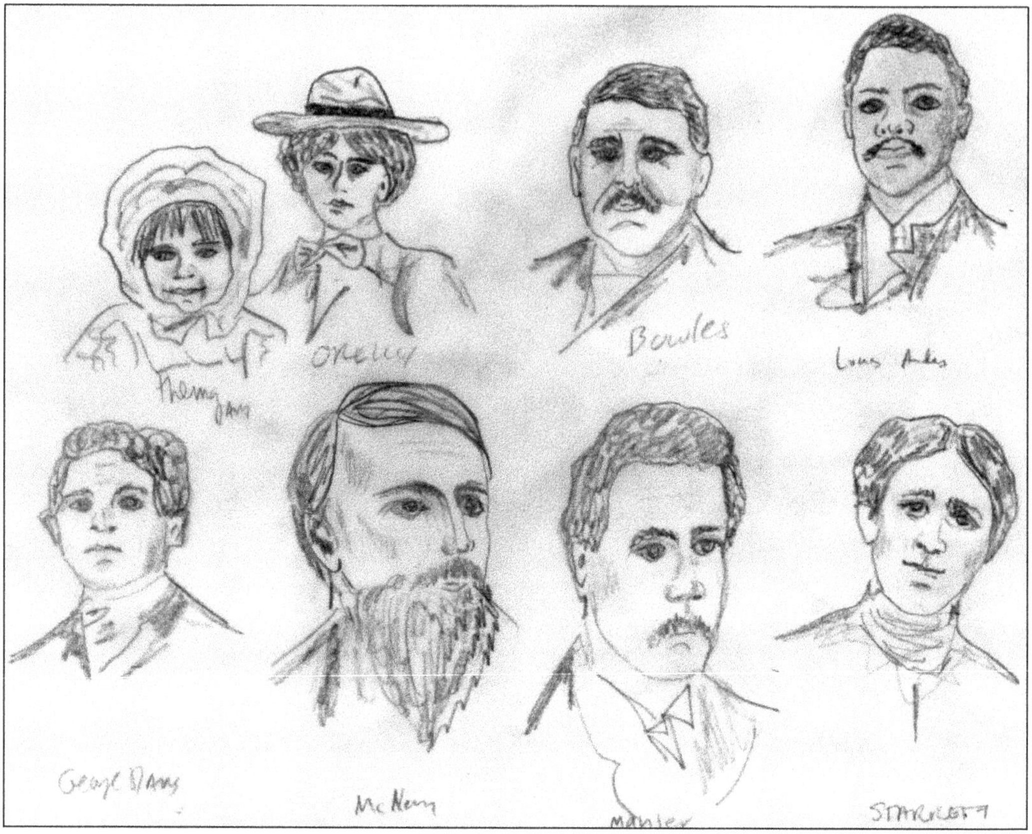

Illustrated here are several passengers and a GN porter; from left to right are (first row) George Davis, James McNeny, Albert Mahler, and Ida Starrett; (second row) Thelma Davis, Catherine O'Reilly, Albert Boles, and Lucius Anderson. Most of the passengers were westbound, headed to Seattle from various places. (Author's collection.)

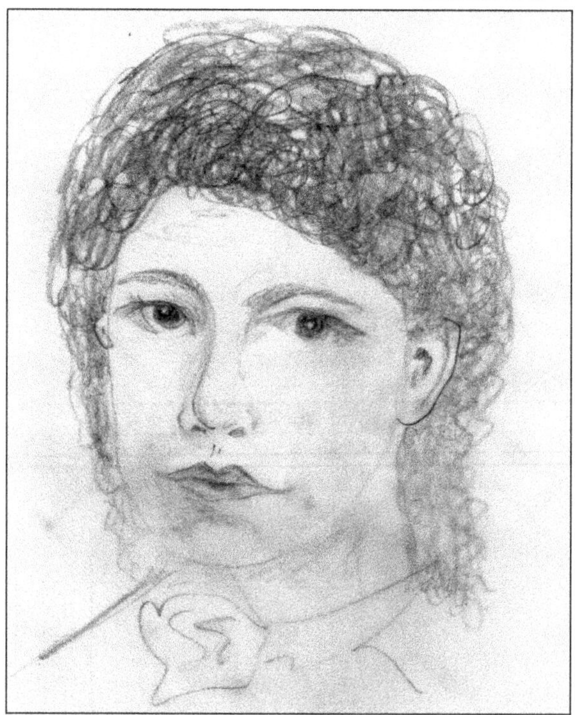

Nellie Sharp was a 26-year-old, high-spirited gal who had big dreams of writing for *McClure's Magazine*. She was recently separated from her husband and was staying with a friend in Spokane, the two women preparing to write articles about the wild west in both Washington and Montana. Her body was found carrying a diamond ring and $100 cash. (Author's collection, from an image courtesy of Karen Frazier.)

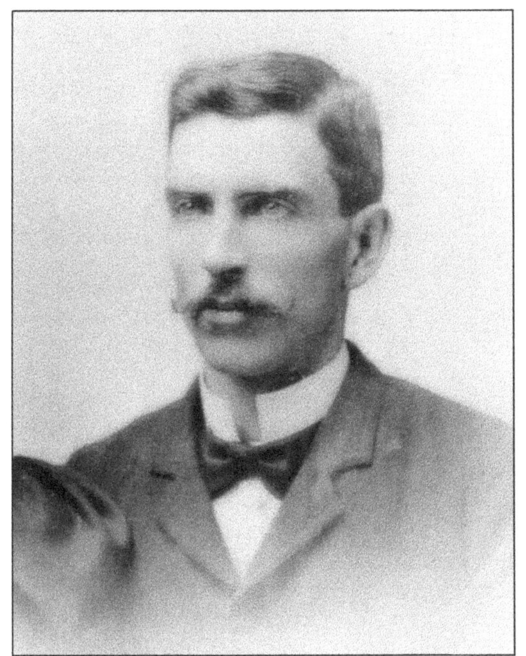

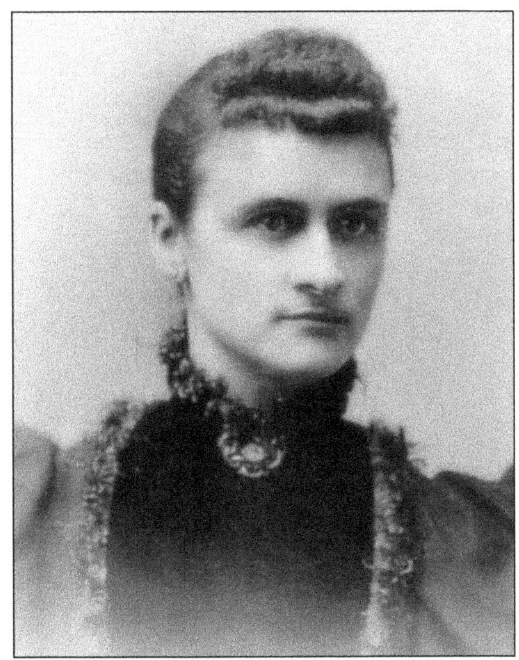

Ada and Edgar Lemman were passengers aboard the Seattle Express No. 25. Edgar tried to rally a meeting in the observation car prior to the disaster to discuss demanding the train be moved back into the tunnel. The men suggested passenger Solomon Cohen be their chairman, but he refused. Conductor Pettit showed up, bringing them food from the hotel and melted snow for water. His offerings did little to offset his bad news that there was no more coal available. The Lemmans' bodies were found together on March 3. Edgar was 47 and Ada was 40. Edgar was a prominent lawyer, and they lived in Hunters, Washington. Their deaths left their teenage daughter in the care of Ada's sister. (Both, courtesy of Laura Mulcahy.)

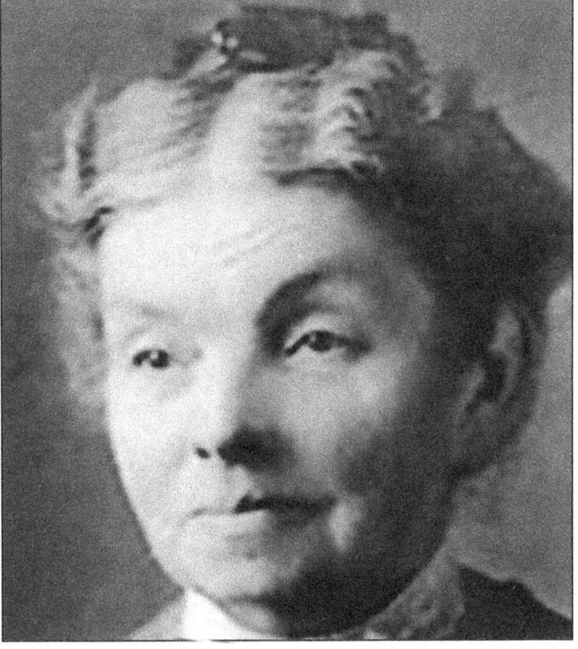

Sarah Covington was 70 years old at the time of the catastrophe and her death. Her diary and letters were found in the snow. One letter reads in part: "I'm with a hundred or so snowbound here . . . No one can tell anything about when we will get out . . . Some are in deadly fear that another landslide will come down on us. . . . A man just came in who had been talking with a woman who has been here 17 years who told him a landslide had never occurred here. We had a service on the cars quite a number present; the reading of Psalm 17 and 27, songs and preaching . . . Another slide reported two killed. A lady borrowed a phonograph and we had some music but people are getting very blue." (Courtesy of the *Seattle Post-Intelligencer.*)

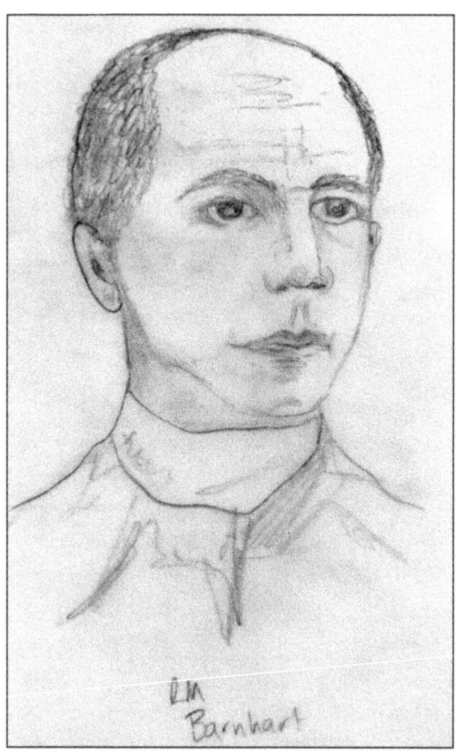

Richard Barnhart was a Spokane lawyer and a passenger on No. 25. He purchased supplies and heavy pants from Bailets Hotel on Sunday, determined to make his way to safety the next day. His plans were in vain as he was dead by morning. Barnhart was only 41 years old and practiced law in Colville. He was one of the best lawyers in the West. This image was published in the *Spokesman Review* on March 4, 1910. (Author's collection.)

A delay turned into a nightmare as the 100-plus passengers became nervous about the snow cap perched high above them. After a few days, problems arose, such as a lack of clean drinking water, sanitation, and food. Pictured are passengers in a Pullman car similar to those used in the trains stuck in Wellington in 1910. (Courtesy of LOC.)

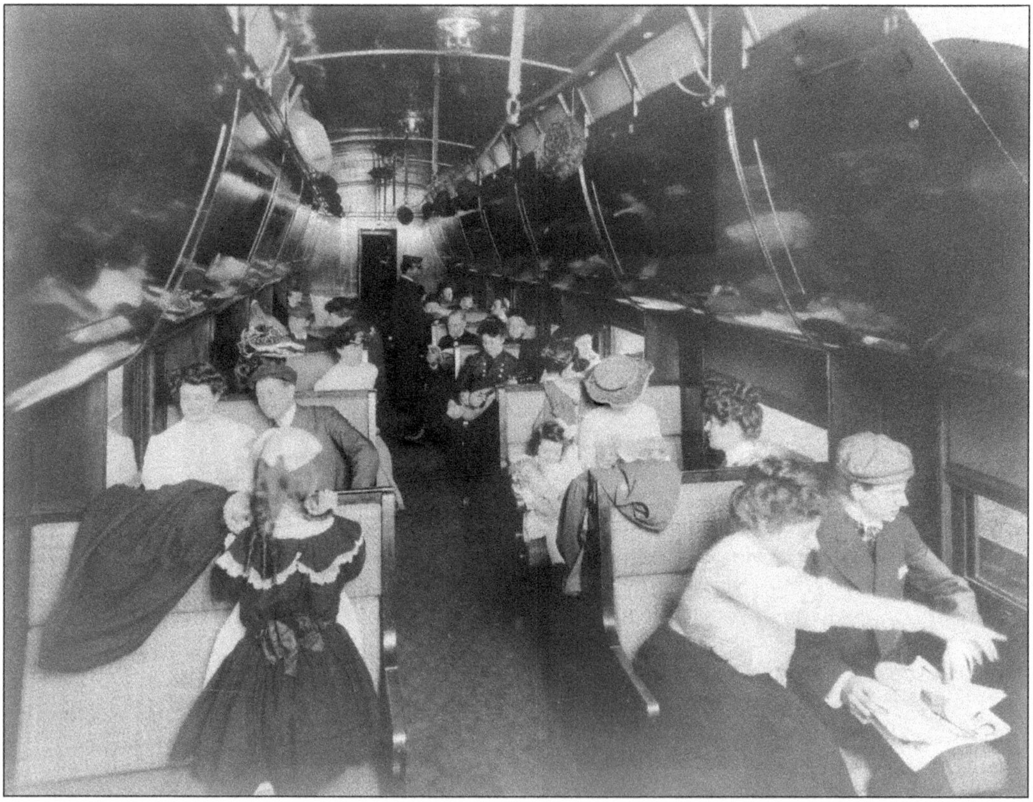

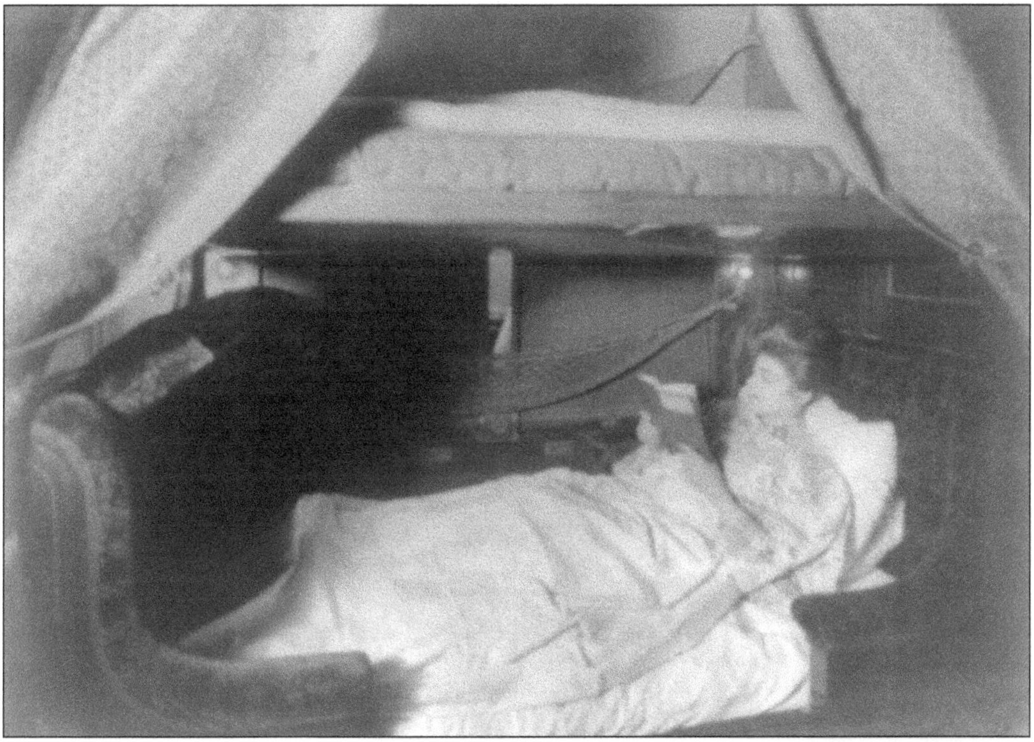

Accommodations on the trains seemed luxurious at first, as seen here. The cars were heated with the last remains of the coal. Most people felt the trains were the safest place, so much so that Susan Bailets and her granddaughter slept on the trains the night before the tragedy. (Courtesy of LOC.)

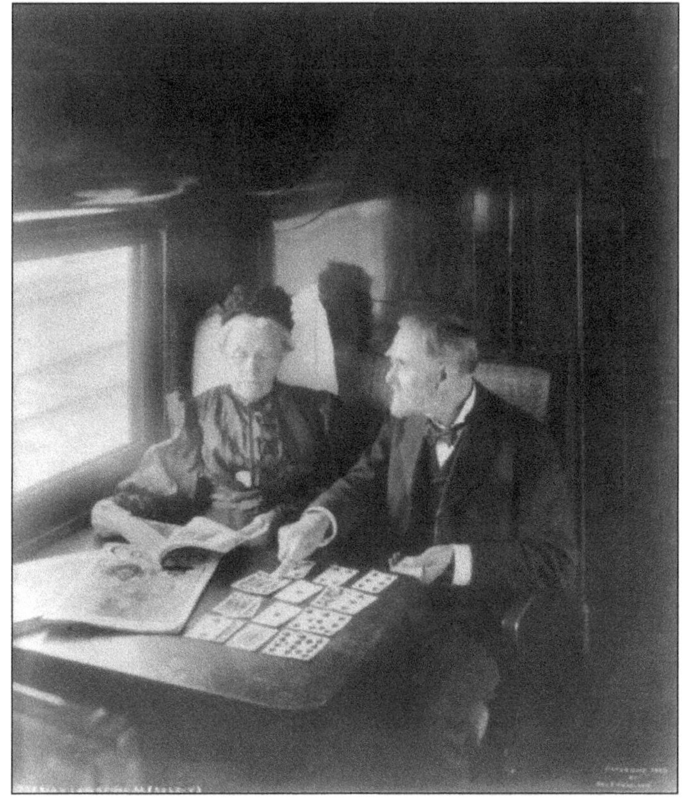

After many hours playing cards together, the passengers grew bored and anxious. On Monday, February 28, the day before the avalanche, they begged the GN crew to move them back into the tunnel for safety. By now, they were down to two meals a day, which consisted of boiled potatoes and bacon. (Courtesy of LOC.)

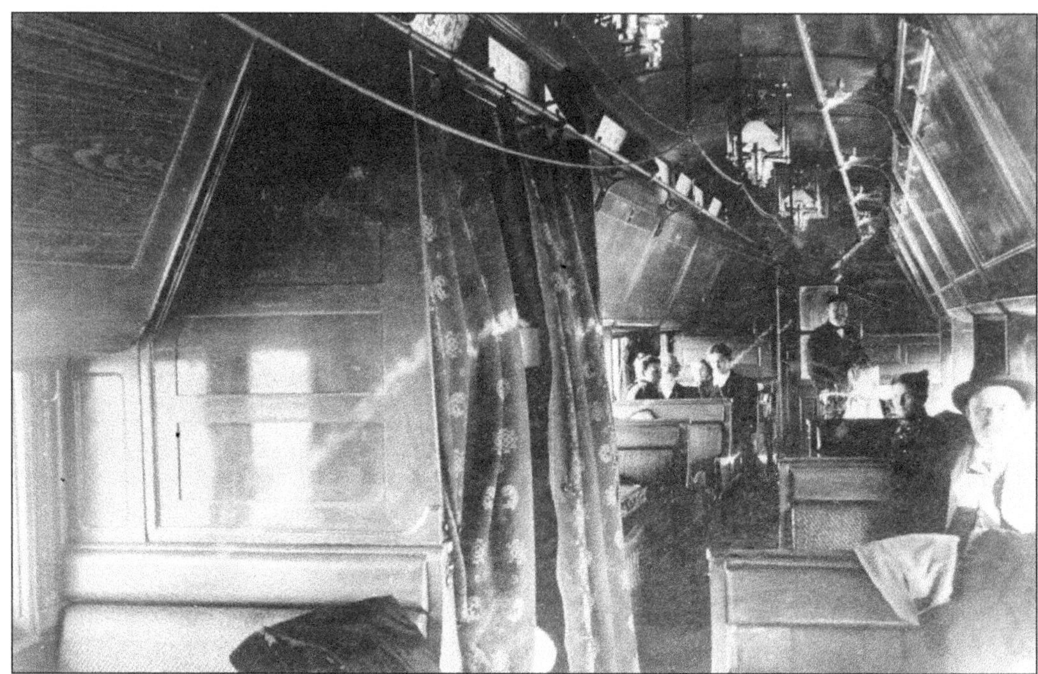

The women made clothes for the children from old dresses to pass the time, and gave each other nicknames. Nellie was "Wild West Girl," Libby Latch was "The Merry Widow," Rogers was "Seattle," and Bethel was "Colonel Cody." Nellie and Libby tried to borrow men's clothes (since their skirts would be too cumbersome in the snow) to escape the train, but did not succeed. These images show the train interiors with unidentified passengers. They wanted to be moved to the perceived safety of the tunnel, but as Alathea Sherlock testified, the snow was the height of a boxcar on the spur tracks near the tunnel, so it would have been impossible to move the trains there after the rotary had headed east. (Both, courtesy of LOC.)

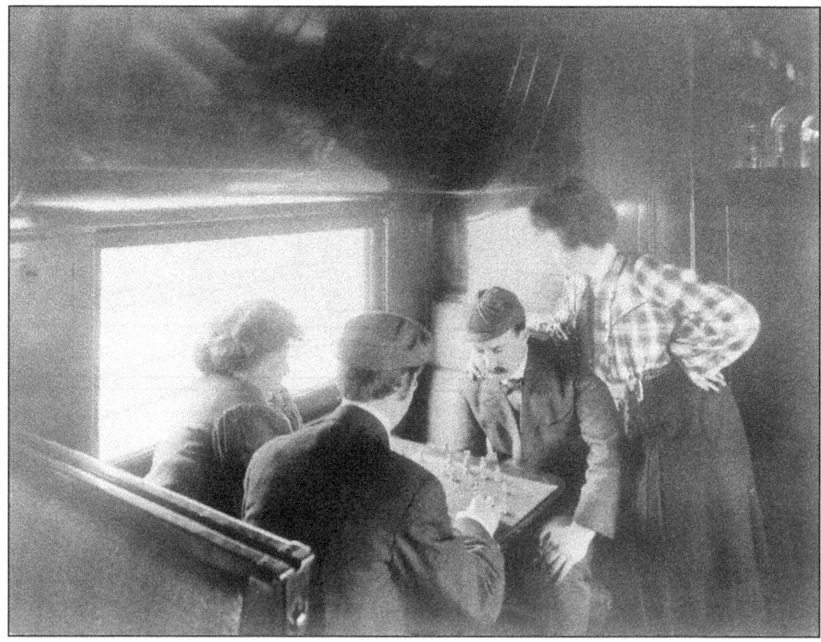

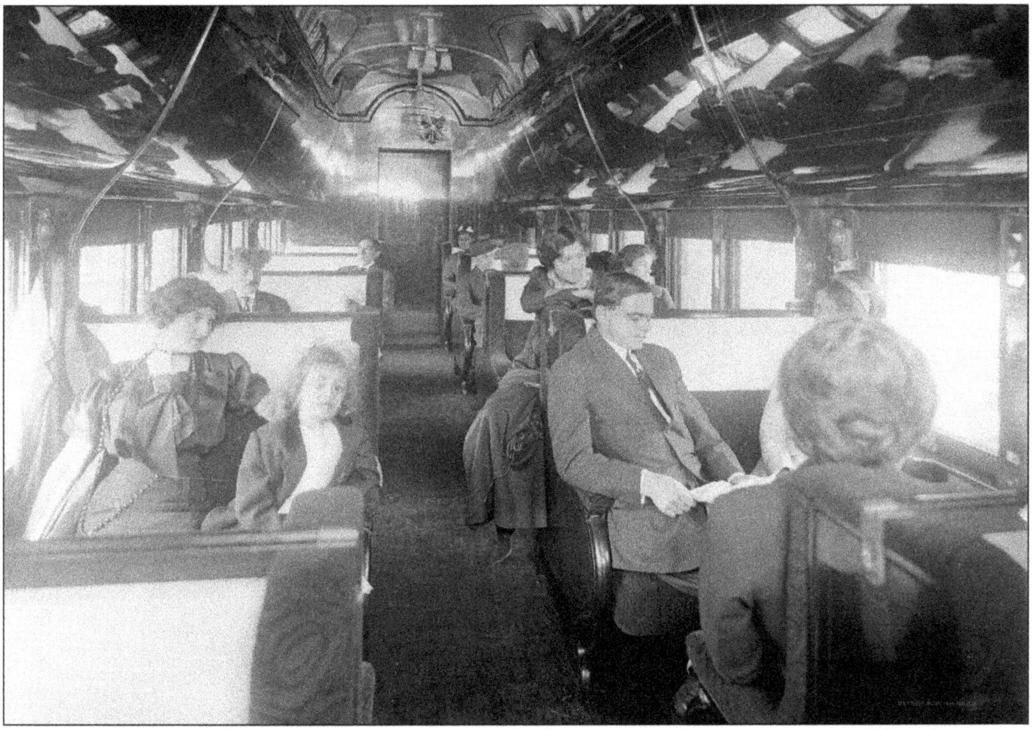

There were three tracks where the trains were parked. Closest to the mountain was O'Neil's car, two boxcars, an engine, and three electric motors; the second held the No. 25 Seattle Express engine, baggage, two coaches, two sleepers, and an observation car. The third had the No. 27. Passengers are seen here relaxing in a Pullman. On February 25, the Friday before the avalanche, passengers approached Conductor Pettit requesting that the trains be moved out from under the snow cap. He calmly explained that the trains were parked in the safest location. (Both, courtesy of LOC.)

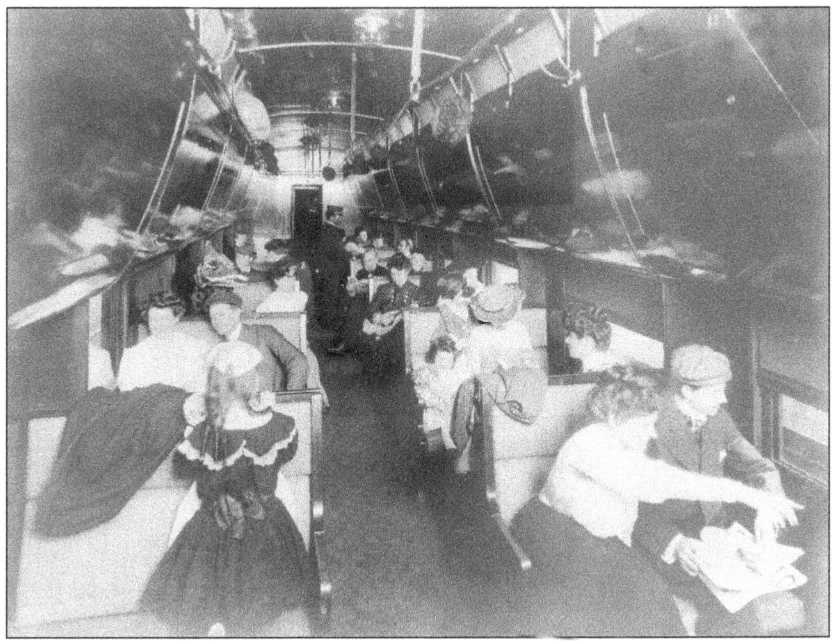

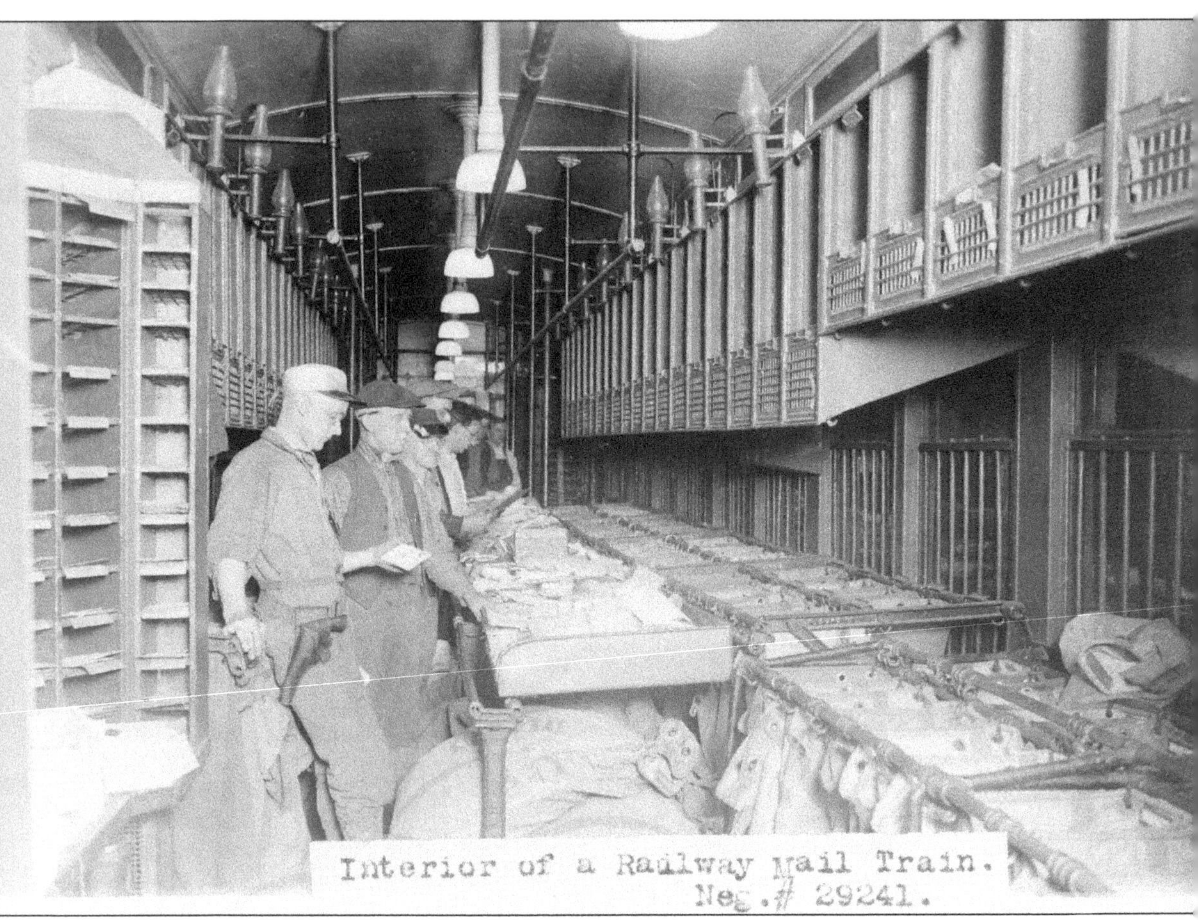

Only one fast mail clerk, Alfred B. Hensel (age 19), survived the tragedy. This example of the interior of a mail car shows workers sorting through the mail. The night of the avalanche, Hensel could not get comfortable in his makeshift bed, so he moved to the other end of the car and prepared a spot to sleep between a few mail crates. The avalanche broke the fast mail car in half, resulting in the other eight men dying instantly, whereas the half Hensel was in was crushed, but he survived with a broken collarbone and a few broken ribs. The car had stopped moving an amazing three inches from his face, and he was rescued barefoot wearing only a nightshirt. The mail cars were finally found on March 6 and 7, and only 150 of the 700 sacks of mail were ever found. Hensel spent 10 days at Wellington before being moved to a hospital in Spokane. (Courtesy of LOC.)

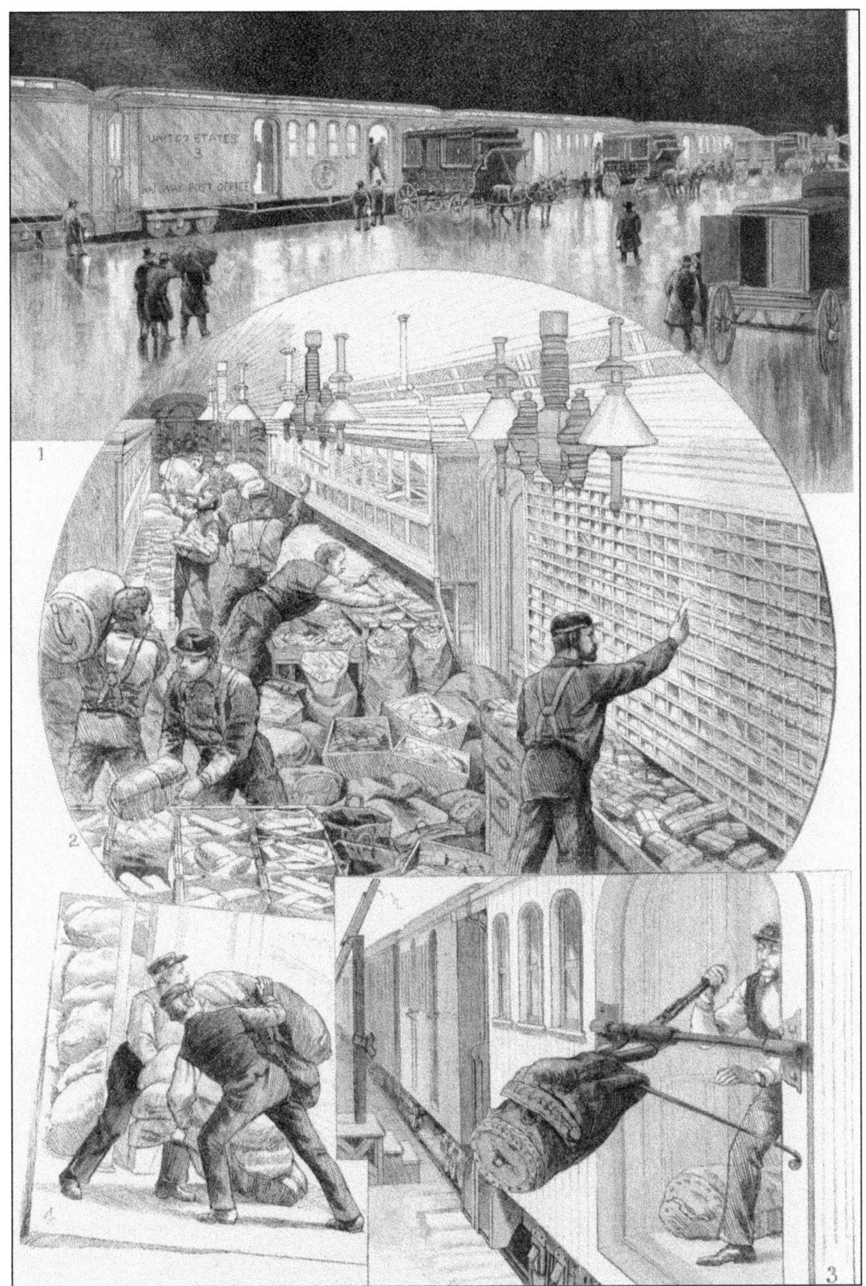

The fast mail service methods of distributing and delivering mail included delivering the mail and newspapers, distributing and sorting the mail, the "catch" as they rolled by a depot to grab mail bags, and the throw-off. Fireman Bates was sleeping in the fast mail car No. 27 during the avalanche. He recalled in the *East Oregonian* issue published on March 3, 1910, "I was under my engine for five hours, it was snowing hard and piling around my head. Twice I gave up and said, 'It's all off,' and then the rescuers came . . . everything was covered in snow and it is hard to tell how many were dead." (Courtesy of LOC.)

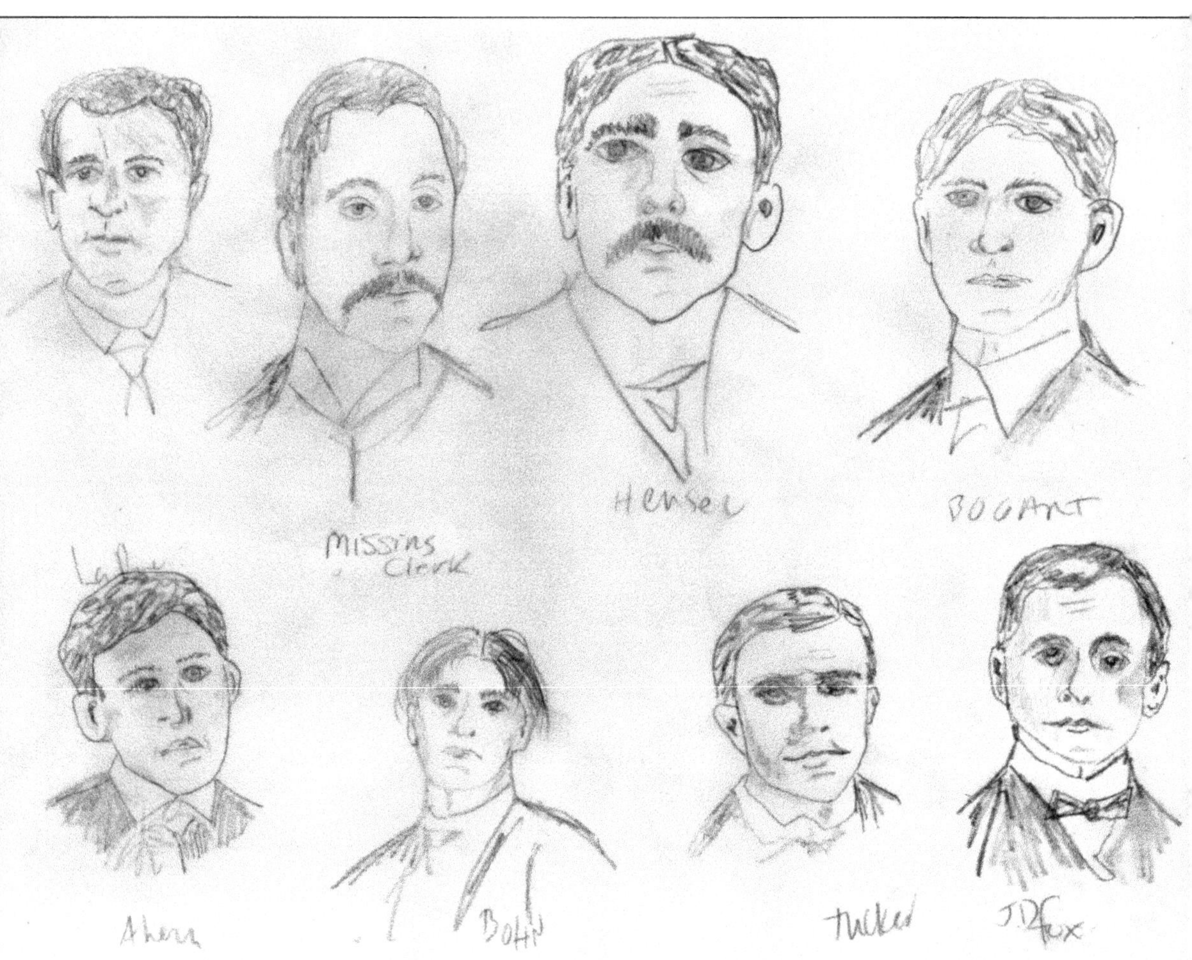

Illustrated here are some of the deceased, as well as the only surviving, fast mail clerks. From left to right are (first row) Lee Ahern, Fred Bohn, John Tucker, and John D. Fox; (second row): Charles La Du(e), an unidentified missing clerk, Alfred B. Hensel (survivor), and Richard Bogart. Fast mail employees George Hoefer and Hiram Towslee were also killed in the disaster. Fast mail conductor Walter Vogel was busy with a rotary at Corea during the slide, so he fortunately escaped harm. The avalanche at Wellington carried approximately 10 acres of wet snow, and the remaining twisted iron debris is evidence of this even today. (Author's collection.)

Seven

The 1910 Disaster and Avalanche

O'Neill had several reasons for not putting the trains back into the tunnel: the possibility of a collision, danger of suffocation, passengers having to walk through the water to get to the hotel for food, and there not being enough coal to both move the trains and heat them, on top of the fact that slides could occur at the mouths of the tunnel, trapping the trains inside.

GN engineer J.C. Wright considered the tunnel the "dirtiest, blackest hole that a man ever went into." Wellington passengers begged for the trains to be moved back into the tunnel, but GN crew members did not forget the 1901 incident killing two of their men. On March 25 of that year, a freight train with two engines moved into the tunnel, but the noxious fumes and gases became so powerful that W.W. Bradley and fireman Wheelon died and the rest were rendered unconscious.

When Pat Ryan, GN laborer of 18 years and a Wellington/Alvin track walker, was asked about the tunnel, he replied, "Well, there have been quite a lot of people killed in there with gas and they suffocated and were killed."

O'Neill really had no choice but to keep the passengers away from the tunnel.

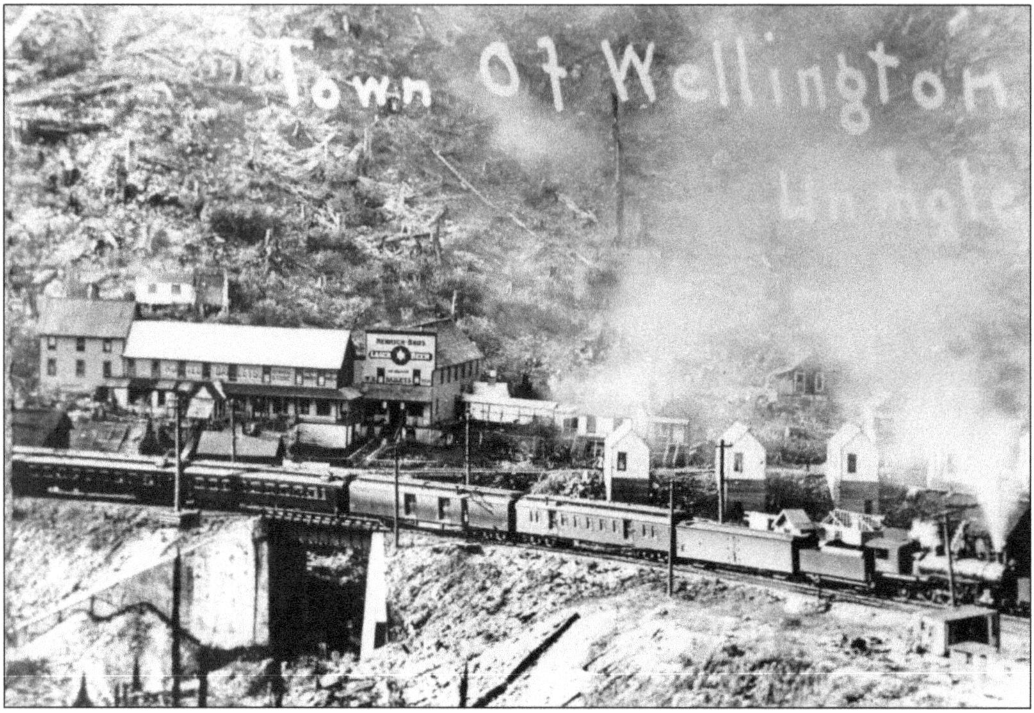

A train rolls peacefully through Wellington in 1910, prior to the avalanche that destroyed part of the town. The concrete bridge wing walls (bottom left) were built so the train could go over Haskell Creek. Bailets Hotel and the tavern are in the background as well as other buildings and cottages. (Courtesy of SHS.)

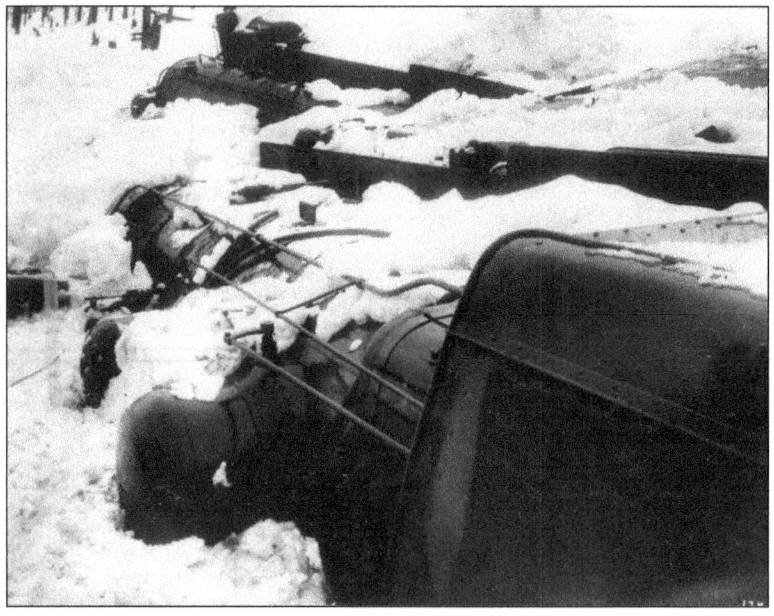

Mackey, a traveling engineer who walked to Scenic with word of the disaster, testified, "I may say that every man and woman in Wellington was up and they had the women at the hospital caring for the wounded, and every man that I knew was doing all they could to rescue the injured." Here, a derailed locomotive lies among timbers and mounds of snow. (Courtesy of WVM, 87-142-10.)

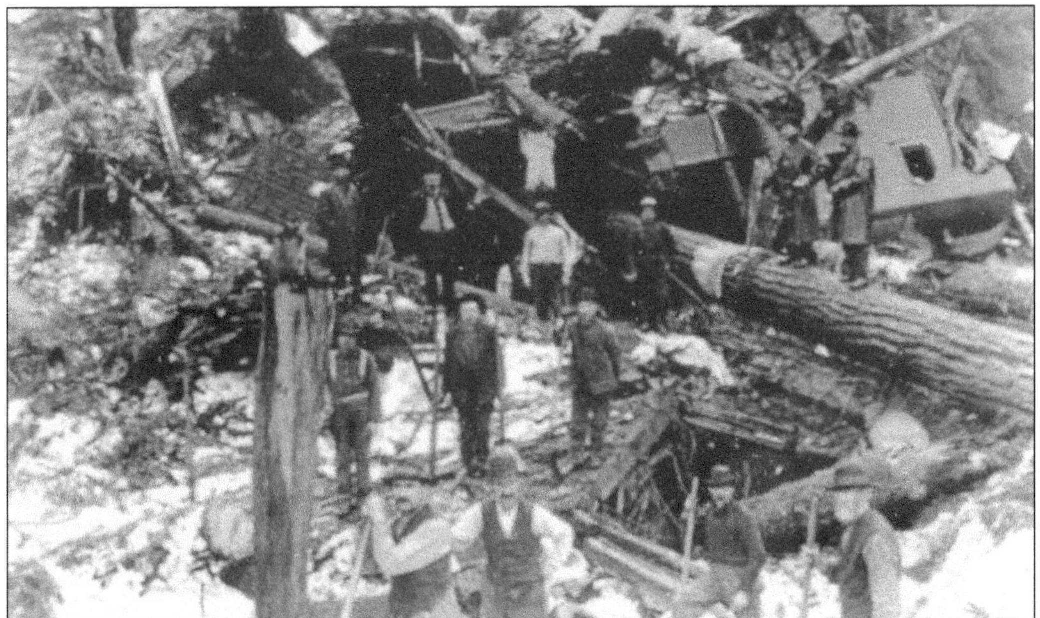

Wellington resident H.R. DeLaplin remarked in the *Oregonian* on March 4, 1910, "I have seen engines and rotary snowplows thrown over many times by slides, but a slide capable of carrying two trains over a cliff must have been an immense avalanche—the greatest in the history of mountain railroading." The men estimated that the avalanche weighed around half a million tons. (Courtesy of Jerrold F. Hilton.)

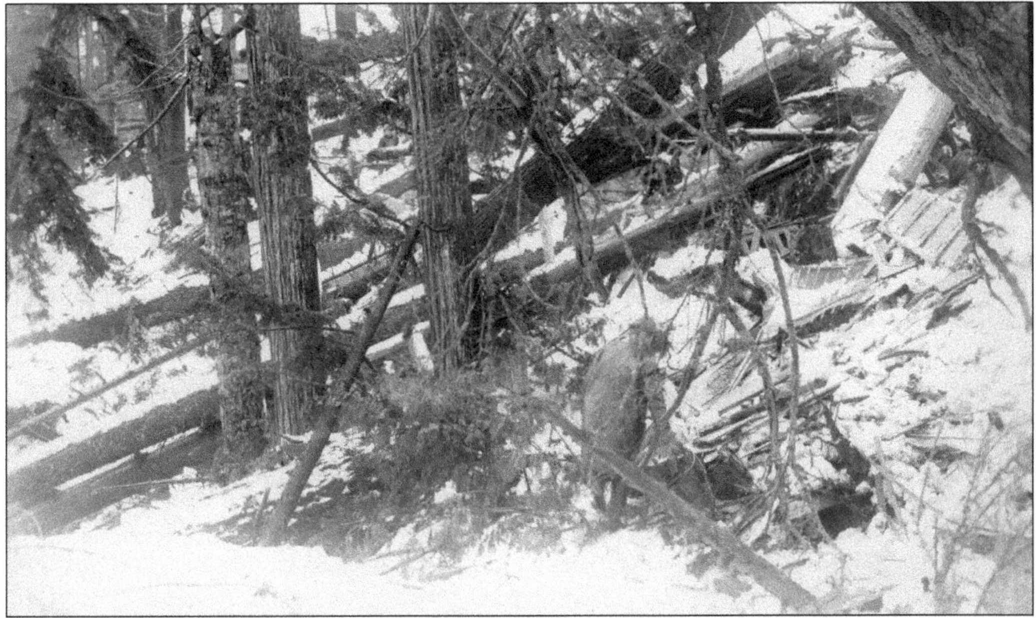

Workers slowly sort through the debris from the wreck. From Scenic, passenger Rogers watched Pettit write a telegram that read, "Tell passengers they can come over the trail," but it never went through. Pettit trudged back to the stalled trains to offer his help. He would have avoided his death if he had stayed at Scenic instead. He was well liked by all, and tragically left behind his wife and five small children. (Courtesy of EPL.)

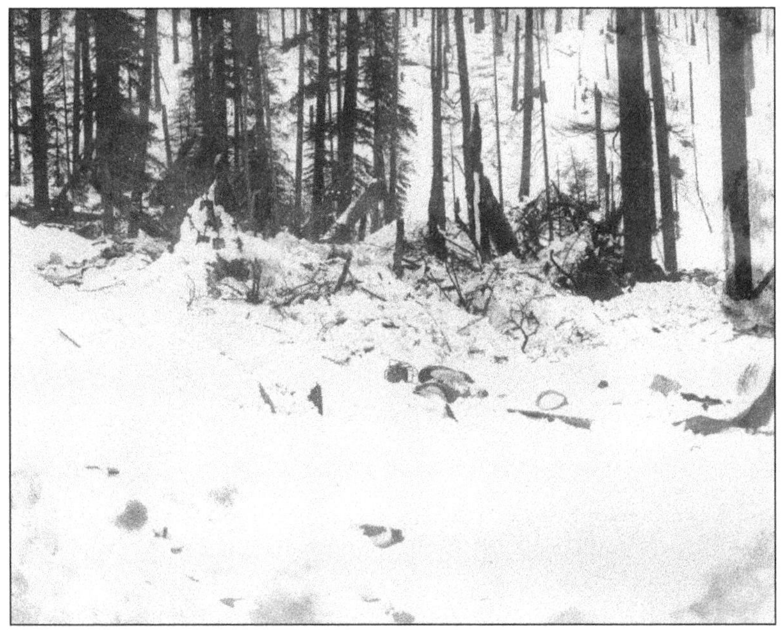

The snow was piled almost 40 feet in the ravine, making rescue efforts almost futile. The men used long sticks to poke into the snow until the pole hit something hard, and then they would call out and listen for a response. Mail orders and registered mail from No. 27 (as well as personal items from the passengers) were guarded by government officials. (Courtesy of EPL.)

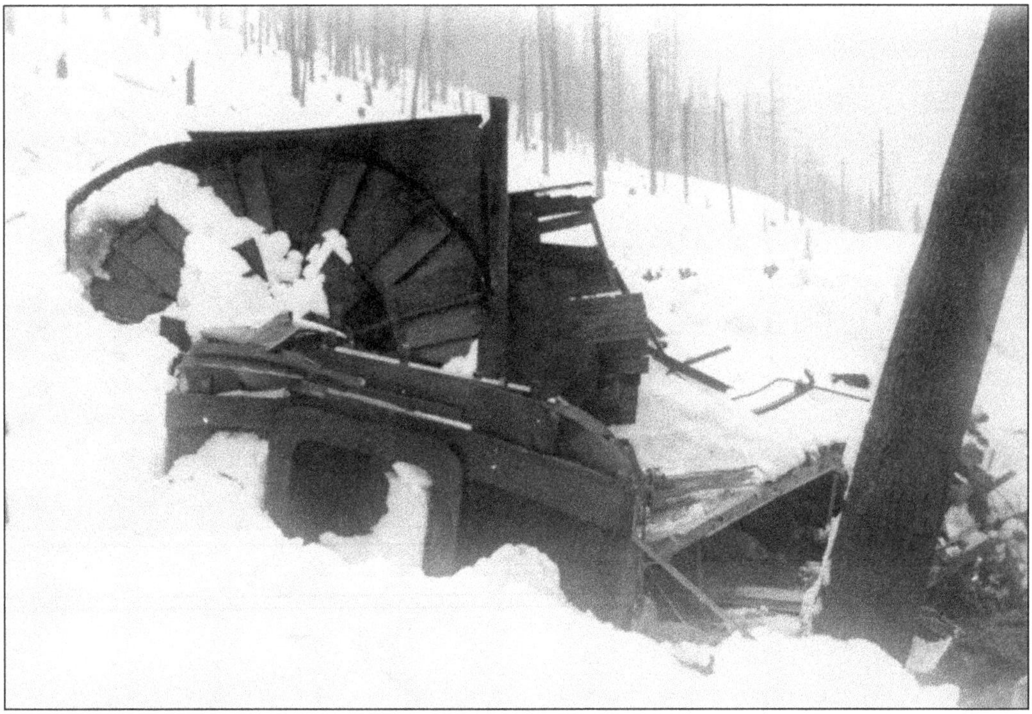

Pictured is rotary plow X807, which was swept into the canyon below during the avalanche. The rotaries were a marvel, but no match for the constant snowfall. The Snow King, William Harrington, endured another slide at Corea in the 1915 storm. The 1915 slide hit the train and killed eight people and injured another 22 passengers. The Corea Station was the first station east of Scenic. (Courtesy of EPL.)

Many GN men wept when the bodies of Earl Longcoy (O'Neill's secretary) and Lewis Walker (his steward) were discovered in the A-16 car at 1:00 p.m. that day. The car had been shoved off the tracks yet covered by so much snow, they could not find it. (Courtesy of EPL.)

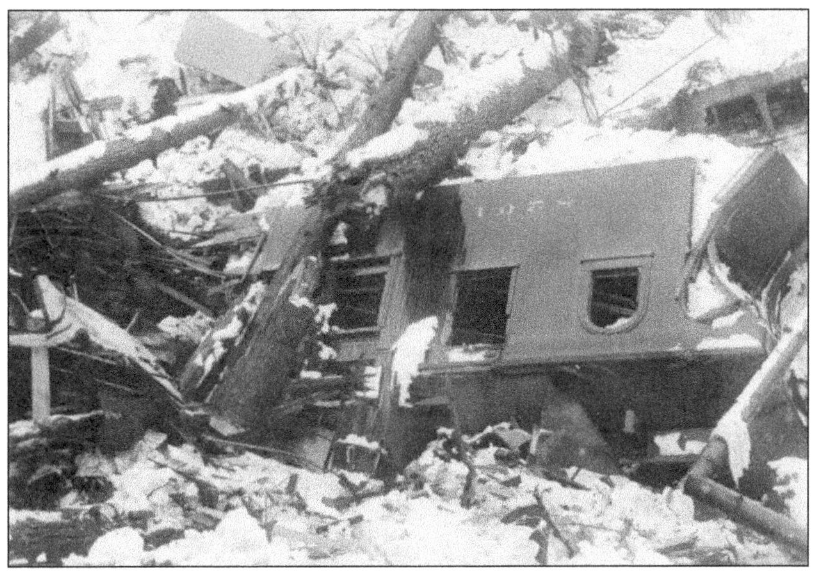

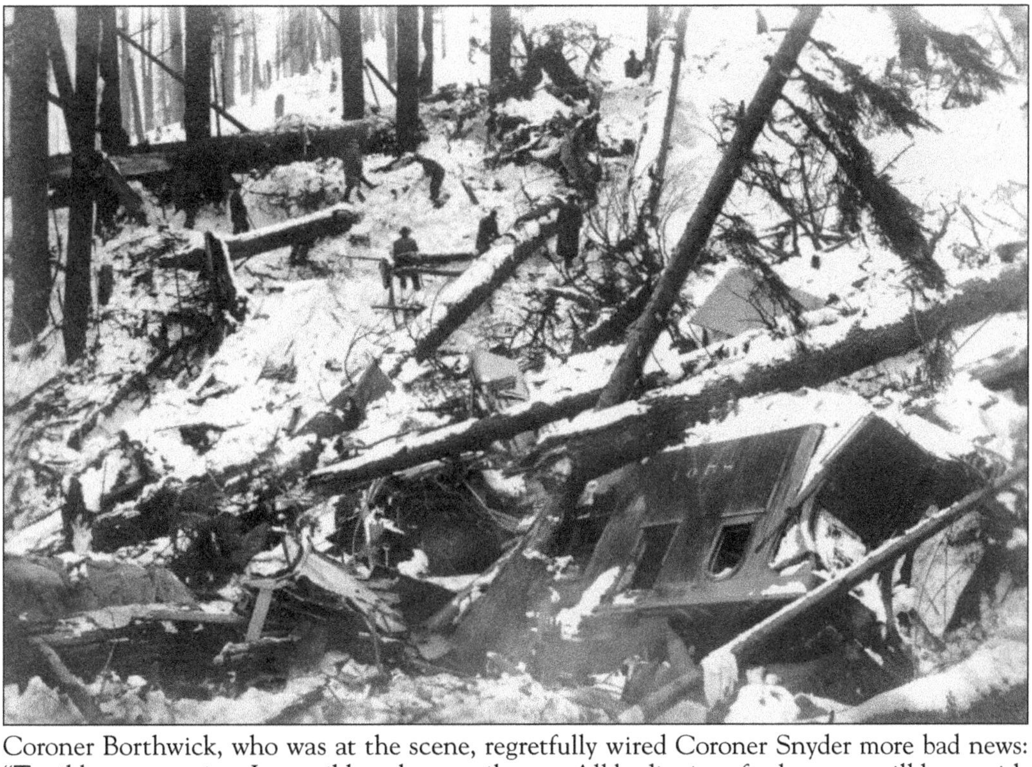

Coroner Borthwick, who was at the scene, regretfully wired Coroner Snyder more bad news: "Terrible storm raging. Impossible to keep trail open. All bodies in safe places . . . will leave with 18 more bodies as soon as possible." When the smoking car was finally located on March 7, it was almost impossible to determine how many people had been inside it. (Courtesy of EPL.)

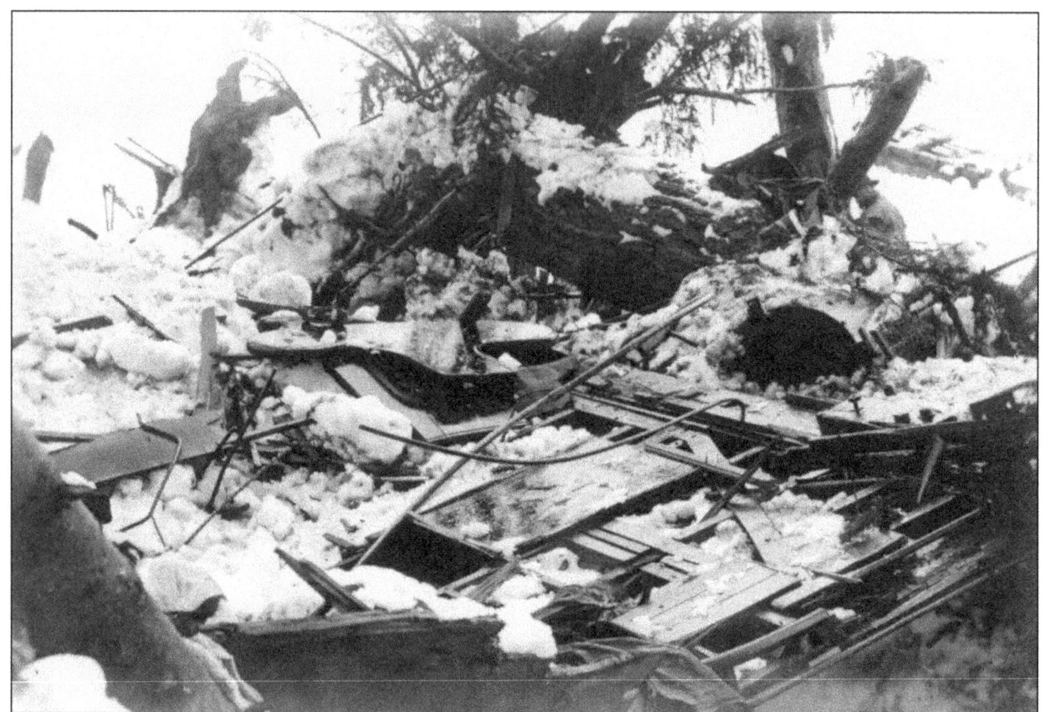

The night before the avalanche, passengers demanded guides and ropes from the GN in order to leave the trains and get to Scenic. Blackburn calmly told them that eight guides would be ready to help them out first thing in the morning, but that no women, children, or invalids could leave the trains, and if they did, Great Northern was not responsible for their safety. (Courtesy of EPL.)

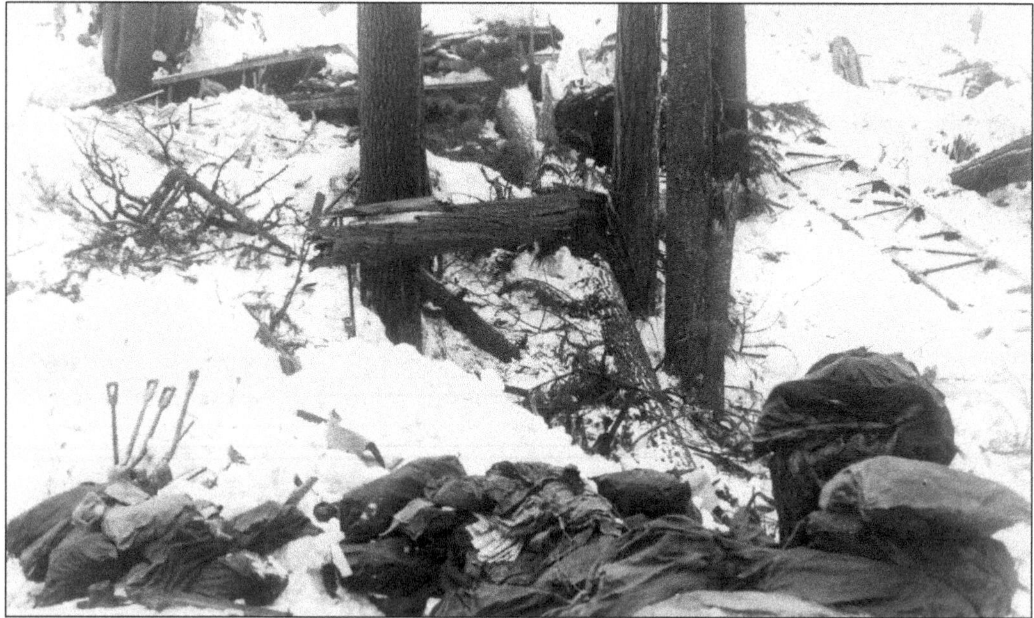

Rescuers' shovels are stuck near the mail sacks as men returned to using long poles to search for more objects under the snow. The night of the disaster, men grabbed axes and lanterns and ran to the ravine and looked for bloody hands poking out of the snow. (Courtesy of EPL.)

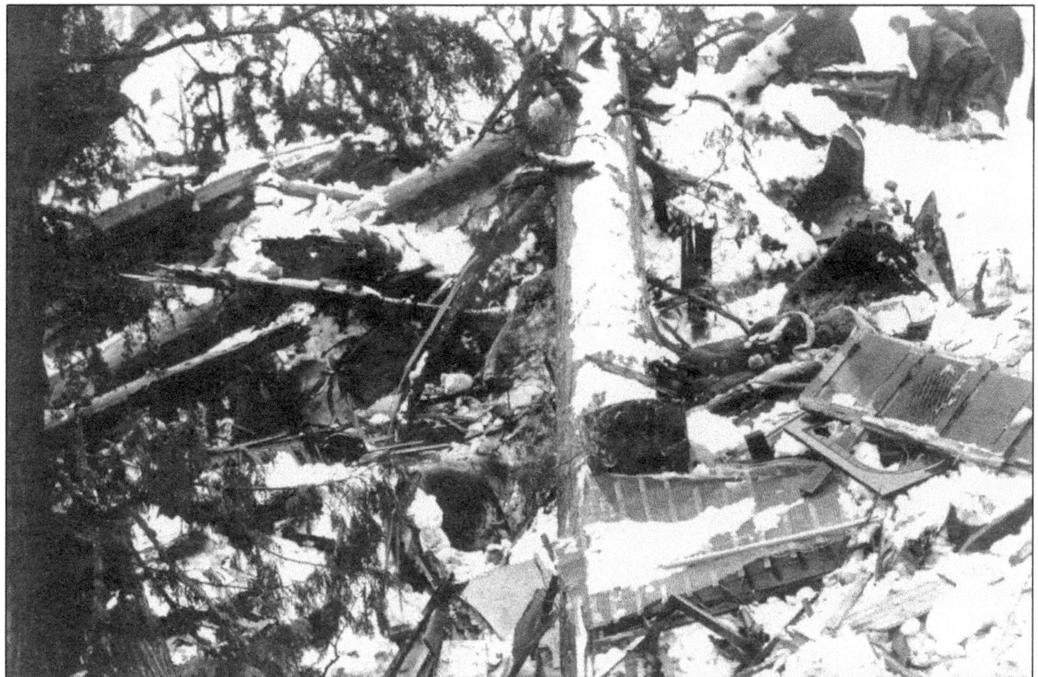

Ida Starrett was traveling with her three children and parents, Mr. and Mrs. William May. Although she and her son Raymond (found with the stick in his forehead) survived, her son Francis (eight months old) and her daughter Lillian (nine years old) died. Ida was pinned beneath a tree trunk for 11 hours before she was found. She was almost frozen to death. (Courtesy of EPL.)

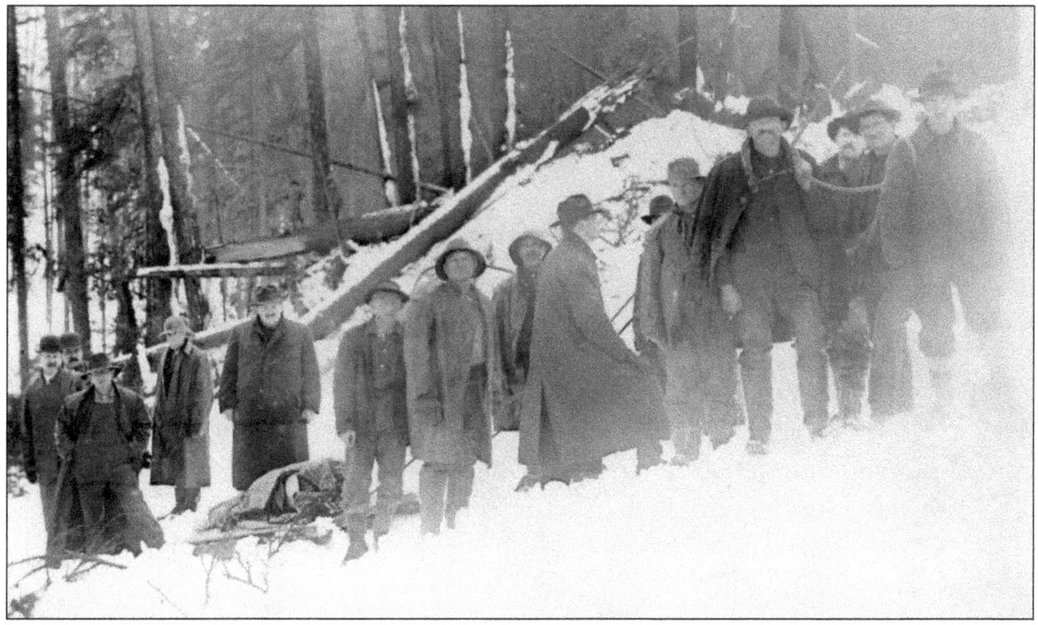

Rescuers wrapped bodies in checkered blankets and hauled them up and stacked them. They dragged the bodies on sleds for miles until they could be hoisted down a slope (Dead Man's Slide) to Scenic. The rope was tied to their feet, and the bodies were lowered head first to the men below, where the bodies would be loaded into a train. (Courtesy of EPL.)

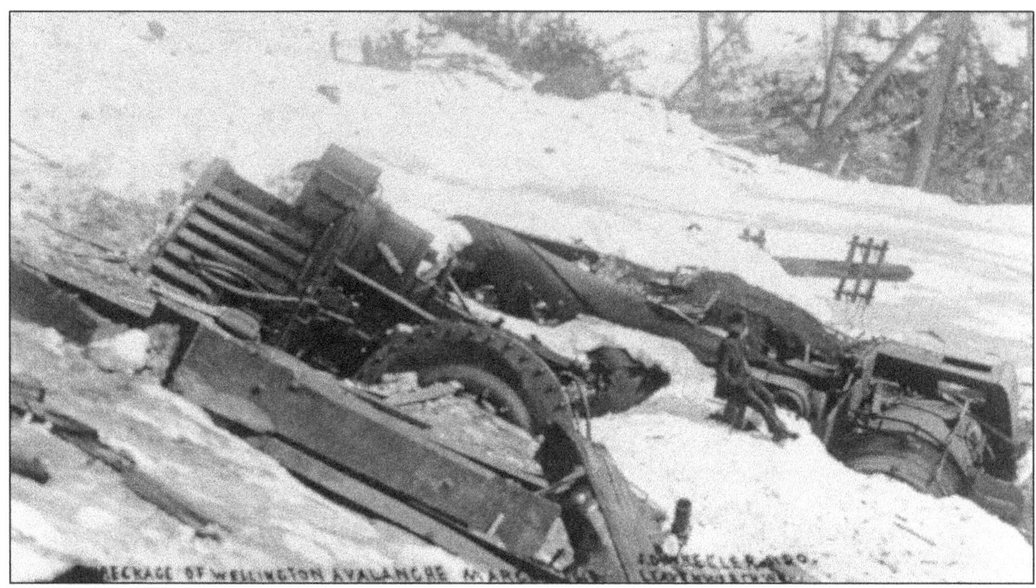
A medical team consisting of a GN physician, Dr. W.C. Cox, Dr. H.P. Howard, Dr. James Chisholm, and nurses Leonora Todhunter and Annabelle Lee (wearing men's clothes for protection) were ready to help. Others, such as Dr. J.A. Durrent from Snohomish, Dr. Gehrken from Monroe, and Dr. E.C. Greason from Skykomish were also eager to provide assistance. (Courtesy of the J.D. Wheeler Collection, SHS.)

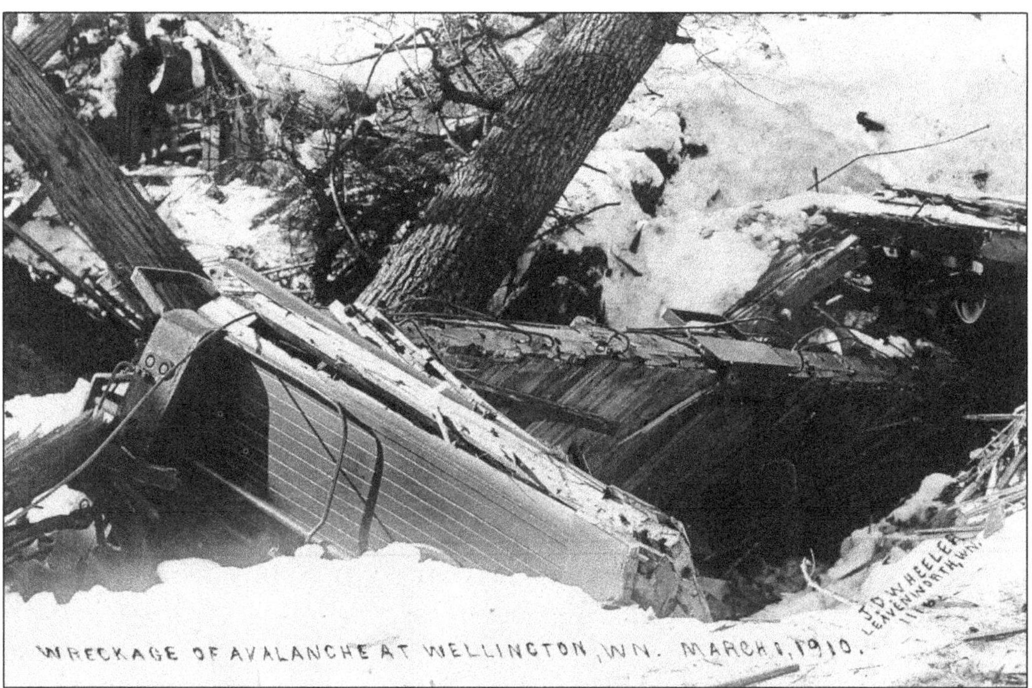

With telegraph wires down, communication became impossible. John Wentzel carried news to Scenic. Exhausted from walking, he yelled, "All gone, they're all gone!" It was all he could manage to blurt out. Men who were willing to help were almost useless, as they could hardly even get to Wellington due to the snow. (Courtesy of the J.D. Wheeler Collection, SHS.)

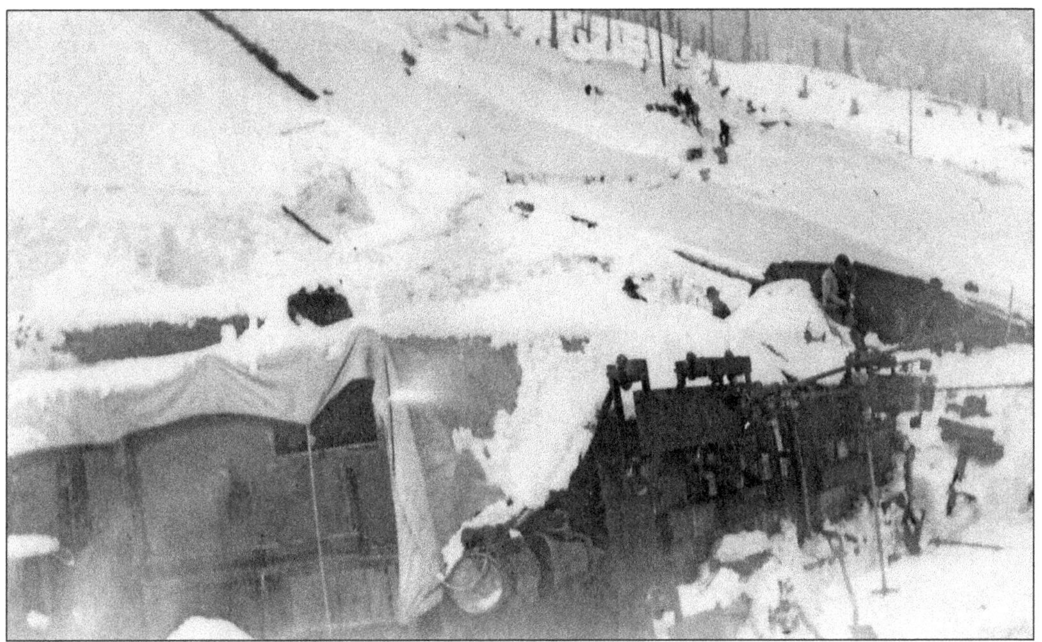

Rescuers pull bodies from the wreckage up the trail (wrapped in blankets, at top center) with ropes, to later be lowered down the slope to Scenic. Chelan County sheriff J.E. Ferguson from Wenatchee offered help, along with Jon Polson, who was in charge of removing the bodies from Wellington to send to the Butterworth & Sons Morgue of Seattle. (Photograph by J.D. Wheeler, courtesy of Hensel Collection, SHS.)

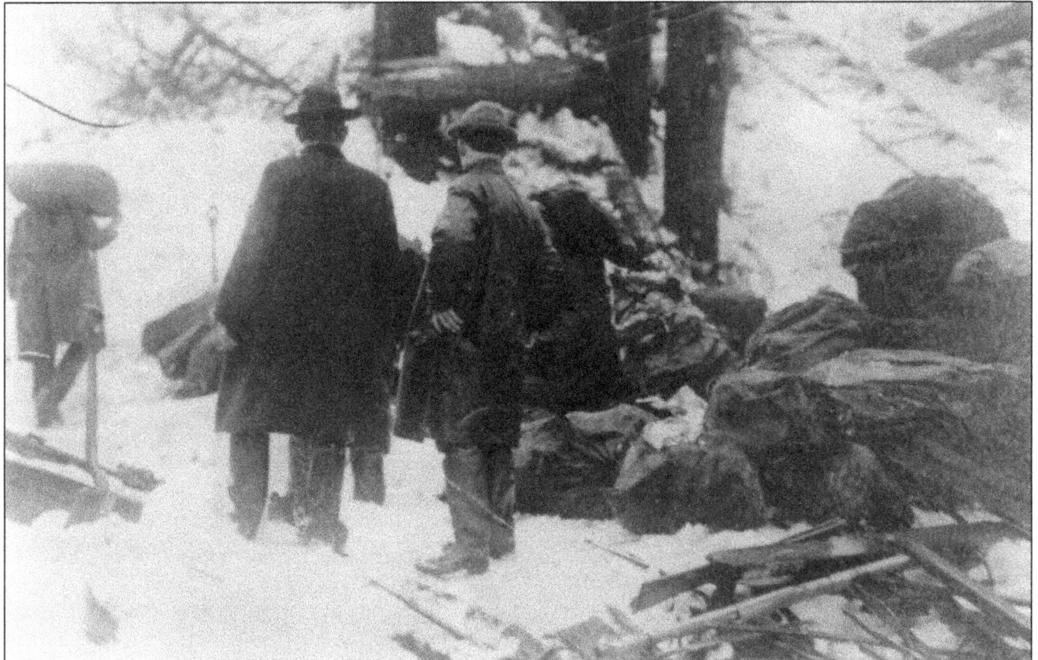

Rescuers sort through baggage, bags of mail, and other debris from the wreckage. More relief doctors soon came from both Snohomish and Everett, and had to hike 10 miles in snowshoes to get to Wellington. (Photograph by J.D. Wheeler, courtesy of Hensel Collection, SHS.)

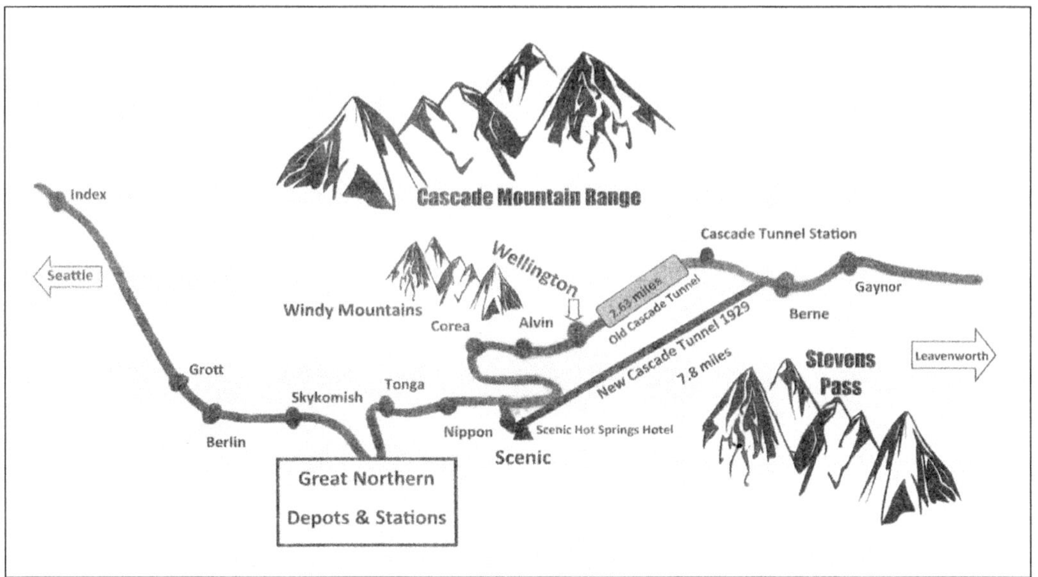

This map shows some of the GN depots and stations, as well as a few of the small towns that were contributors to the Wellington story. It also indicates the locations of the two tunnels and their lengths. The old Cascade Tunnel can be explored on foot at the Iron Goat Trail off Highway 2 near Stevens Pass, mile marker 63. The new Cascade Tunnel is still in use today. (Author's collection.)

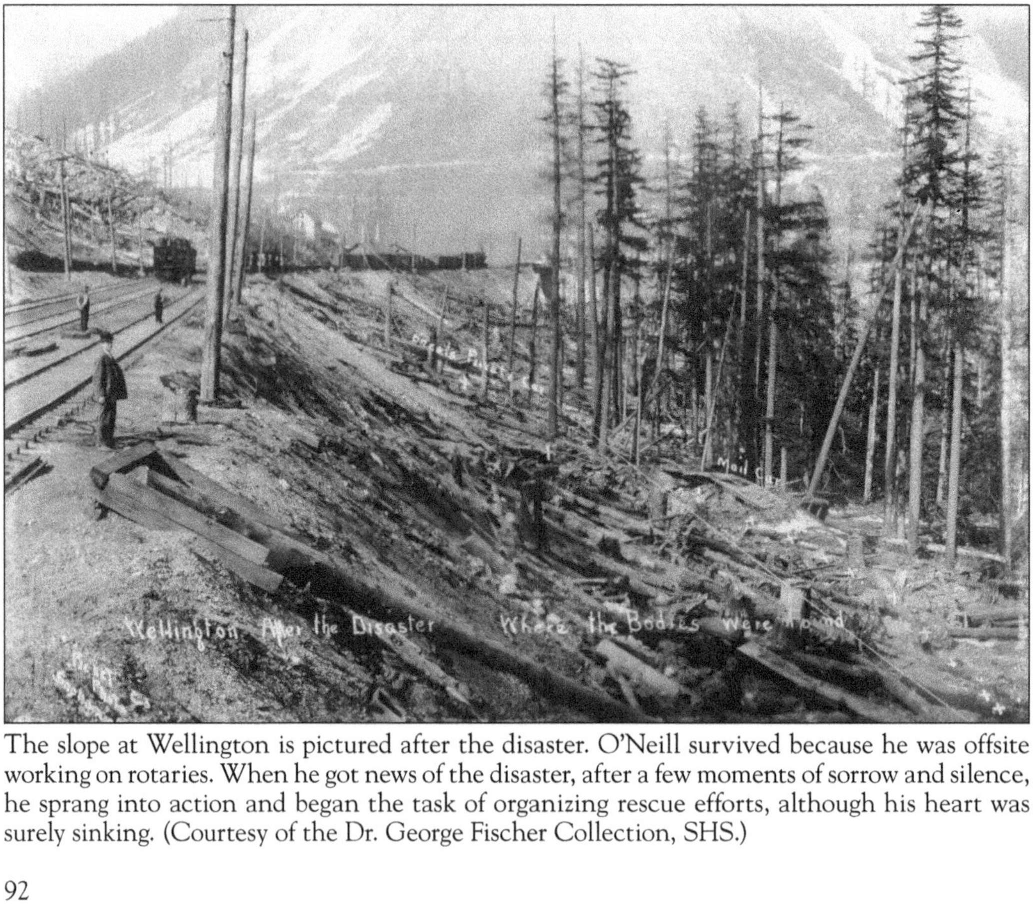

The slope at Wellington is pictured after the disaster. O'Neill survived because he was offsite working on rotaries. When he got news of the disaster, after a few moments of sorrow and silence, he sprang into action and began the task of organizing rescue efforts, although his heart was surely sinking. (Courtesy of the Dr. George Fischer Collection, SHS.)

Men help with rescue efforts by digging into the deep snow several days after the avalanche. One can be seen at the bottom with snow up to his neck. The men are digging pits to place black powder in to explode and loosen the snow. (Photograph by J.D. Wheeler, courtesy of SHS, Hensel Collection.)

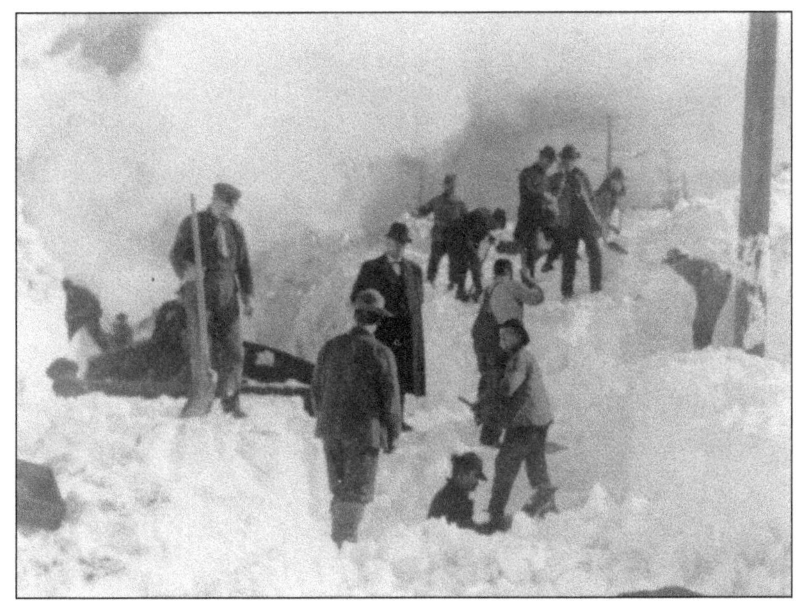

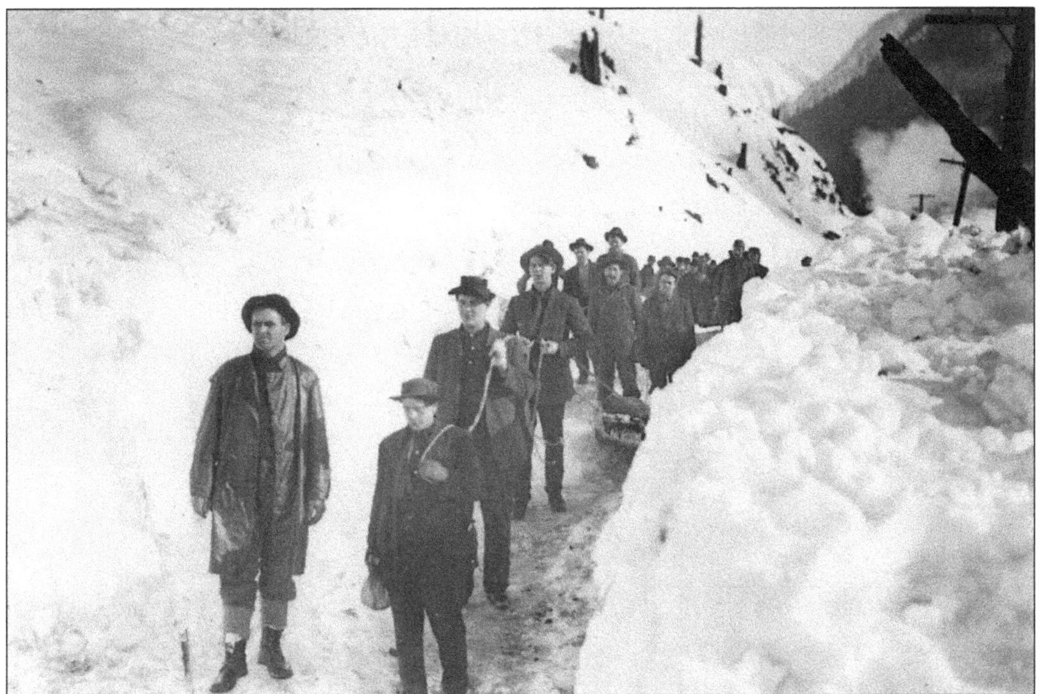

Men are pulling bodies out in sleds using long ropes. Before the disaster, on Saturday, February 26, another slide fell at snowshed 3 that was 800 feet wide, 35 feet deep, and full of green timber, which meant it had to be cleared by hand. All the rotaries were out of commission. One was disabled, two were stalled between other slides, and the fourth was stuck at the east end of the tunnel. (Photograph by J.D. Wheeler, courtesy of SHS, Hensel Collection.)

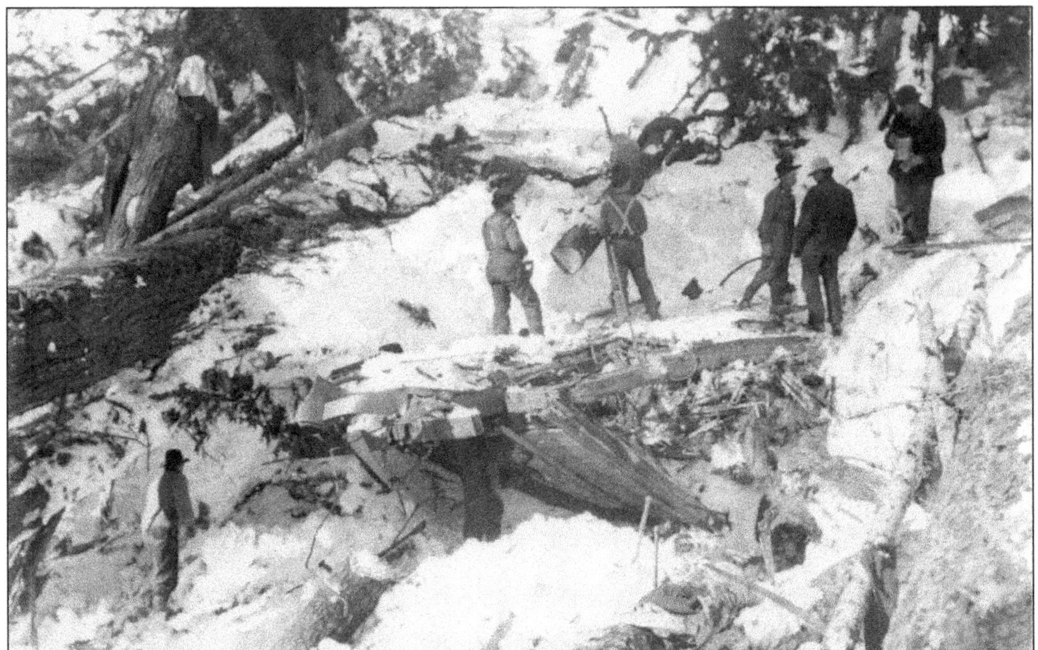

A rescue team searches for more victims. On March 4, twelve more bodies were found, including conductor J.M. Parzybok as well as four unidentified mail clerks and the Beck family. The final body, that of 23-year-old brakeman Archibald McDonald, was found months later. (Courtesy of the Jerrold F. Hilton Collection, SHS.)

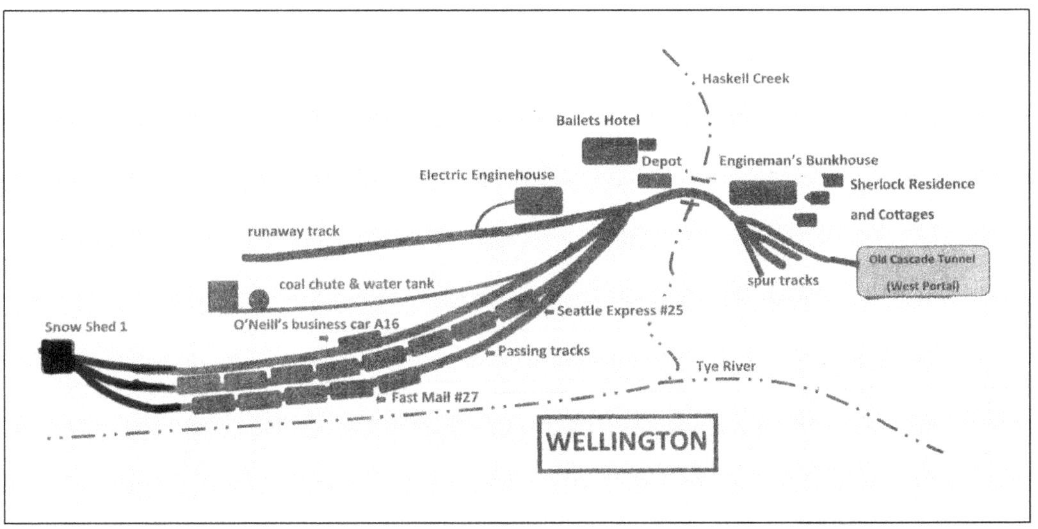

This illustration shows the approximate locations of buildings, tracks, and railway cars before the avalanche. The fast mail was parked on the passing track closest to the ravine, the Seattle Express was on the middle track, and James O'Neill's business car was parked on the track closest to the mountain. (Author's collection.)

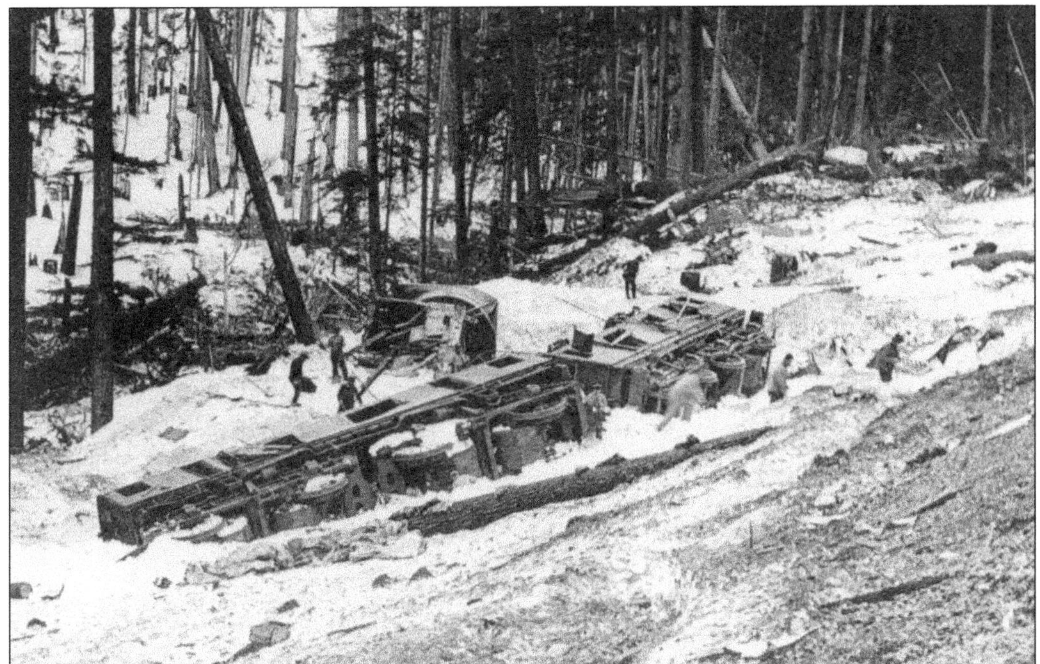

A GN electric locomotive is shown lying on its side down in the gully with the car still attached as rescuers carefully search through the debris. During this already horrendous and stressful accident, the fact that the telegraph lines were down again did not help the situation. (Courtesy of the Jerry Quinn Collection, SHS.)

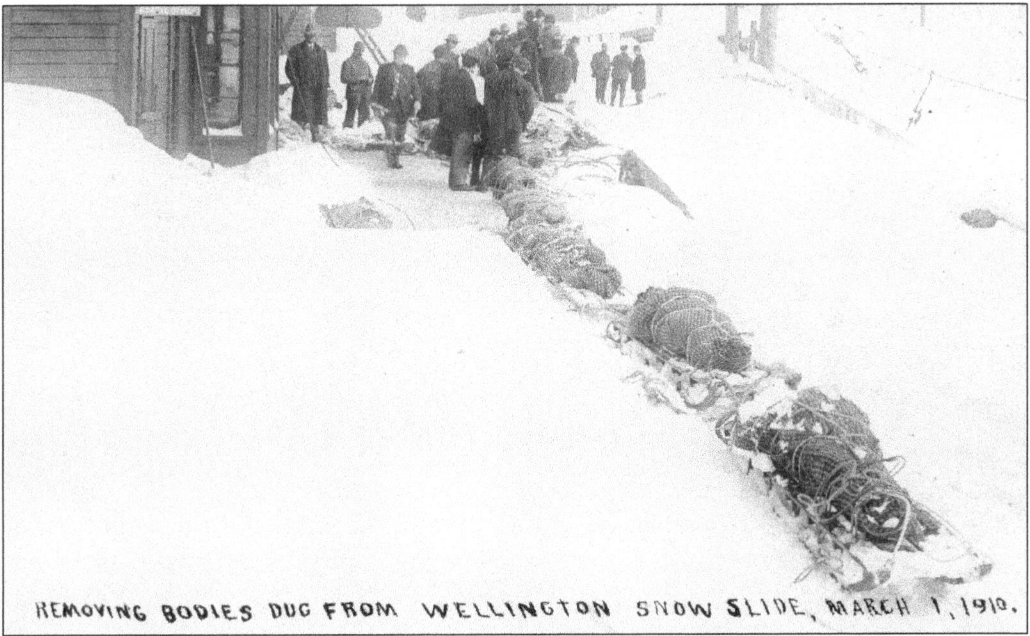

Since the avalanche took place at 1:42 a.m., most passengers were dressed in only their nightclothes. Any survivors who escaped by their own accord were dazed and confused, walking aimlessly, bleeding and half-naked in the storm. Victims are seen here lined up outside the Western Union office. (Courtesy of EPL.)

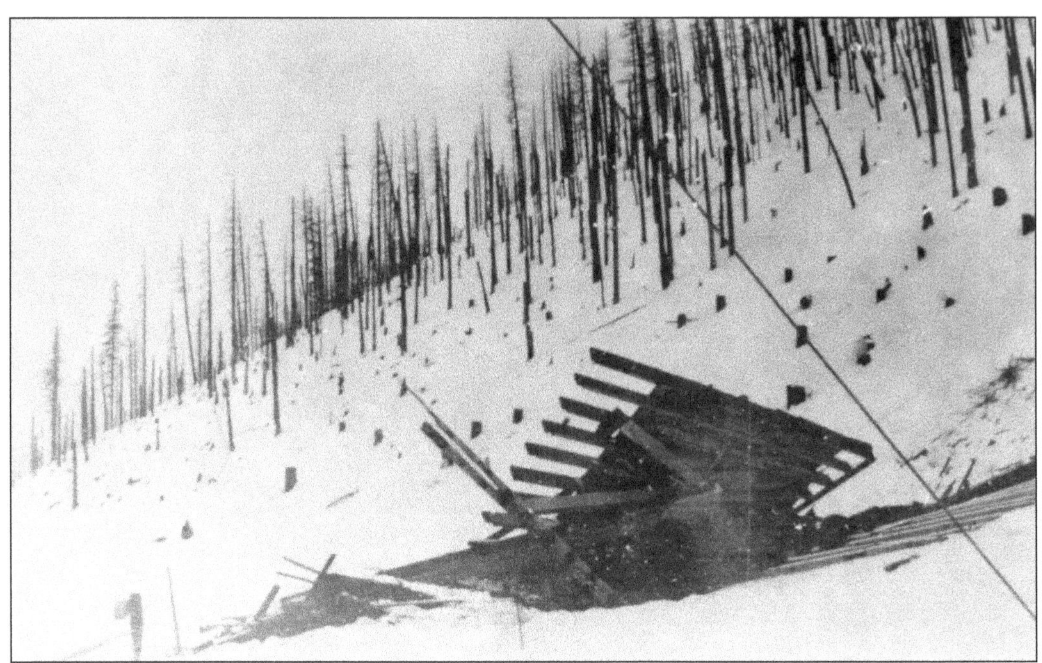

The remains of a building are pictured near the motor shed at Wellington. A coded telegram sent to Louis Hill, president of Great Northern, by H.H. Parkhouse, a GN official on the scene at Wellington on March 4, reported, "So far as loss of life and damage to property is concerned, I believe this is the worst experience we have had." (Courtesy of WVM, 87-142-37.)

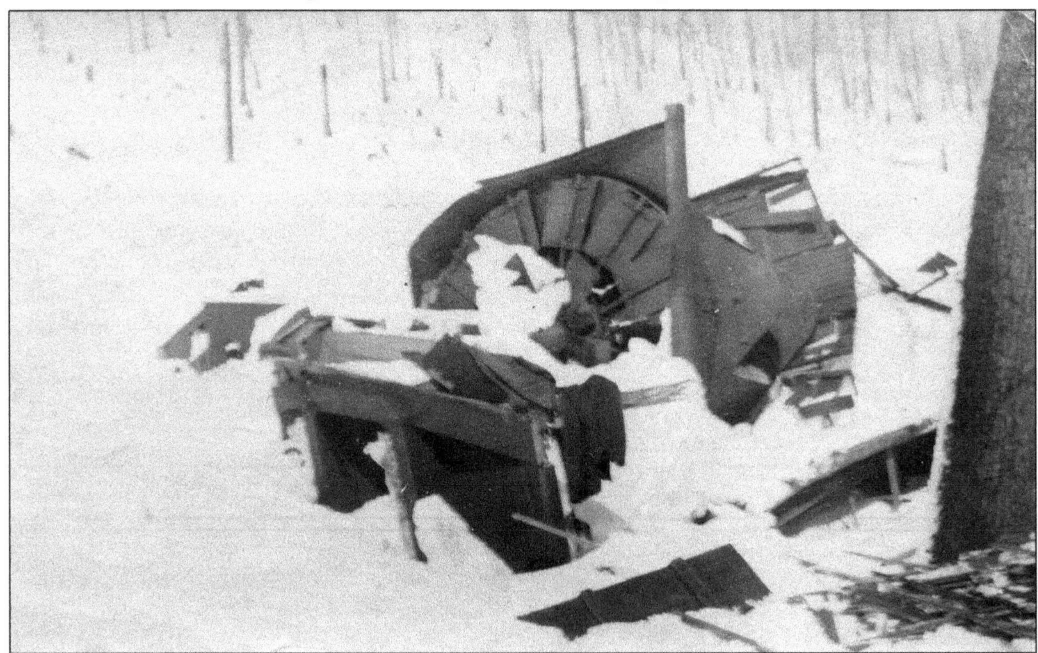

The weight of the snow pushed the extremely heavy rotary plow down into the ravine. Some of the wreckage was buried under 40 feet of snow. Dr. Cox, a GN physician, along with Dr. Rockwell, helped the survivors and three of the injured leave on the first relief train: R.M. Lavelle, Ray Forsyth, and GN fireman S.A. Bates. (Courtesy of WVM, 87-142-36.)

Eight

Wellington after the Disaster

Word of the disaster spread like wildfire once the telegraph lines were working again. Newspapers had a field day reporting on it—some truths, some myths—but there was no sugarcoating the fact that it was about as bad as it could get for everyone at Wellington. When Will Smith, the division superintendent of Kalispell, Montana, heard of it, he worked his rotary toward Wellington to offer his assistance.

It was not until late April that the crews finally got the last pieces of the engines and rotary hoisted up and onto a flatcar to be hauled down to Skykomish.

William Harrington, the assistant trainmaster, nicknamed the Snow King, later recalled the force of the avalanche: "I just felt the crash, an awful crash, that was all, and it struck the—just when the slide hit the side of our train we just felt an awful crash—it was done in an instant, and then we went down the bank."

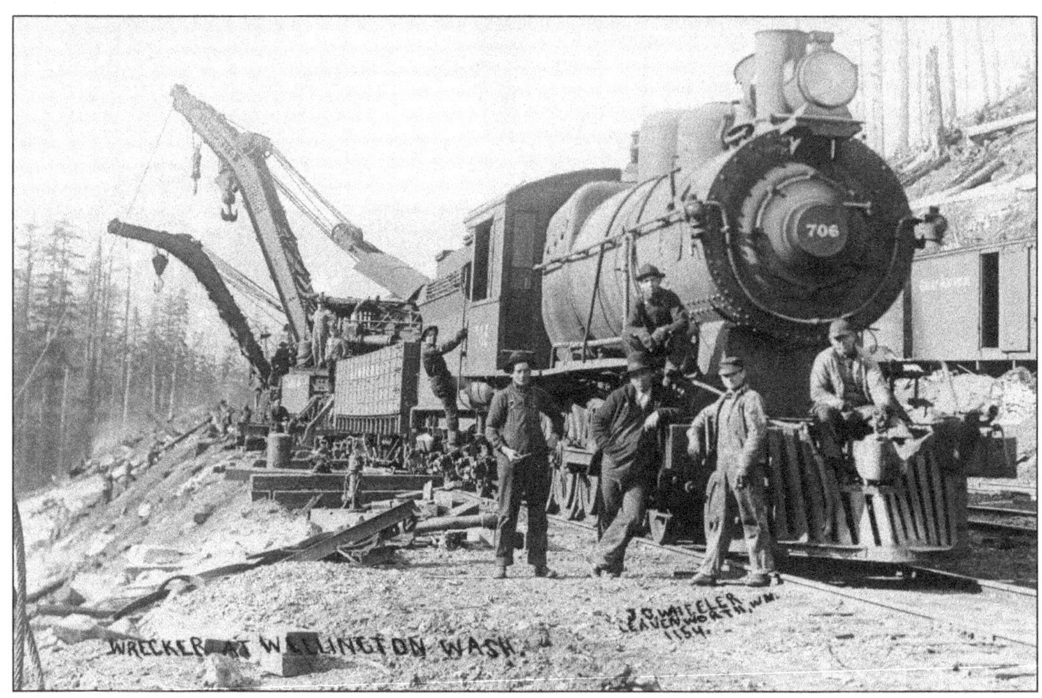

The Great Northern reported that 150 men were working at the disaster site to recover the victims and help remove the debris. On March 4, forty dead passengers, crew members, mail clerks, and laborers had been recovered from under the acres of snow. A wrecking outfit complete with a dining car and 250 men rolled in to help. Another carried fuel, food, medical supplies, and a bunch of dynamite. The work was so unbearable with the freezing rain, heavy fallen timbers, and more snow that rescue efforts were soon abandoned, and it was not until after the snow had finally melted that it was possible to retrieve the last of the bodies. (Both photographs by J.D. Wheeler, courtesy of the Jerry Quinn Collection, SHS.)

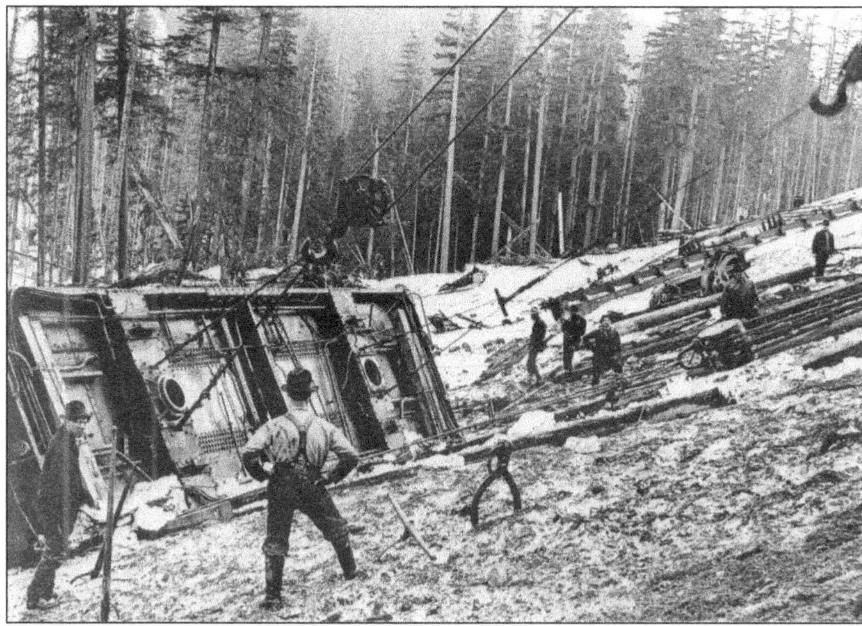

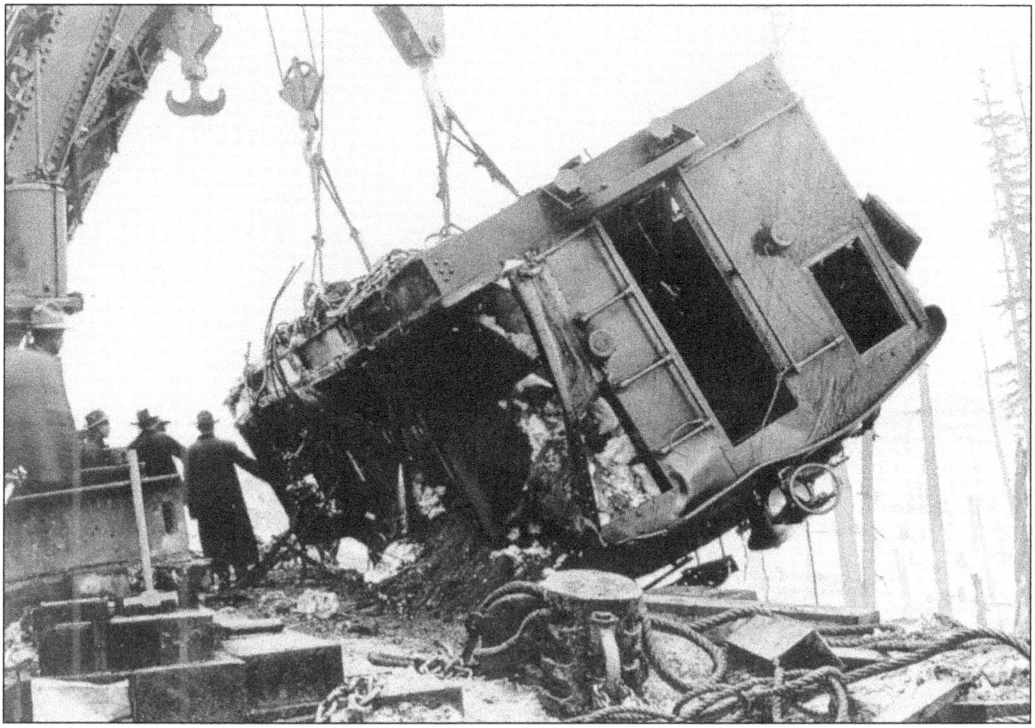

Above, a GN crew uses a winch to pull wreckage from the ravine. The photograph below, taken after the disaster, shows the top of Bailets Hotel, and the tavern peeking out under snow that buried most of the other buildings. Master mechanic J.J. Dowling was at Scenic during the avalanche but was put in charge of the rescue party while O'Neill walked nine miles to the Nippon Station (later called Alpine) to try to telegraph GN officials of the disaster. Dowling, Mackey, and 40 other men from Scenic pulled mangled bodies out of the deep snow for over 12 hours. (Above, courtesy of the Dr. George Fischer Collection, SHS; below, courtesy of WVM, 87-142-8.)

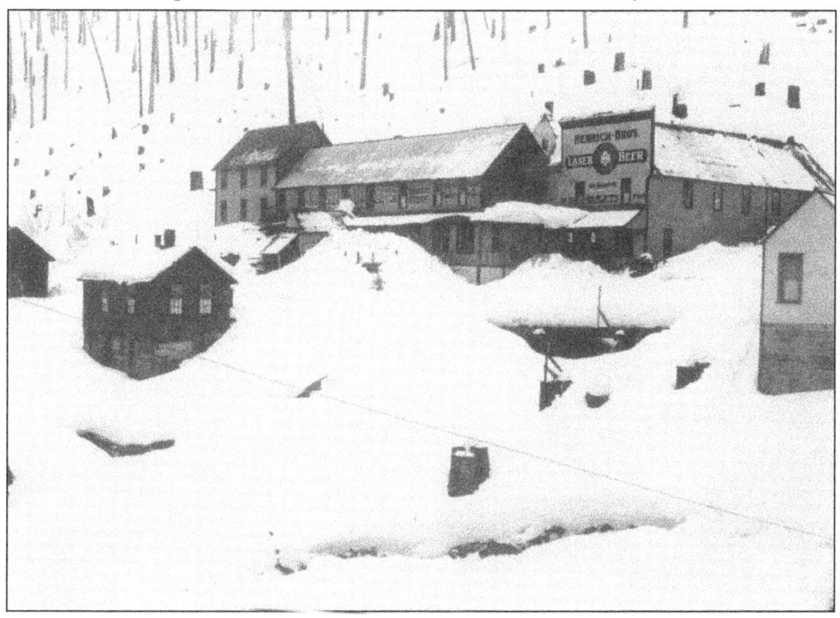

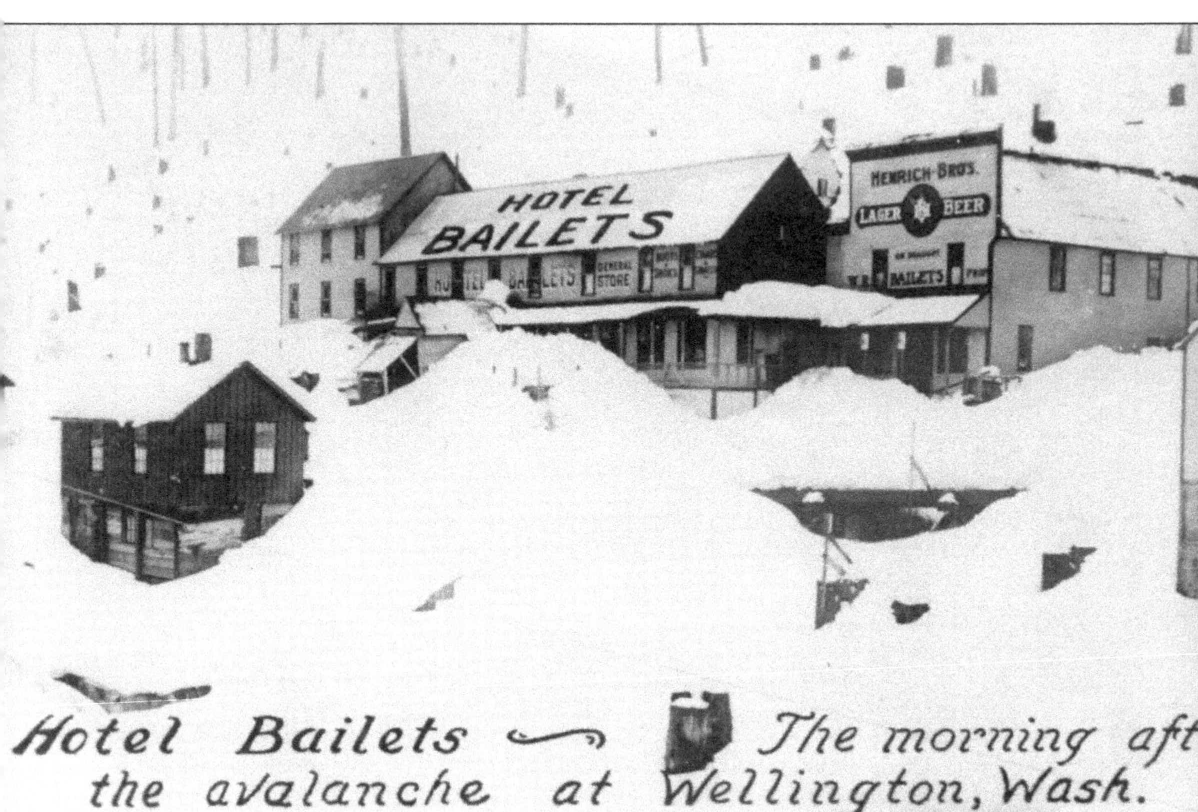

Wellington appears almost peaceful blanketed under piles of snow the morning after the deadly avalanche. Passengers would get their meals at the Bailets Hotel. Some of the buildings at the bottom are completely entombed in snow. "Hotel Bailets" was hand-written on the photograph along with the information at the bottom. (Courtesy of SHS.)

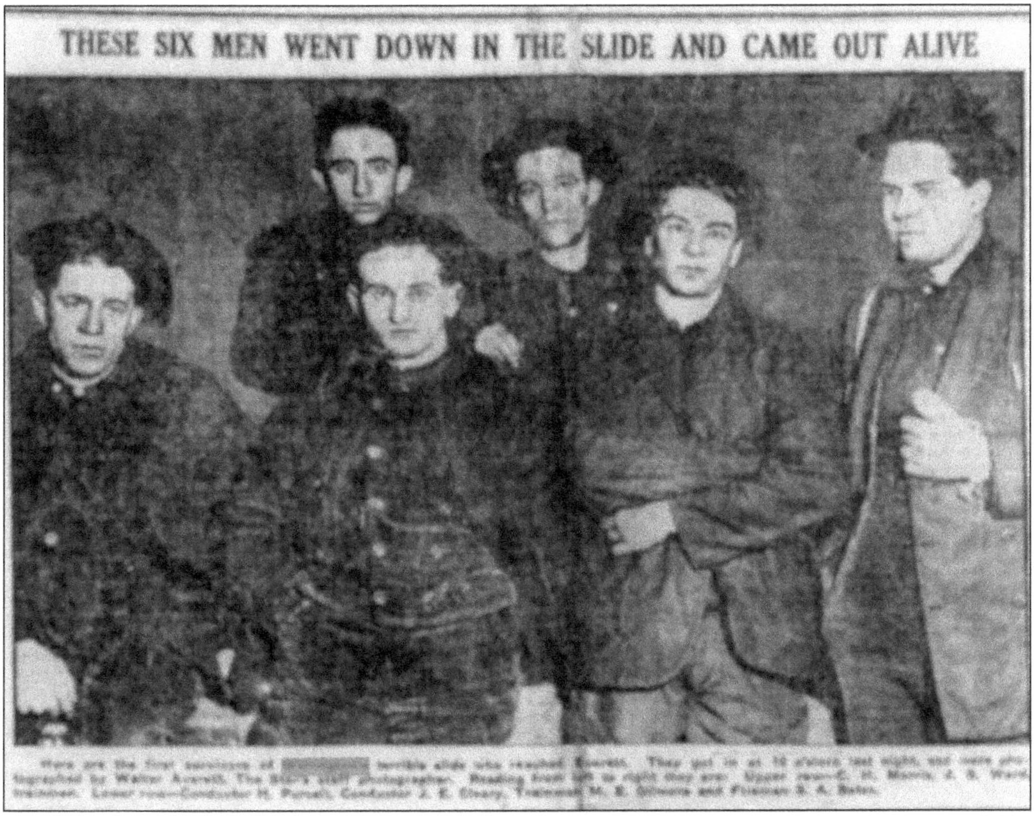

THESE SIX MEN WENT DOWN IN THE SLIDE AND CAME OUT ALIVE

Seen here are the six men who made it out alive. From left to right are rotary conductor Homer Purcell, trainman C.H. Morris, conductor J.E. Cleary, trainman J.S. Ward, brakeman M.E. Glimore, and fireman Samuel Bates. Bates was trapped for over five hours before he was finally rescued. This image is from the *Seattle Star* of March 3, 1910. (Courtesy of SHS.)

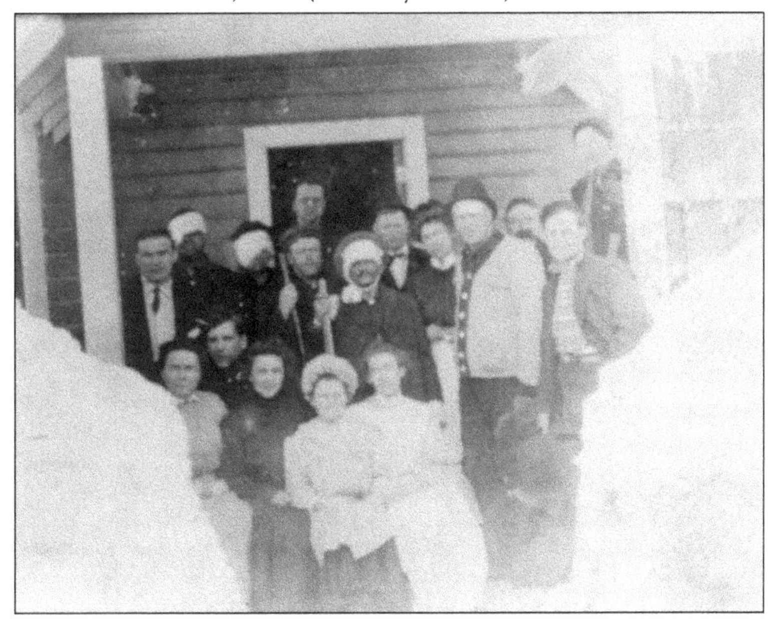

Possibly three of the five women pictured here among the unidentified men are Alathea Sherlock (first row, second from left), Mrs. Miles (wife of GN engineer Bob Miles), and Mrs. Shelton (the wife of the night telegraph operator), who were listed among those who immediately tended to the injured. They turned the motorman's bunkhouse into a temporary hospital. (Courtesy of WVM, 87-142-38.)

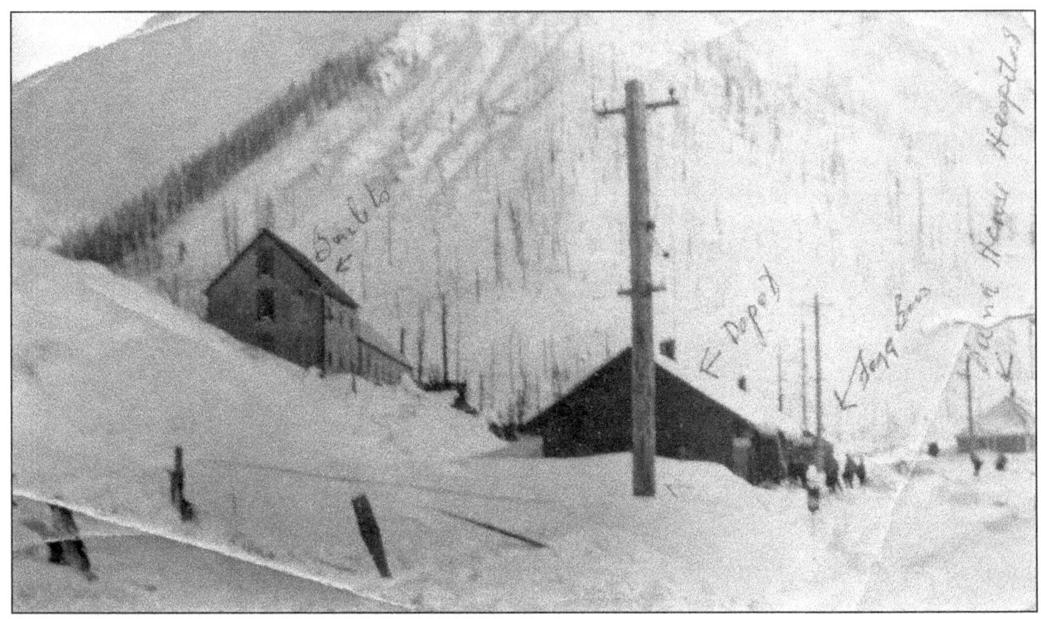

Looking into Wellington at the edge of the deadly avalanche, from left to right are Bailets Hotel, the train depot, Foggs Bros. Tavern, and the engineers' bunkhouse that was turned into the makeshift hospital. The telegraph pole marks about where the avalanche tore through, just missing the buildings by several feet. (Courtesy of WVM, 87-142-34.)

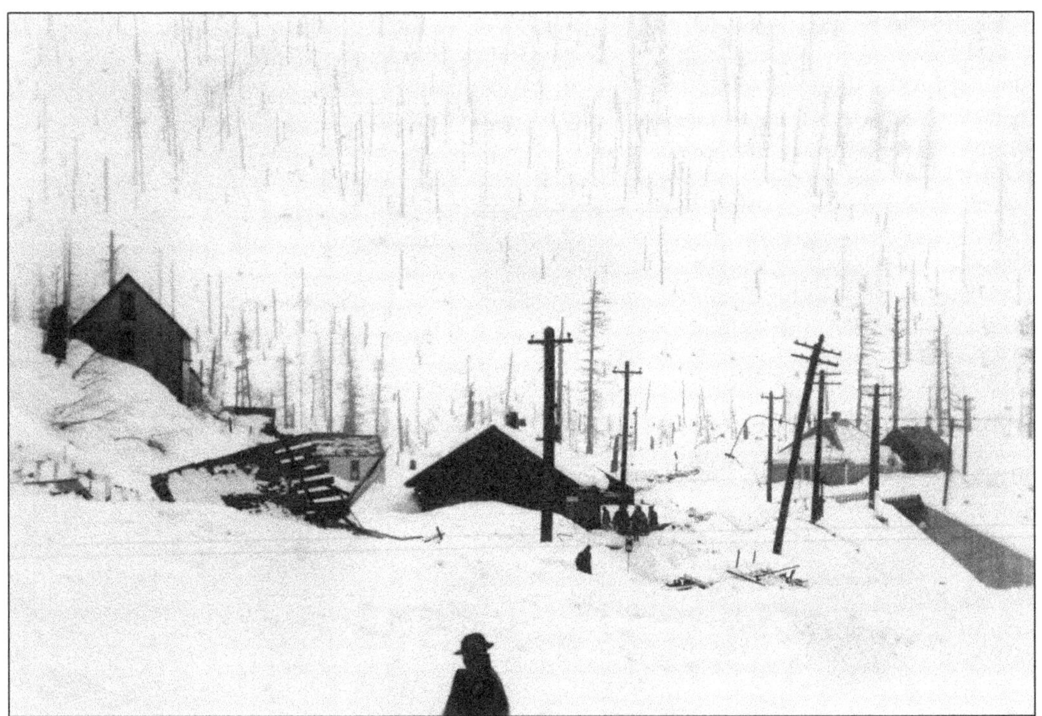

This is a similar shot to the above photograph, but with more details visible. Prior to the disaster, a large group of passengers left the trains determined to hike to Scenic, but they quickly got discouraged by the snow and made their way back to the "safety" of the trains. (Courtesy of SHS.)

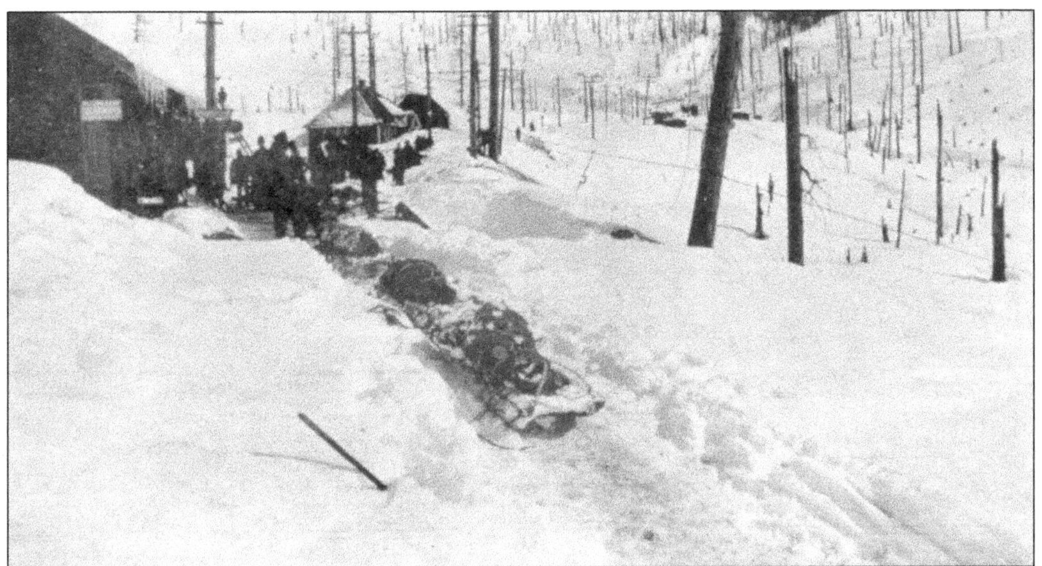

Transporting the dead out of Wellington was quite a complicated procedure. There were no trains running at Wellington, so the bodies had to be taken out on Alaska sleds by hand, pulled by men a treacherous 12 miles toward Scenic, where trains were coming through. (Courtesy of WVM, 87-142-30.)

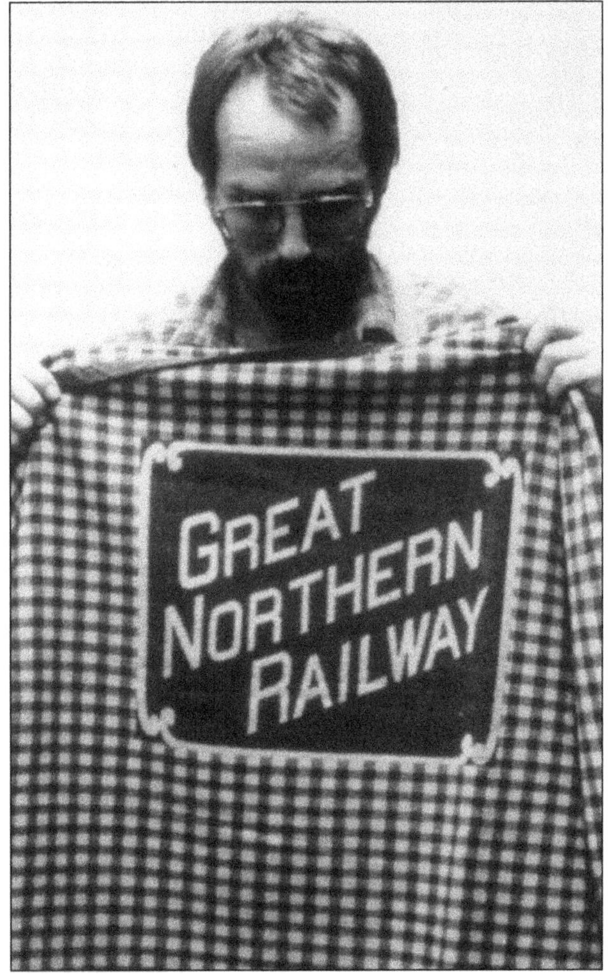

Wellington author Don Mood is shown holding up one of the original blankets from the disaster. Later, the coroner rented a large hall in Seattle for the public inquest, and after two weeks and eight hours of deliberation, the 11-person jury made a verdict. The inquest jury placed fault with the GN, and so did the Superior Court, but the Washington Supreme Court determined that the disaster was an act of God, and GN was not at fault. (Courtesy of the Richard E. Bell Research Collection, WVM, 012-51-952.)

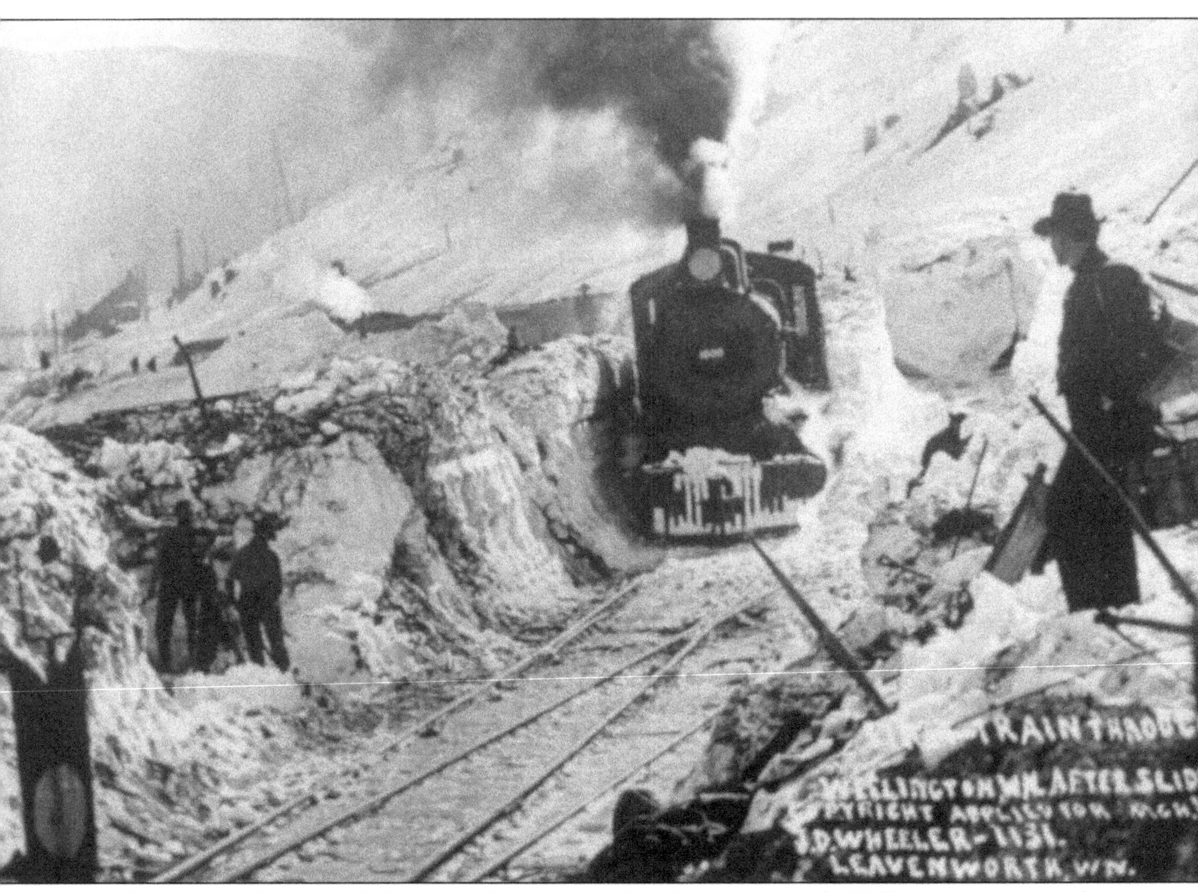

Photographed on March 12 is the first train to finally run through Wellington since its closure on February 23. Men put their shovels down momentarily and stood to the sides of the tracks as the locomotive pulled through. It took the Great Northern a long and laborious three weeks to finally repair the tracks before trains could start running over Stevens Pass and the Cascades again. Along with the concrete snowshed at Wellington built by GN, officials estimated their loss was about $2.5 million, with Wellington being $1.5 million of that figure. (Photograph by J.D. Wheeler, courtesy of WVM, 87-142-29.)

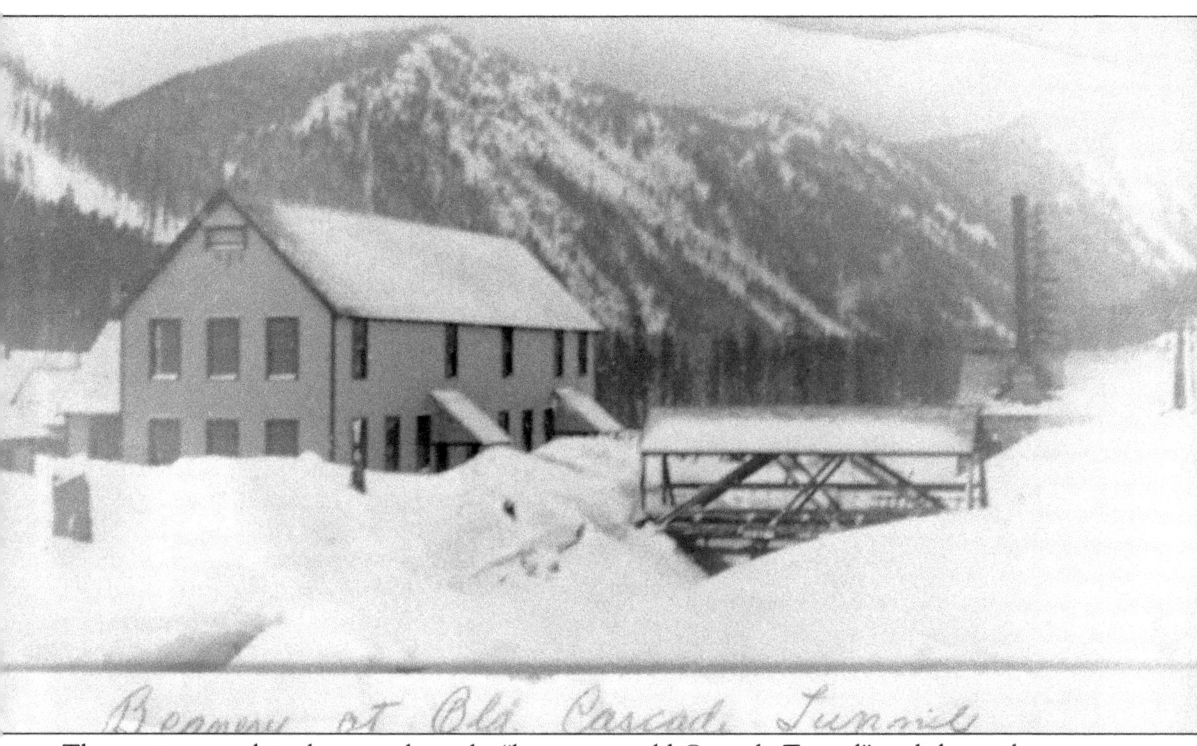

The writing on this photograph reads, "beanery at old Cascade Tunnel" and shows the new beanery and bunkhouse built near the old Cascade Tunnel after 1910. It also shows a covered bridge over Haskell Creek. The original beanery (destroyed in a slide days before the March avalanche) can be seen on old maps, but no photographs of it have been found. According to H.L. Wertz, a passenger who hiked out on Monday, "Coming from the west side of the tunnel, it was very smoky and gas, and the passengers got up in the smoking car and shut all the windows to keep the gas out of the car." (Courtesy of SHS.)

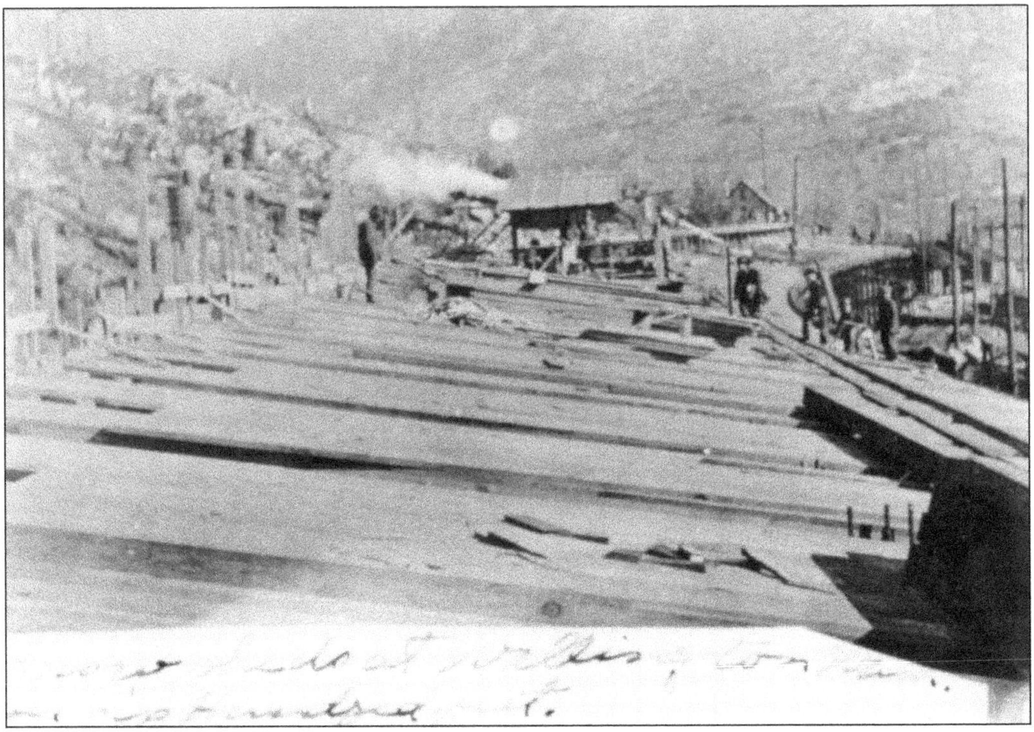

The much-needed snowshed at Wellington was built after the avalanche, costing the Great Northern a small fortune. This new concrete shed utilized the new ferroconcrete process, which needed 30,000 barrels of cement and 2,400 tons of steel. The technology was state of the art and very innovative at the time. The abandoned snowshed is now part of the Iron Goat Trail and can still be seen from Highway 2 near Stevens Pass. (Both, courtesy of the J.D. Wheeler Collection, SHS.)

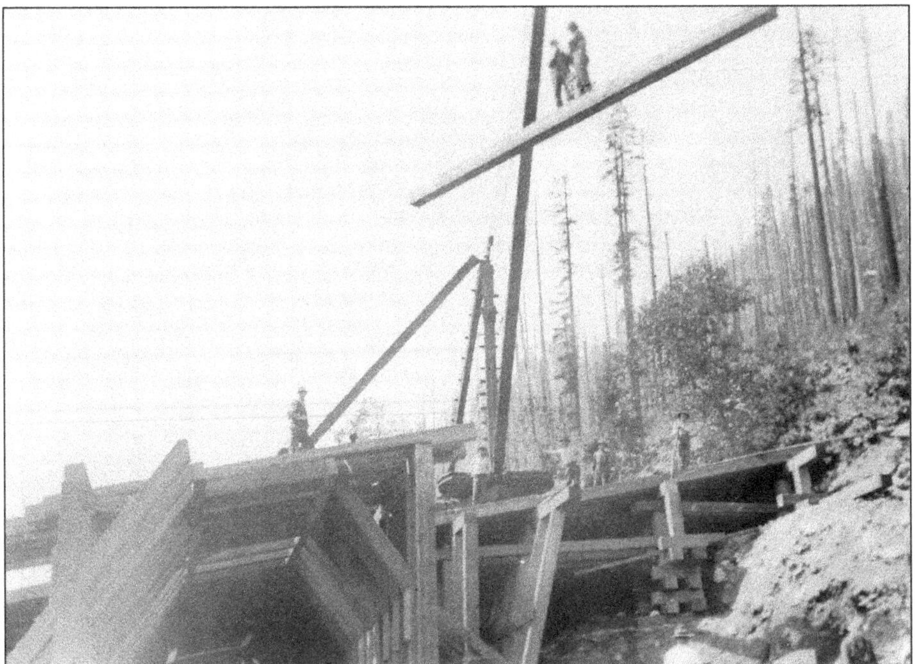

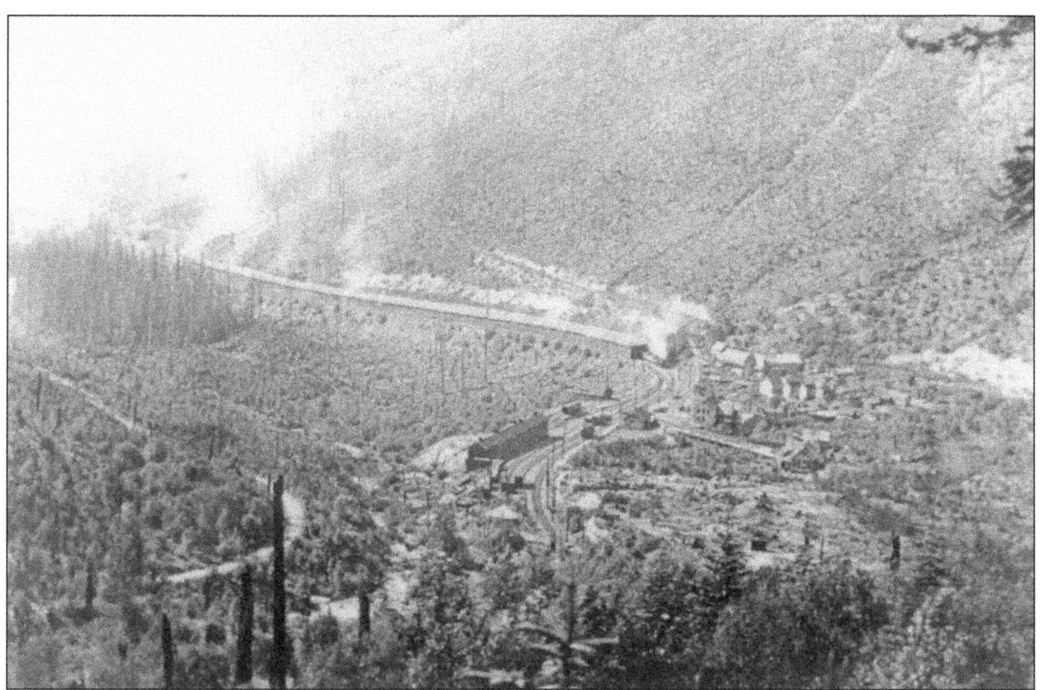

Construction on snowsheds continued in full swing, keeping many laborers very busy for a long time. This photograph is of Tye during 1913 and shows the steep mountain area the slide came down. The snowshed at Wellington was the first of its kind to be built with reinforced concrete, and the GN estimated its cost at about $1.58 million, which also included new buildings to house laborers, to train men, and to store equipment. (Above, courtesy of SHS; below, courtesy of SHS, Batchelder Collection.)

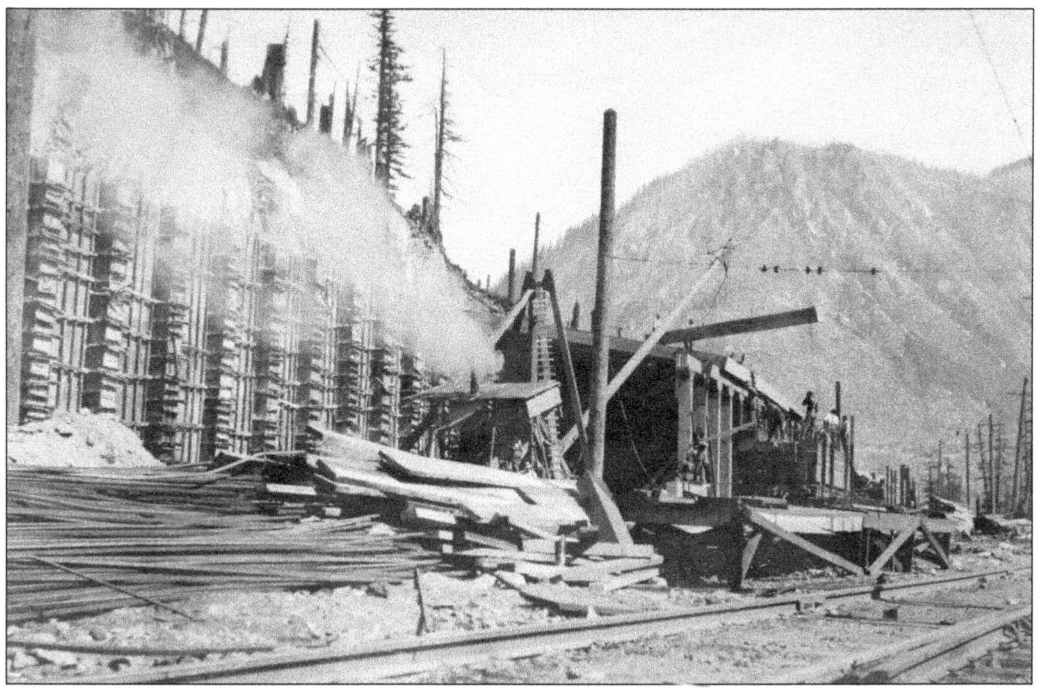

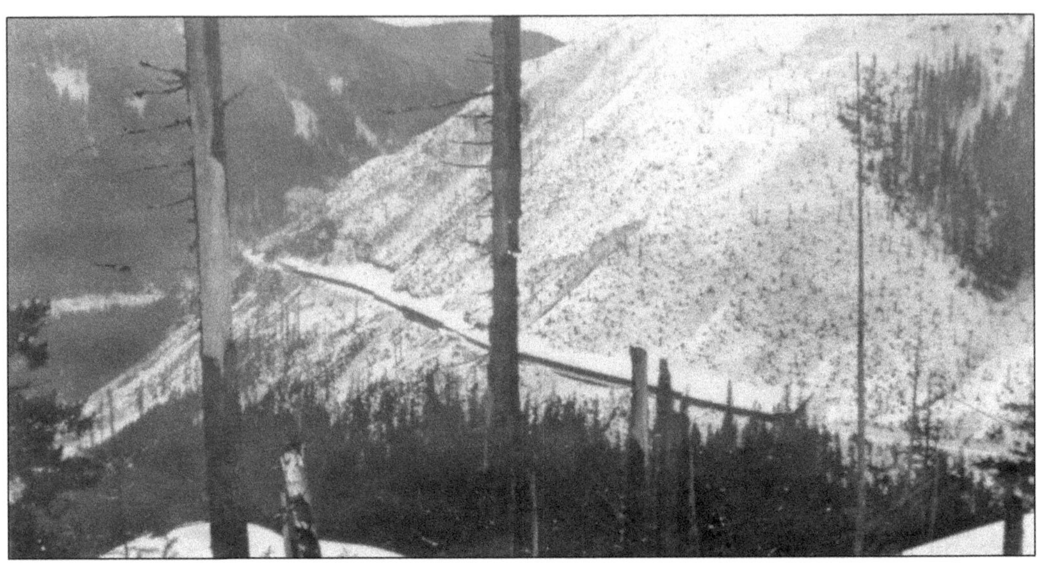

After the Wellington disaster, the Great Northern invested millions to build a snowshed at the disaster site. Above, the long-abandoned shed covered in fresh snow can be seen looking north from Highway 2 near Stevens Pass. The GN wanted to ensure it would never risk another train or its passengers and crew members in an avalanche again. Costs for the snowshed included: changing the line, $660,000; new timbers, $370,000; new buildings, $85,000; and more, totaling an estimated $1.58 million. The photograph below shows the shed up close when it was still in use. (Above, courtesy of WVM, 87-142-32; below, courtesy of the Batchelder Collection, SHS.)

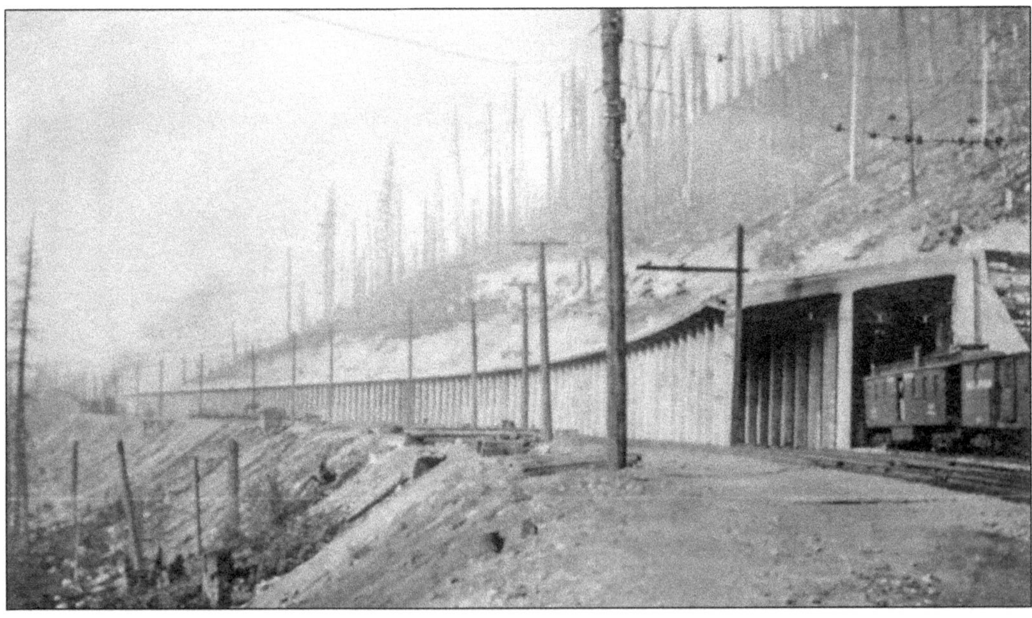

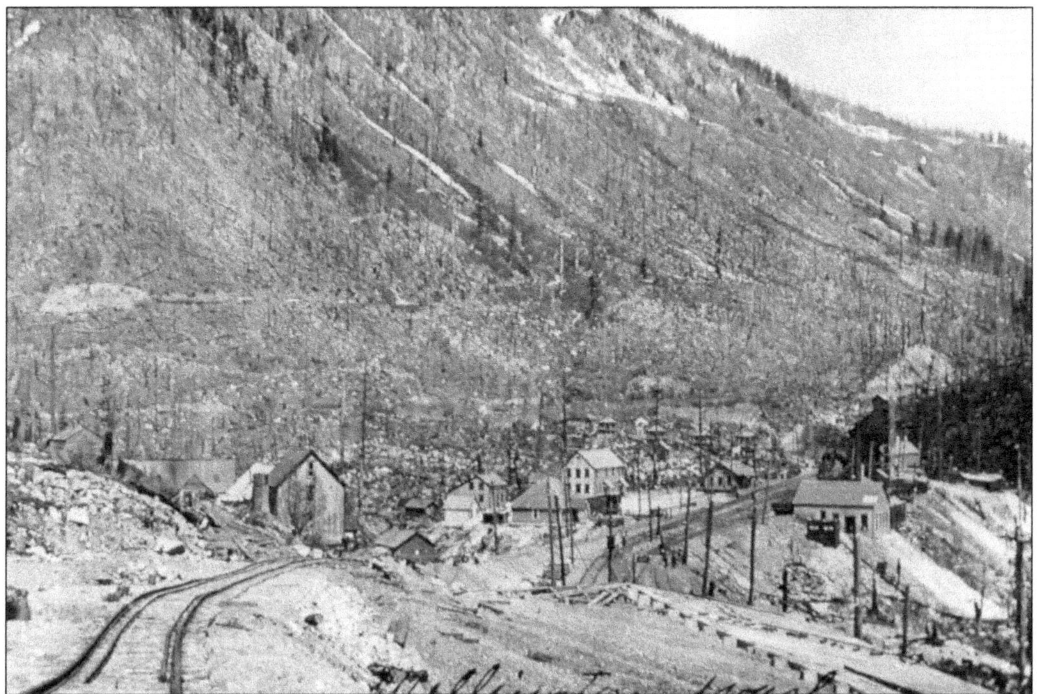

This photograph of Wellington on May 28, 1911, shows the rearrangement of the facilities after the avalanche. At the right bottom is the snowshed. The tracks on the left are the runaway track. The new section house, eating house and bunkhouse, coal tower, and heating plant are all finished. The Tye Depot is at center in its new location, and the four homes are the dispatcher cottages. (Photograph by Mike Shawver, courtesy of SHS.)

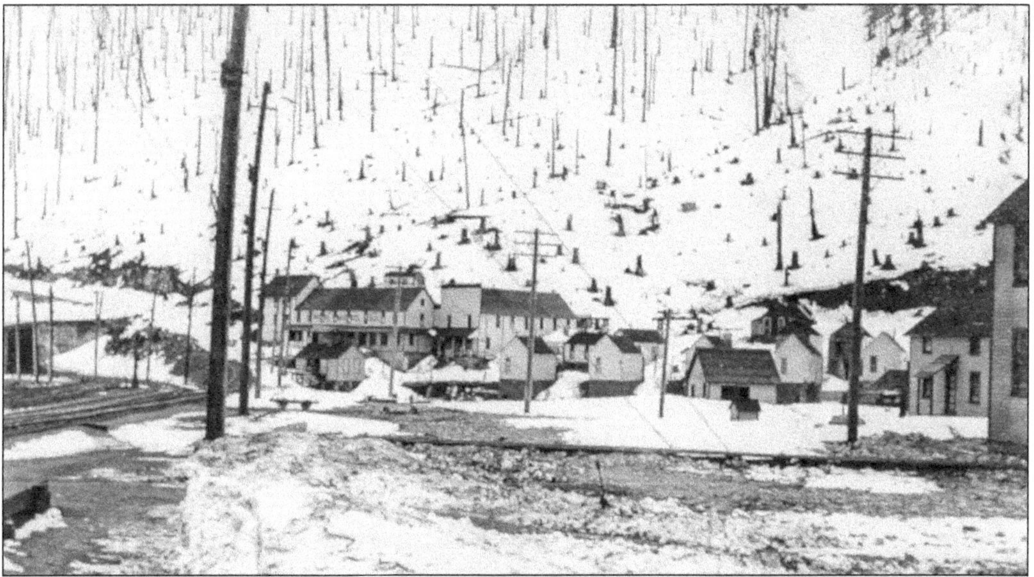

The snowshed is seen here with Bailets Hotel, the tavern, and small buildings. The trees are still sparse. William Bailets later testified, "I was not afraid. I slept in the house every night. I was not afraid of it at all, but some of the rest of them was." (Courtesy of the Batchelder Collection, SHS.)

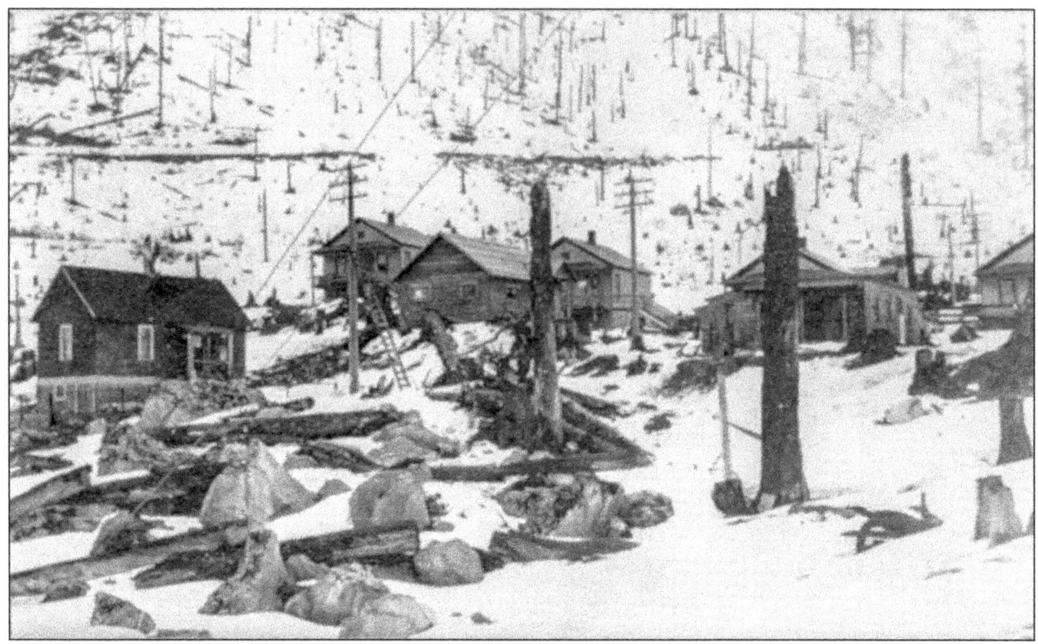

Several dispatchers' cabins were built at Wellington. Dispatchers were in charge of controlling the movement of the trains, such as when they would meet other trains and when to wait at certain locations, as well as any possible problems. At the time, the rulebook and the timetables were used religiously, supplemented by train orders. Dispatchers used Morse code over telegraph wires to relay messages. (Courtesy of the Batchelder Collection, SHS.)

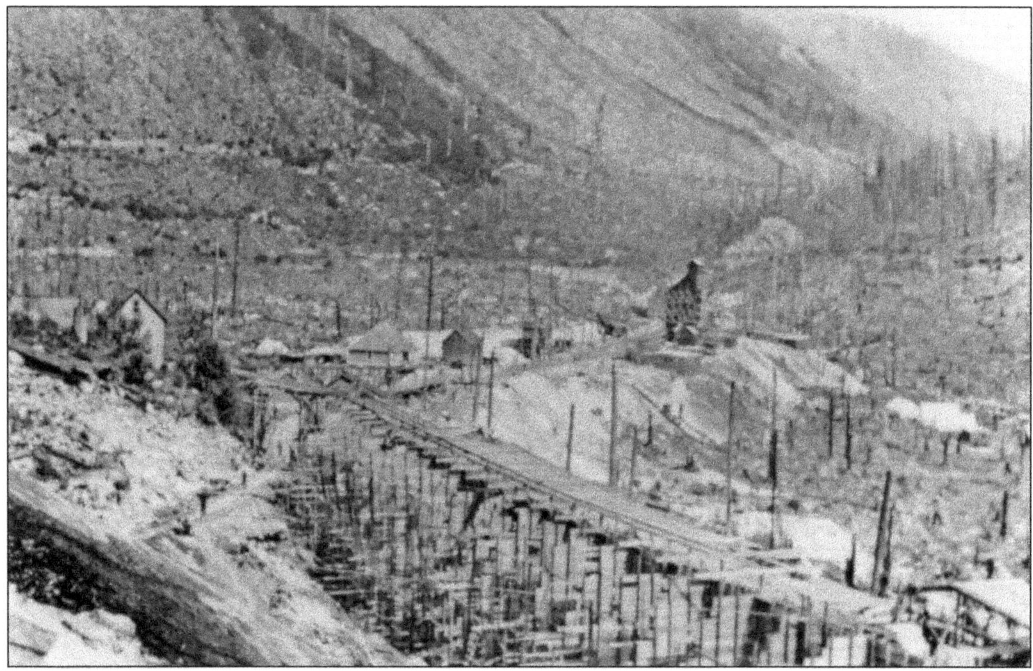

This image shows the new coal tower at top right, and the massive snowshed as it appeared during construction. The snowshed at Wellington was a double-track snowshed and formed a continuation of the mountainside. (Courtesy of SHS.)

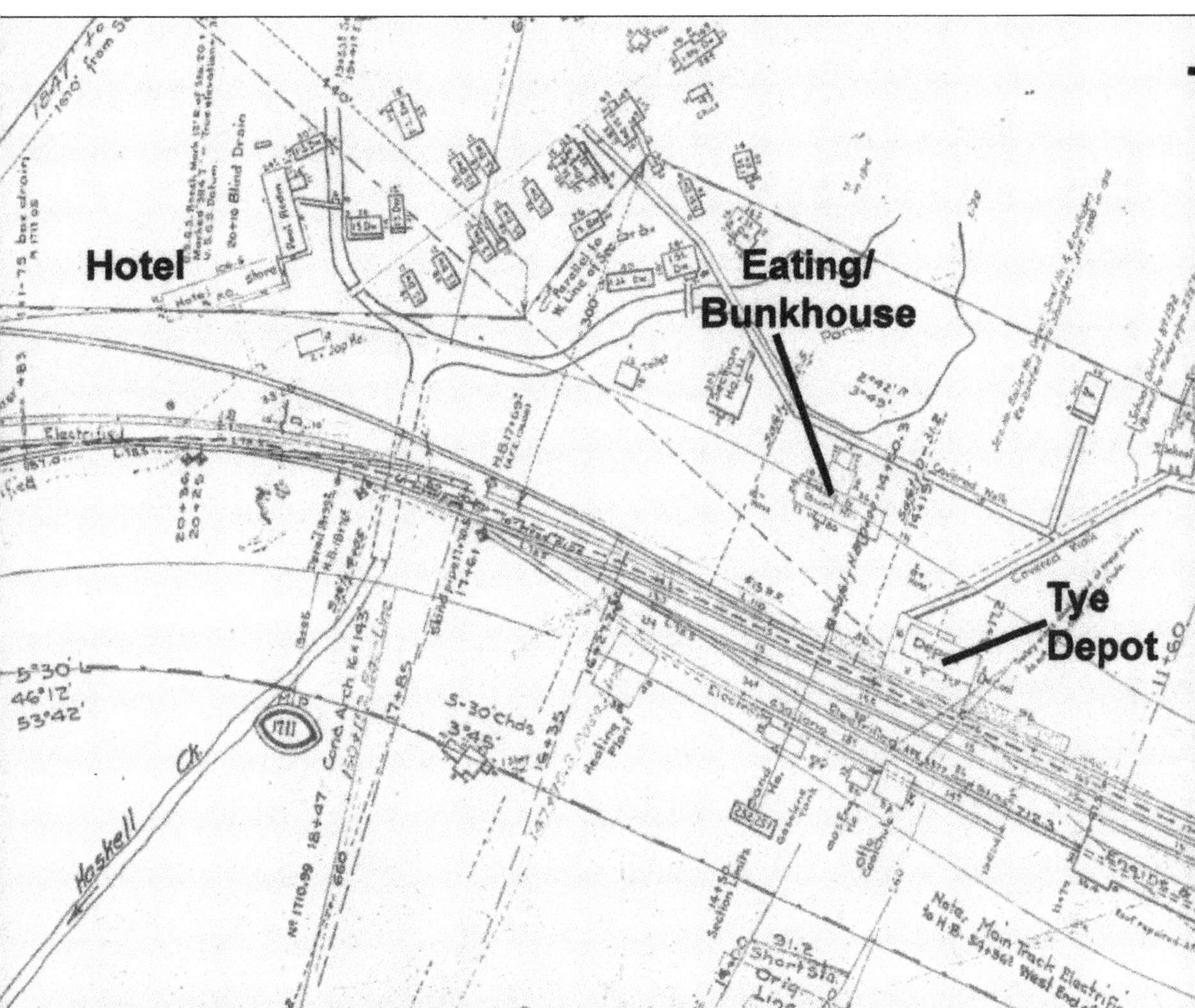

After the avalanche, the town of Wellington was renamed Tye by the Great Northern in the hopes of removing any bad associations from the area as well as memories of the disaster in the minds of tourists. Here is a map of Tye showing the various buildings and details such as the electrified main track, Haskell Creek, the sand house, the depot, the new eating house and bunkhouse, covered walks, the school, the section house near a small pond, the town toilet, Bailets Hotel, the post office and pool room, the heating plant, gasoline tanks, the coal chute, and the engine house. (Courtesy of SHS.)

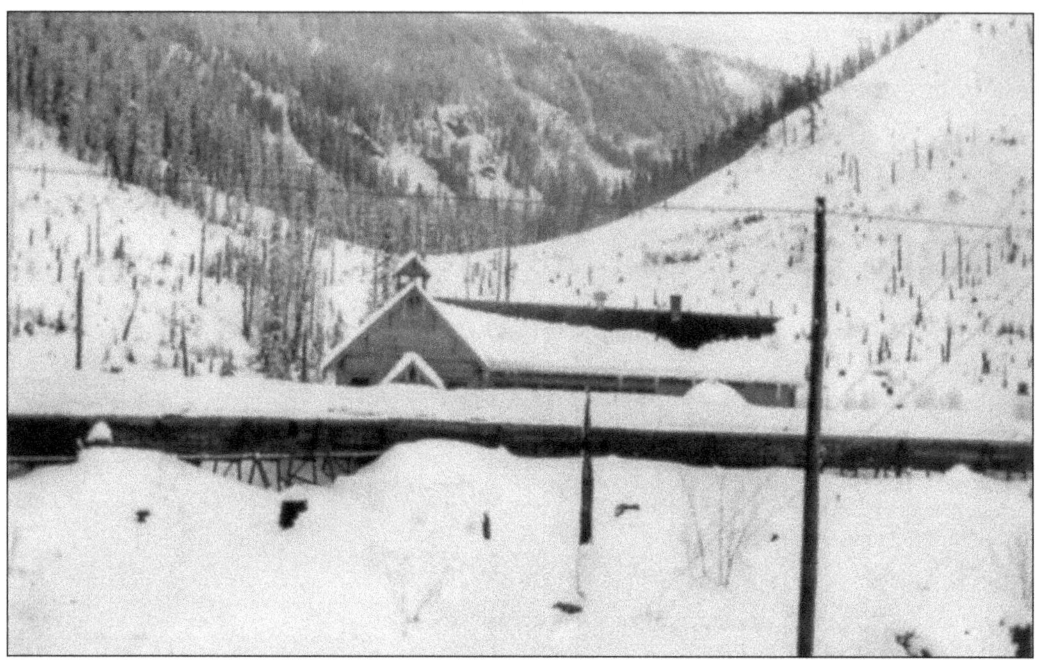

Extreme snow was a regular occurrence in the area. In October 1923, the Tye schoolhouse was almost buried beneath a blanket of white. During that era, many children did not continue their education past grade school, especially in a town as remote as Wellington. Most teaching was done by repetition and memorization. (Courtesy of the Howard Johnson family.)

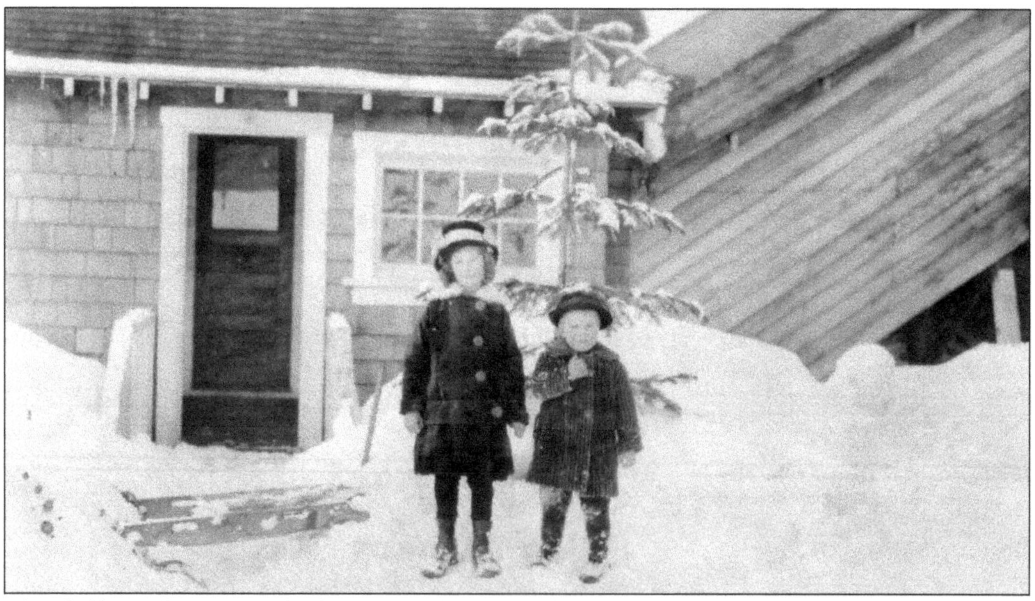

The children of Mamie and Alfred Strandrud stop playing in the snow long enough to pose for the camera in the winter of 1917 in front of their house in Tye. Entertainment for children consisted of marbles, kites, building blocks, simple board games, tag, and dolls. Many hours were consumed by chores both before and after school. (Courtesy of the Howard Johnson family.)

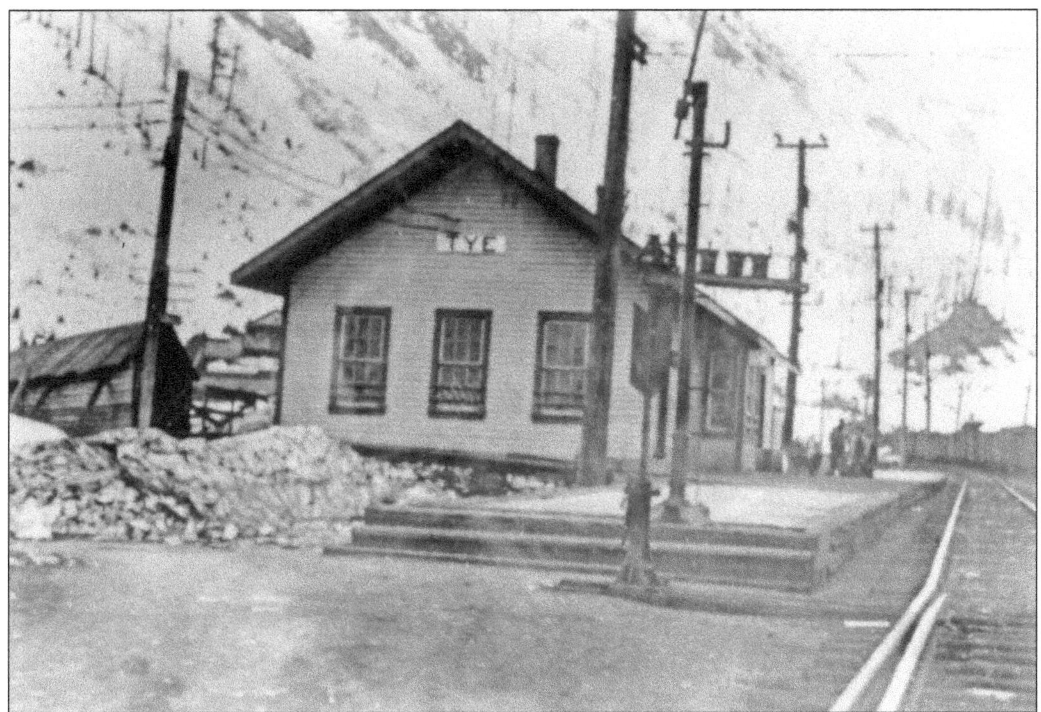

The train depot promoted its new name of Tye after the disaster, hoping to erase the memory of the avalanche and alleviate possible fear in future travelers, thus increasing tourist and passenger flow. The original depot sign for Tye is now in the hands of the Skykomish Historical Society after being lodged and forgotten underneath a house for 30 years and then hidden another 40 years by a fan in Minnesota. The image below shows Tye looking east toward the summit, with the old railroad switchbacks visible on the hillside, sometime between 1922 and1928. (Above, courtesy of SHS; below, courtesy of WVM, 87-142-7.)

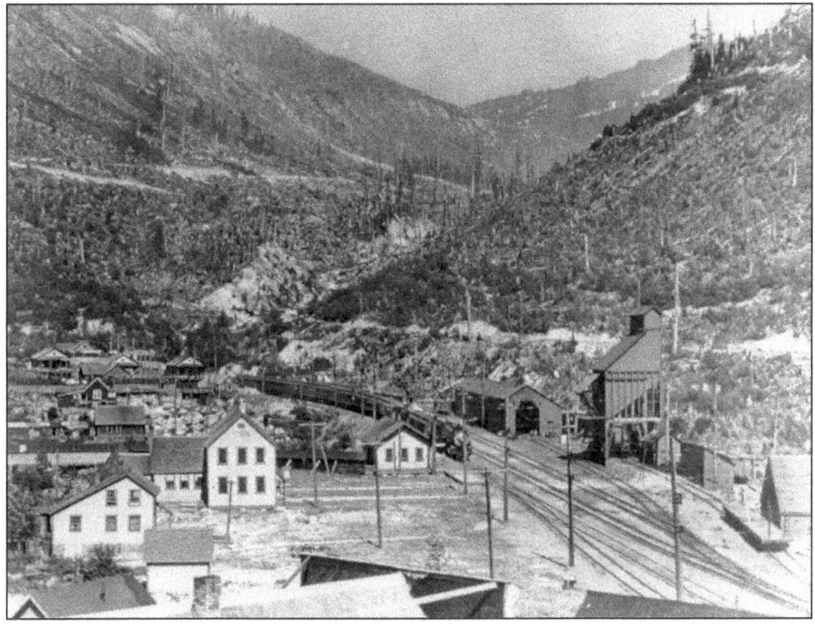

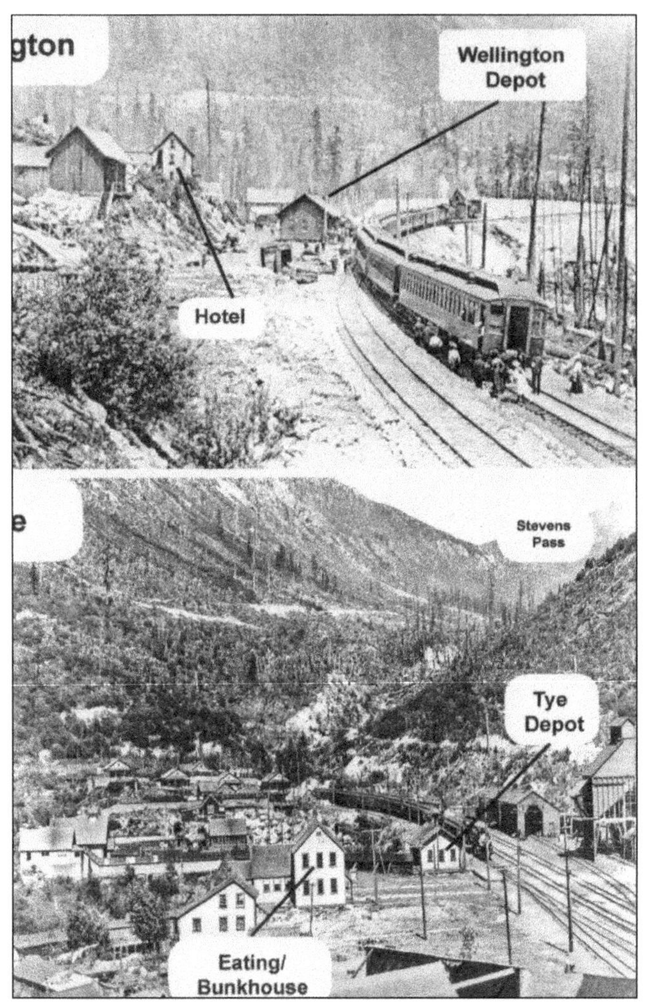

These two images show the differences in Wellington before and after the slide. After the disaster, several buildings were moved, rebuilt, and reorganized by GN and locals. The new two-story eating bunkhouse was a great improvement over the old one. Some survivors and locals moved away after the tragedy; others stayed on at Wellington. (Courtesy of SHS.)

Several GN crew members stand in front of the Tye depot for a photograph. From left to right are W.R. Alexander, B.F. Lang, W.S. Pascoe, unidentified, F. Peterson, E. Burke, C.E. Andrews, and J. Green. The sign on the corner reads, "Great Northern Express Co.," and there is about five feet of snow built up behind the men. (Courtesy of the Dr. George Fischer Collection, SHS.)

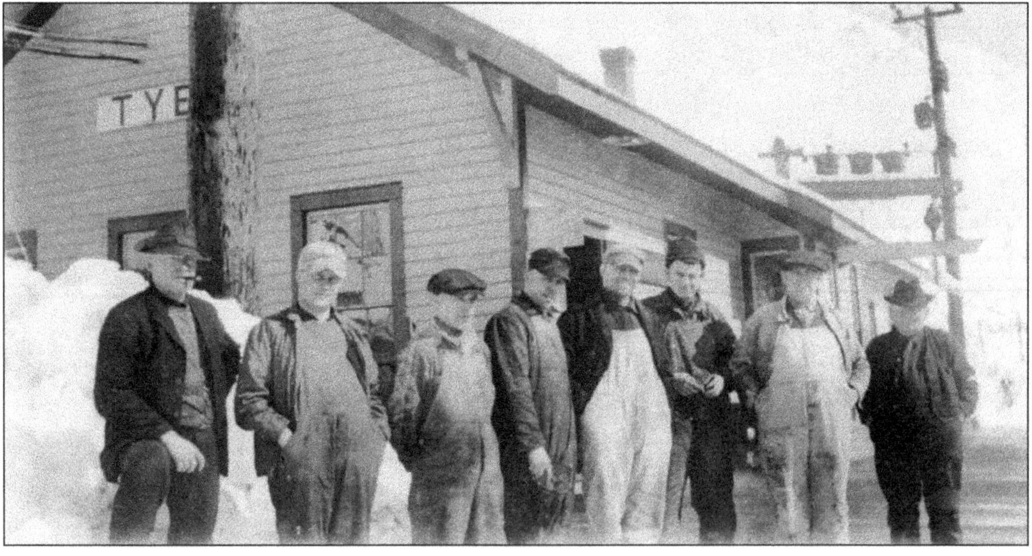

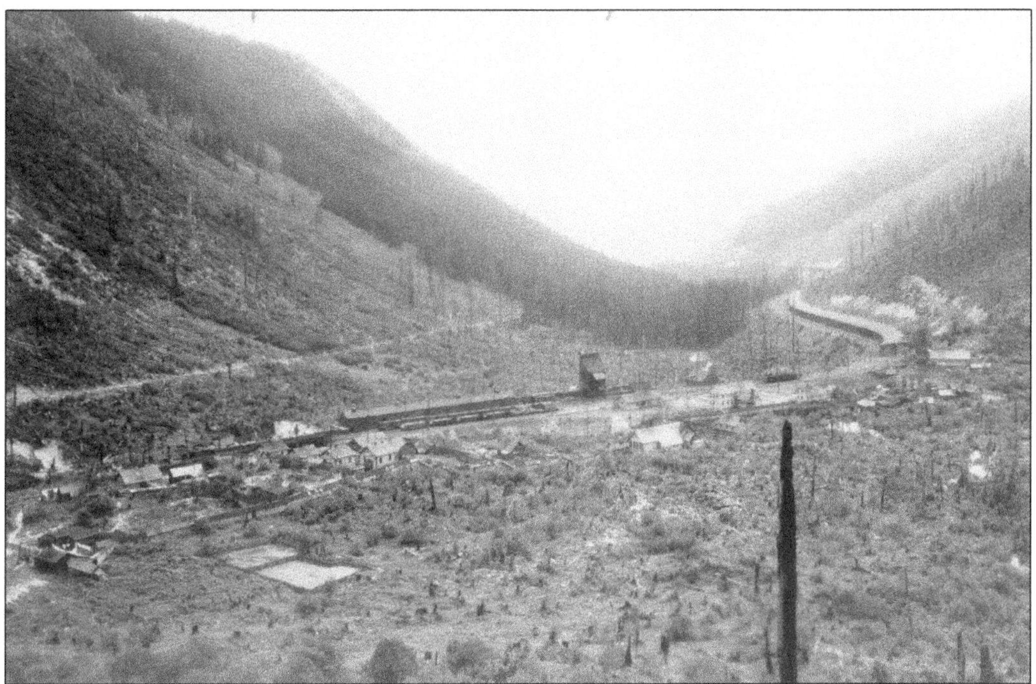

The long-abandoned town of Tye consisted of just a few remaining buildings, which were soon burnt down. A fire destroyed 14 dwellings on one fateful Saturday afternoon. It started in the schoolhouse and quickly spread all the way to the west portal of the tunnel, taking everything in its path, even the telegraph wires. (Both, courtesy of SHS.)

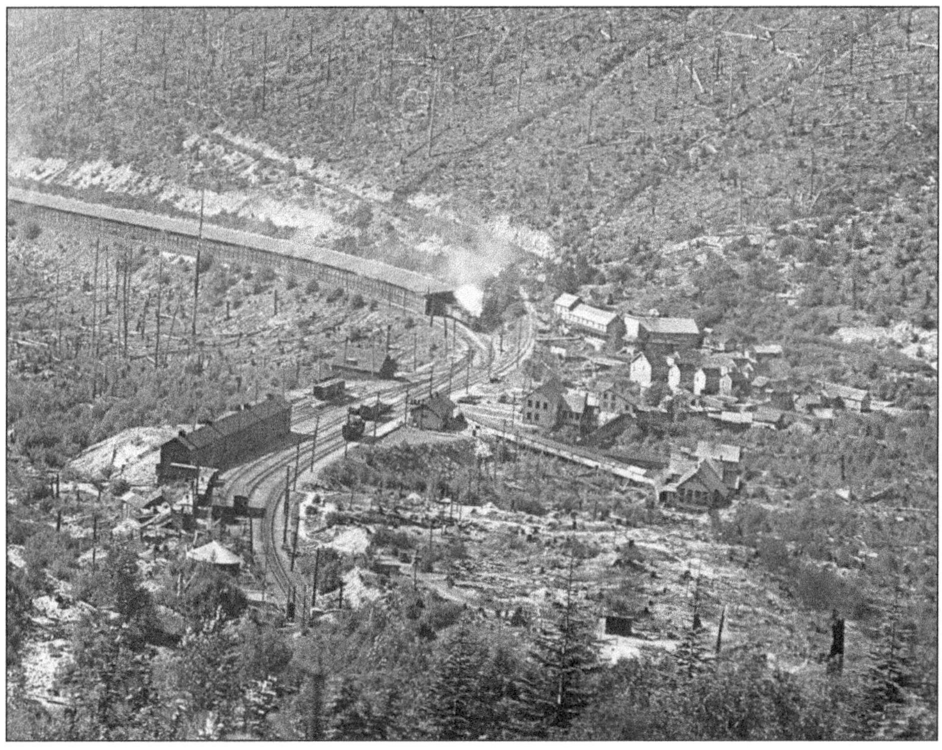

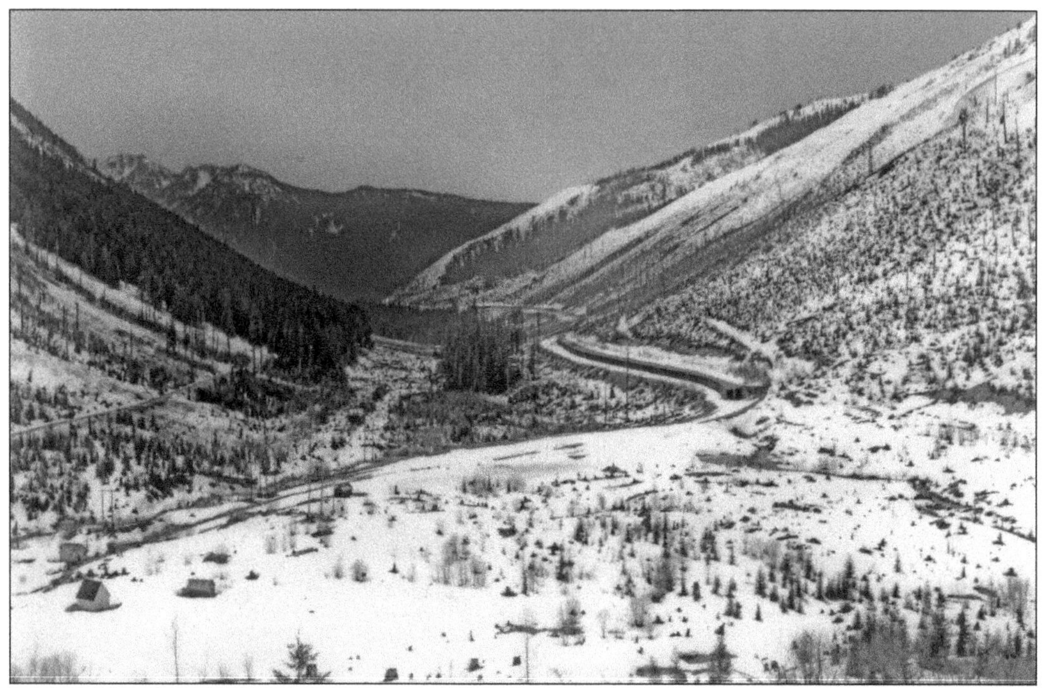

The snowshed was made using 10-foot roof slabs supported by girders that were 24 feet wide by 89 feet deep and 1,100 pounds per square foot. They used eight cubic yards of concrete and 1,500 pounds of steel per running foot. Although crumbling today, the shed was quite an accomplishment at the time. The photograph above shows the snowshed and what remained of Wellington later, with very few buildings still standing. (Above, courtesy of SHS; below, author's collection.)

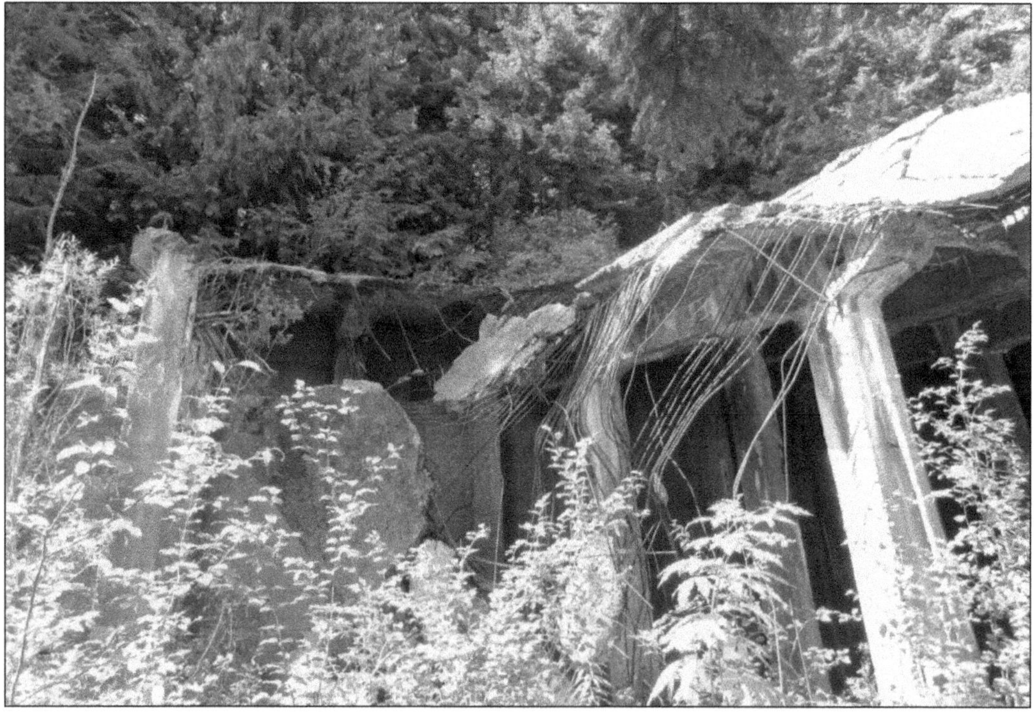

Nine

The Cascade Tunnels

The constructions of the two Cascade Tunnels are without exception some of James Hill's most considerable feats. The ability to survey and construct the tunnels with such archaic equipment at the time and to stay within an inch is no less than outstanding.

During the storm of 1910, some of the passengers wanted the trains to be moved back into the old tunnel for safety. Although this was not a very feasible idea, it caused quite a fuss among the passengers and GN crew during their stall. When the surviving porter of the sleep car *Winnipeg*, Lucius Anderson, was questioned a few years later, he told the jury, "I told them that the condition where they were would be better, because in going to and from their meals they would have to wade through water in the tunnel to get out, and the smoke in the tunnel would be very bad, and it would be very unsanitary in the tunnel . . . I told them they were absolutely safe, because there had never been a slide there."

Porter Anderson, along with many other GN men and Wellington locals, were all wrong. The spot where the trains were parked ended up being the deadliest of all places.

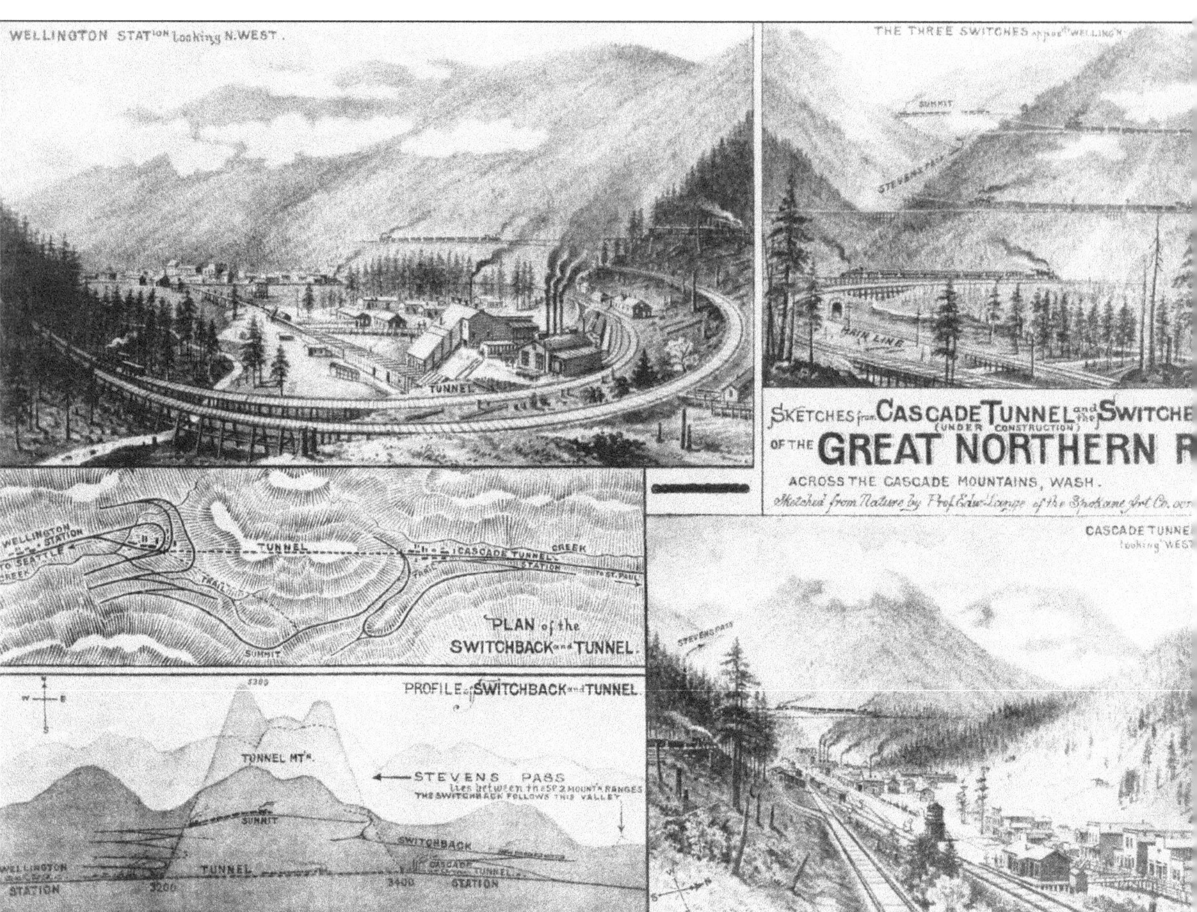

This postcard from 1899 shows the town of Wellington, the switchbacks, and the proposed Cascade Tunnel (profile and plan), as sketched by Spokane artist Edward Lange. Clockwise from top left is Wellington in a view looking northwest; the summit, three switchbacks, the main line, and the tunnel; the Cascade Tunnel and Wellington looking west; a profile of the switchbacks and the tunnel; and the switchbacks and tunnel plan. The first Cascade Tunnel was begun in 1897, took three years, and was part of Hill's grand scheme to beat his competitor, Northern Pacific, on the route from St. Paul to Seattle. The engineer hired was the famous John Stevens, the man who engineered the Panama Canal project. The tunnel replaced the time- and coal-consuming switchback route. (Courtesy of the Dr. George Fischer Collection, SHS.)

This postcard image shows a GN electric engine slowly emerging from the 2.6-mile Cascade Tunnel near Wellington. The GN built a dam near Leavenworth at the mouth of the Tumwater Canyon so electric engines could pull trains through the tunnel, thus reducing the risks of suffocation due to fumes and gases. (Courtesy of Dr. George Fischer Collection, SHS.)

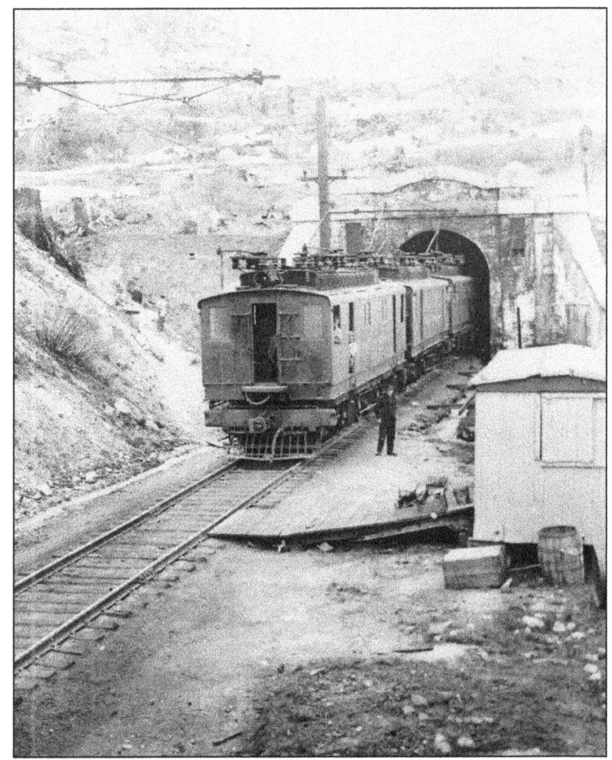

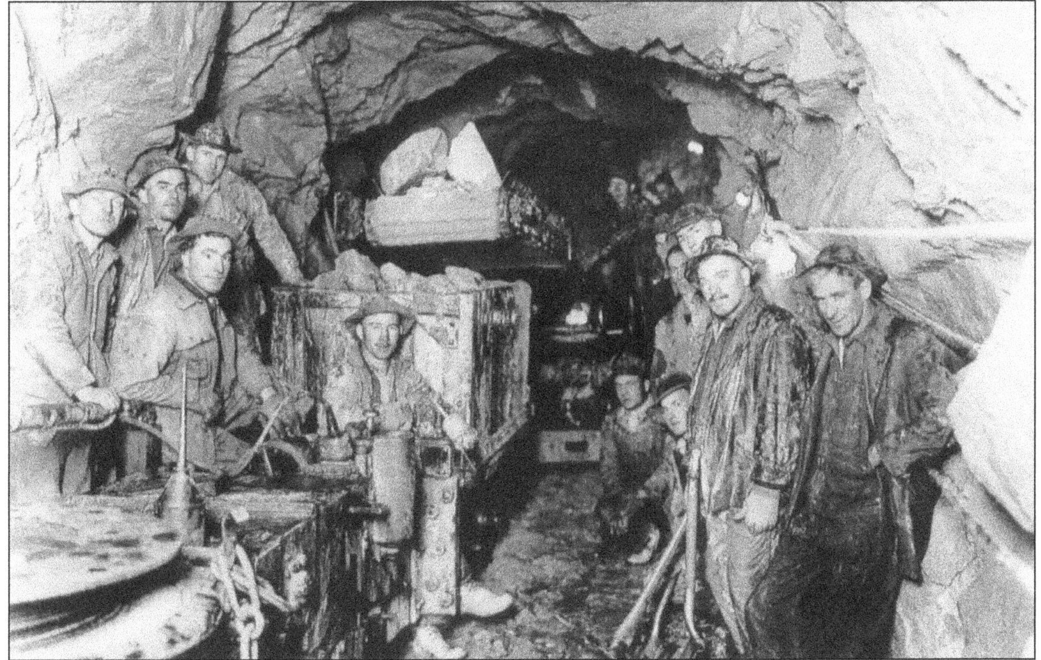

These hardworking men stop to pose for a picture while undertaking the grueling task of removing stones from the west portal of the 2.63-mile Cascade Tunnel. It was this tunnel that the passengers wished to be moved back to, but unfortunately, the tunnel was extremely unsafe, and they could have suffocated. (Photograph by Curtis & Miller, courtesy of SHS.)

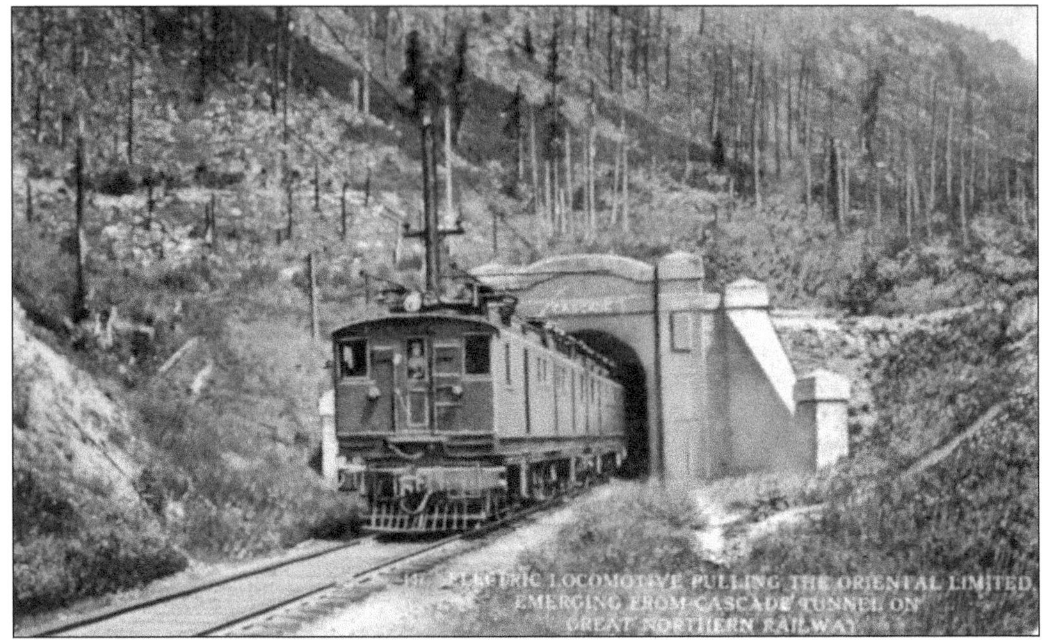

A Great Northern promotional postcard shows the old Cascade Tunnel in its glory days with an electric locomotive pulling an Oriental Limited. The same tunnel today is dilapidated and suffering from water damage—a crumbling reminder of Wellington past. The tracks are gone, and the tunnel is partially filled with boulders and boarded up for safety. Below are hikers near the mouth of the tunnel in a more recent photograph. (Above, courtesy of SHS; below, author's collection.)

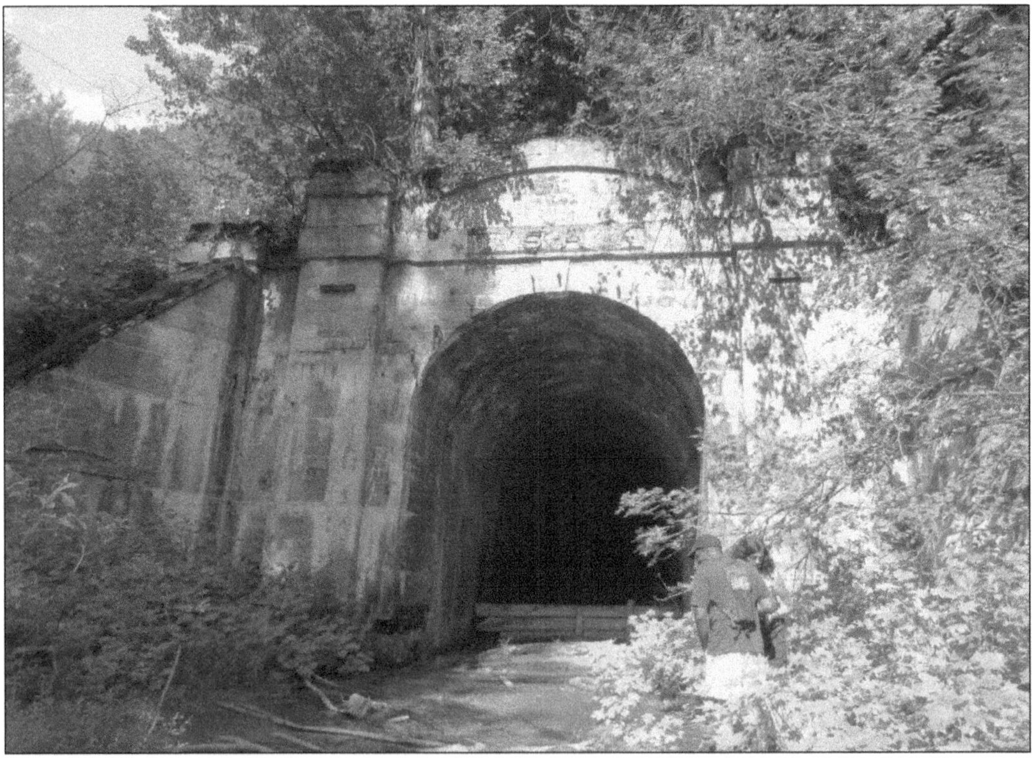

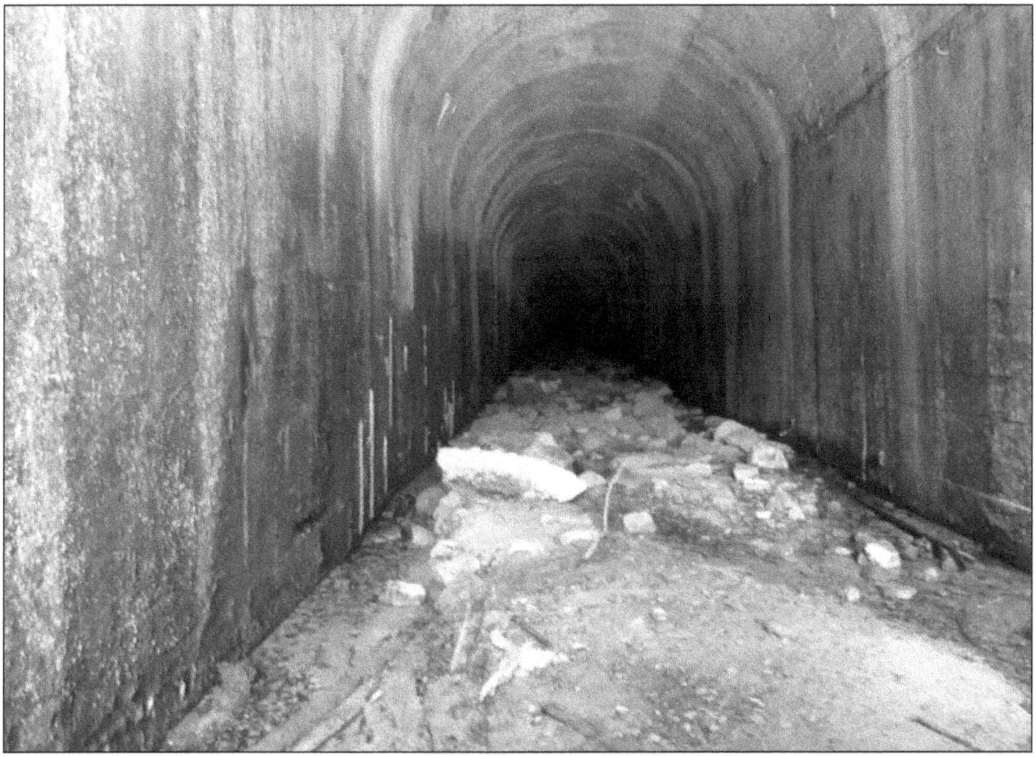

These photographs show the views looking into and out of the old Cascade Tunnel, which closed in 1929 when the new tunnel was built. Seeing daylight after traveling through the dark and dangerous 2.63-mile hole would have been a welcome sight. Ventilation was a huge problem, as crew members got sick and several died. In 1909 the tunnel was electrified, which helped the problem. The tunnel was originally built to avoid the perilous switchbacks (part of the original route over Stevens Pass from 1893, with eight time-consuming zig-zags). O'Neill testified at the inquest that if a man put his hand on the walls inside the tunnel, it would sink several inches into a thick layer of black grime. In 2007–2008, part of the roof collapsed, and the tunnel became unsafe. (Above, author's collection; right, courtesy of WVM, 87-142-17, Oliver Loch Chapple Collection.)

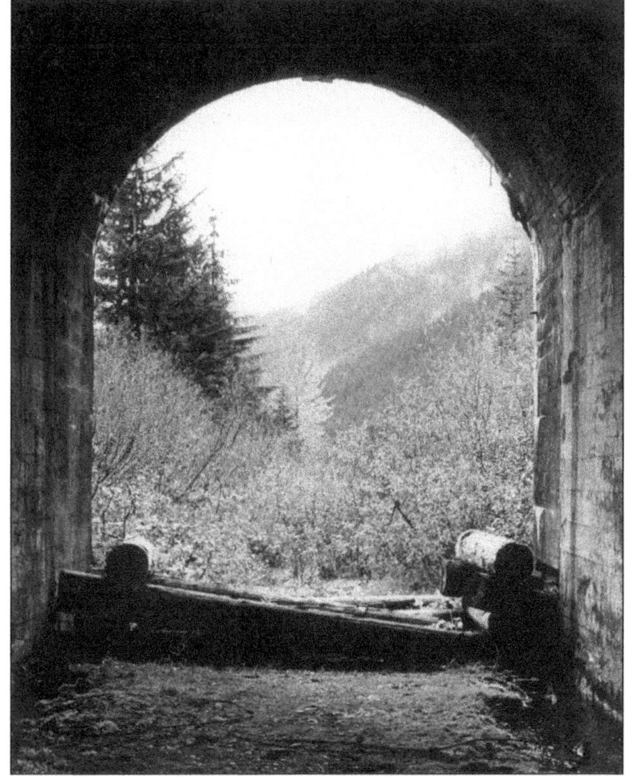

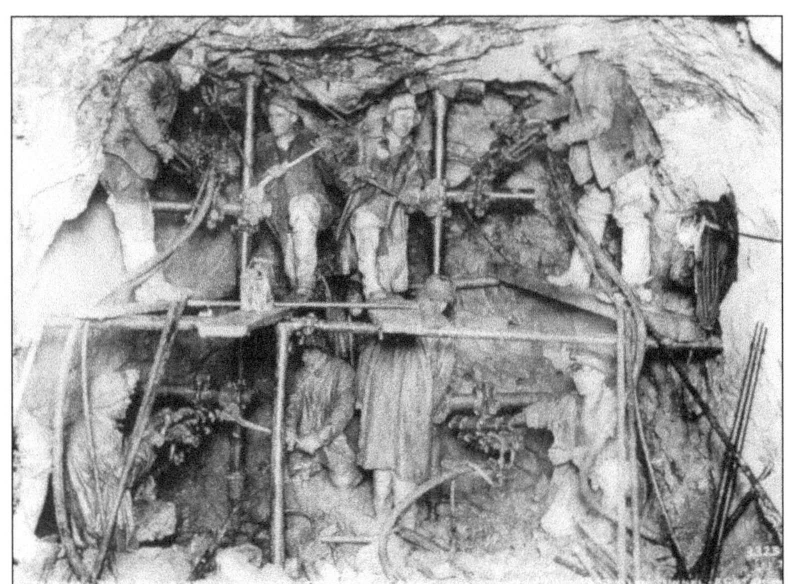

Men are drilling on the new eight-mile tunnel at the east end with Ingersoll Rand drills. The construction of the tunnel was extremely grueling, and the crew had a 50 percent–plus turnover rate each month. Wellington cooks had to feed hundreds of extra mouths during this phase. (Photograph by A. Guthrie, courtesy of Wikimedia Commons.)

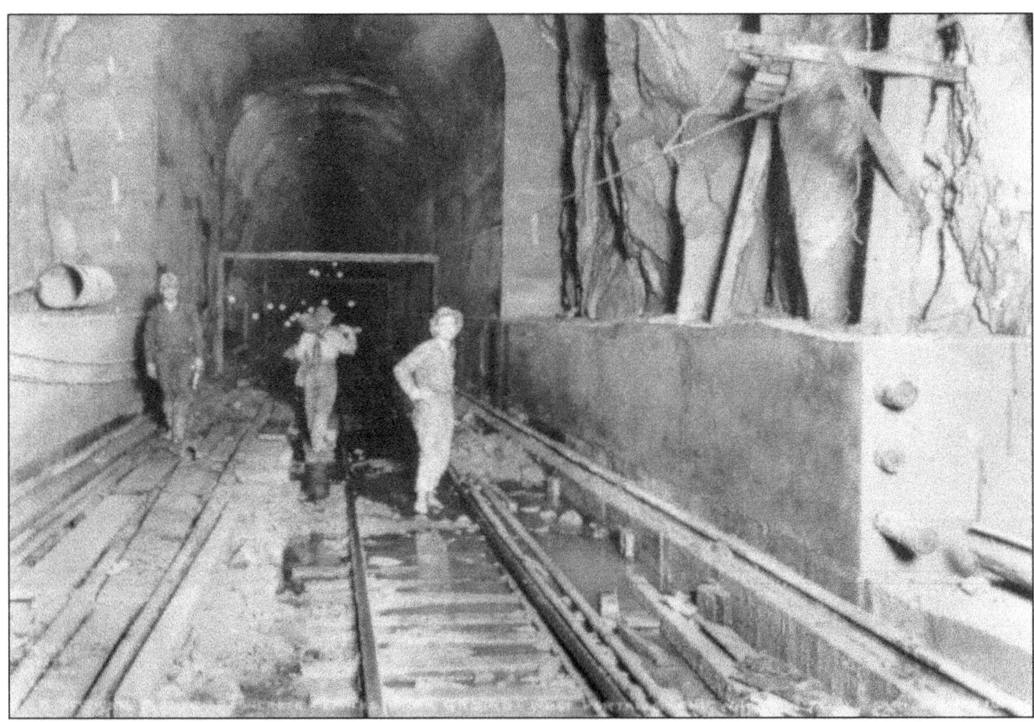

This is a photograph from a GN train entering the new Cascade Tunnel. Wellington still thrived as a railroad town until 1929, when the new 7.8-mile tunnel was built, redirecting the trains. The men were famed for changing shift crews without even letting go of the machines! (Courtesy of Washington State Archives.)

Ten

The Iron Goat Trail and Wellington Today

The town of Wellington today is nothing but a crumbling snowshed lined with hundreds of rotten railroad ties and the old Cascade Tunnel—both eerie reminders of the disaster and those who lost their lives. In the actual ravine where the trains were tossed, a plaque was erected listing the deceased, standing among the litter of rusted scraps of metal and pipes left behind after the clean-up crew pulled up what they could. Although a federal offense, many people over the past 100 years have looted souvenirs from the wreckage, while other pieces made it to museums like the Skykomish Historical Society.

The US Forest Service developed the site into beautiful hiking trails called the Iron Goat Trail, which can be enjoyed most of the year. Long, memorable walks through the snowshed and around the area are both scary and exciting. Though most people are unaware of the 1910 disaster that took almost 100 lives, the plaques with photographs along the trail tell of the long-forgotten avalanche, its victims, and a brief history of Wellington and its inhabitants.

The forgotten, isolated town of Wellington is now just another piece of Washington's and the Great Northern Railway's fascinating history. America's deadliest avalanche and the horrible train disaster that became part of its legacy will hopefully never be forgotten, and hopefully, nor will all of those involved in the battle of the storm, the running of the trains, and the feeding and caring of the passengers and crew. The hundreds of kindhearted people who walked miles to help with relief efforts and assist with the removal of the bodies should not be forgotten either.

But most of all, the faces and stories of the Seattle Express No. 25 and the fast mail train No. 27 passengers and crew who lost their lives that cold, dark night should not be forgotten.

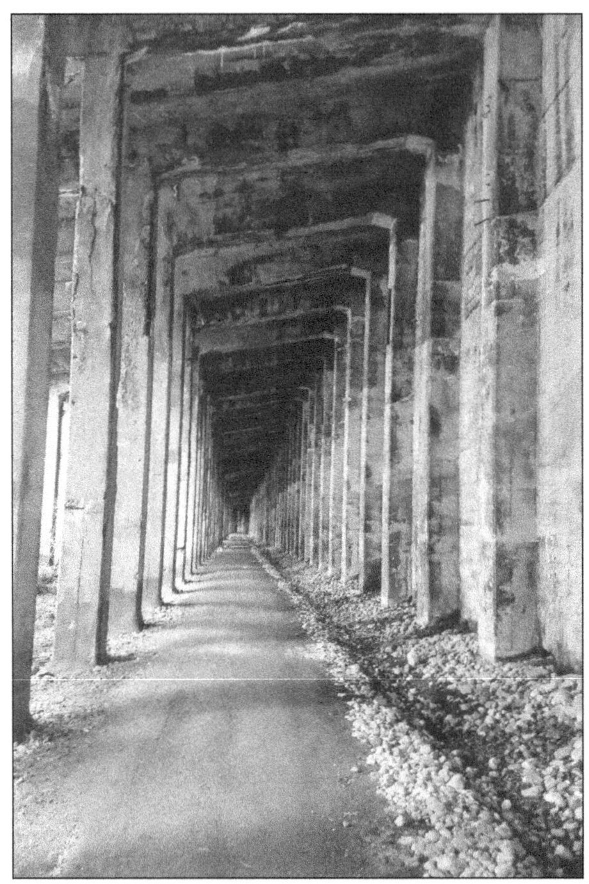

The beginning of the trail is seen from the Wellington side before entering the snowshed from the Iron Goat Trail. There is a white signpost with the number "1711" off to the right of the trail. This is a recreation of the old mileage signs that marked the original rail line and means that this point is 1,711 rail miles from St. Paul, Minnesota. (Author's collection.)

This big piece of the wreckage (possibly an air reservoir tank from one of the coaches) from a locomotive still lies on the ground, probably not far from where it was broken off from the rest of the train a century ago. Fallen trees still bear the marks of metal against wood as they lie rotting in the ravine. (Author's collection.)

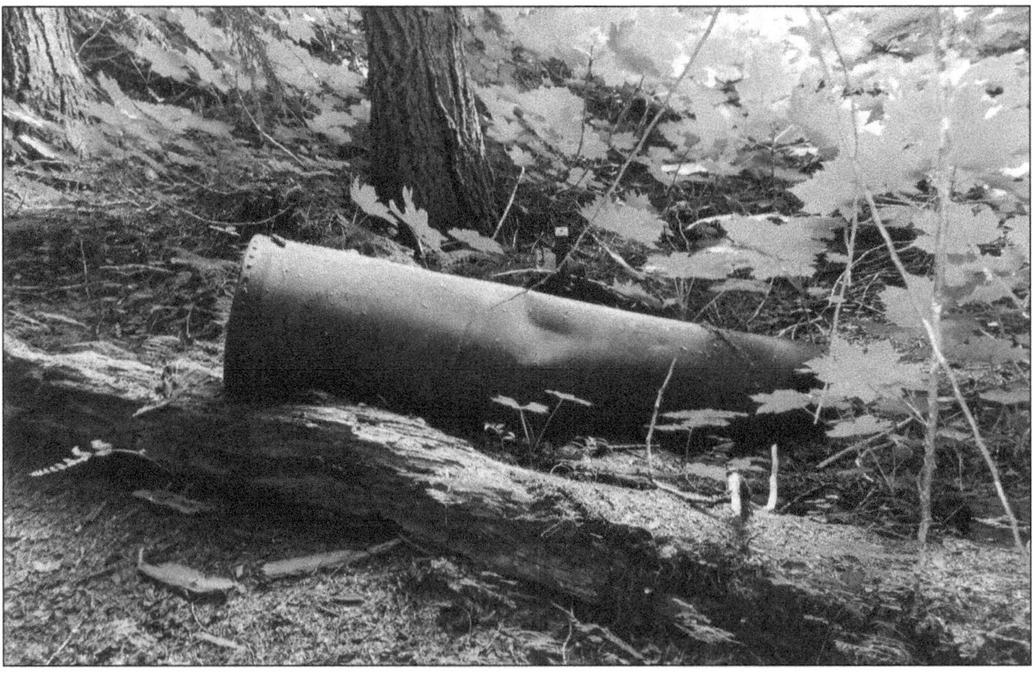

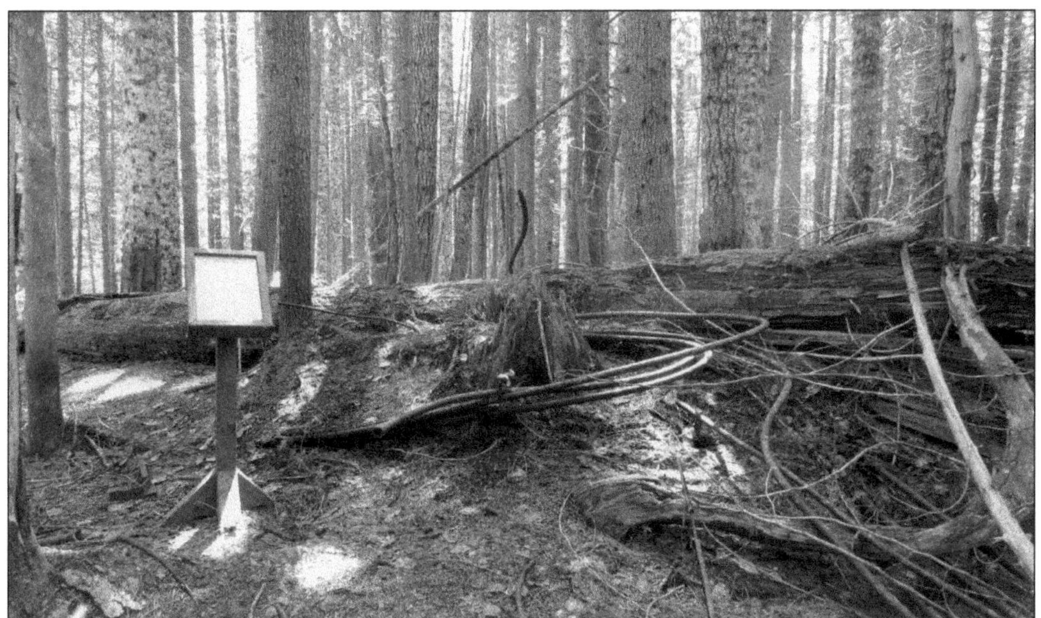

Today, a memorial rests in the ravine with a little history and the names of the victims of the avalanche. Nearby, twisted steam pipes and cables still wrap around trees, much as they were found after the accident in 1910. Final reminders of the avalanche are littered amongst the forest floor—broken glass here, rusted pieces of metal there—all evidence of the century-old tragedy. (Author's collection.)

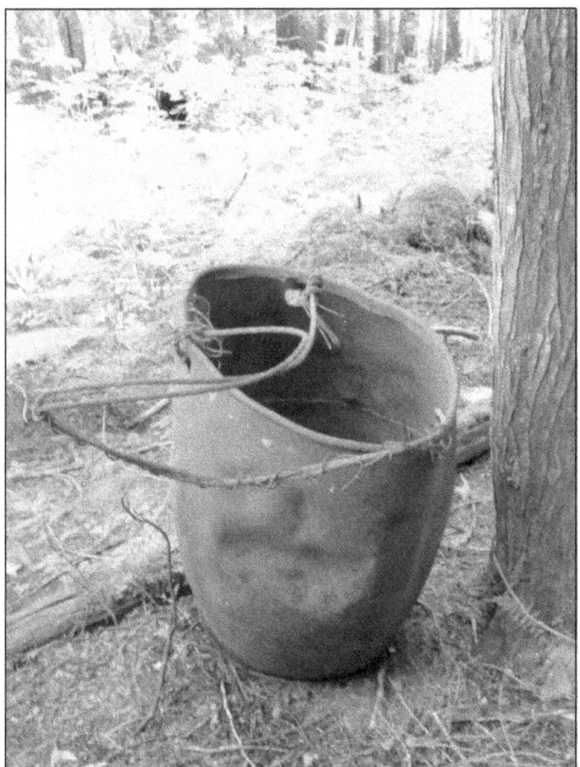

A metal barrel stands upright in the swampy part of the ravine surrounded by huge timbers long ago snapped in half from the force of the avalanche. The splintered remains still poke up from the ground as new growth towers over the moss-covered spikes. Many pieces from the trains have grown into their surroundings, refusing to let go of their final resting place among the departed. These barrels were originally used by GN crews for holding oil and kerosene. The ends were sometimes also removed and used for lifting various things. (Author's collection.)

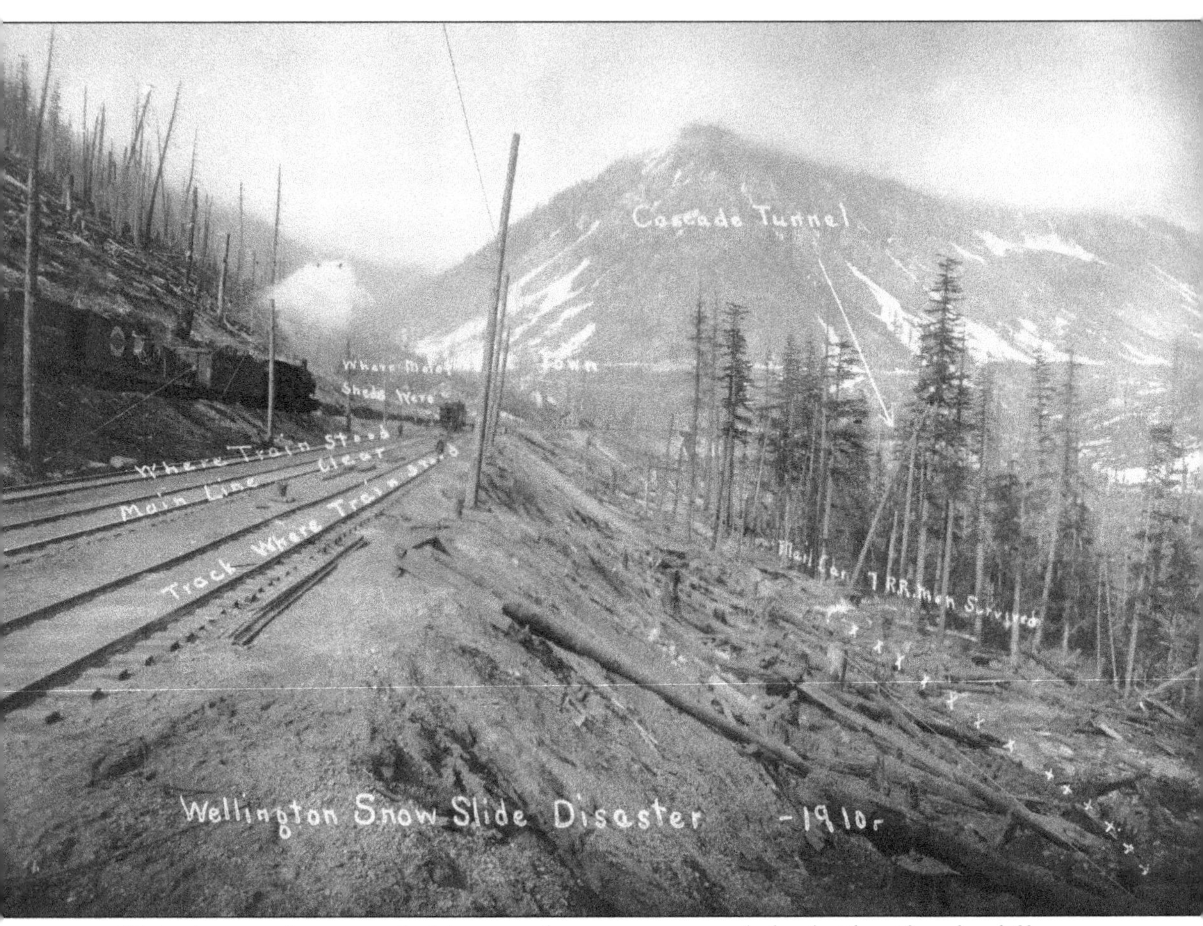

This photograph was marked by an unknown person and clearly identifies the different spots from the disaster: the Cascade Tunnel, with the towering Cascade Mountains in the background; the town of Wellington, where the motor sheds once were; the two tracks where the trains stood during the storm; the main line, and where the mail car was found. The Xs indicate where the wreckage and most of the bodies were located. O'Neill's private car was found just below the tracks instead of down in the ravine. O'Neill was an outstanding superintendent—a final story that sticks about his moral character tells of a couple of men who boarded one of his trains with the intention of robbing the passengers. O'Neill grabbed them by the collars, shoving them both off trackside, yelling, "You two should be ashamed of yourselves—scaring women and children that way!" (Courtesy of the Dr. George Fischer Collection, SHS.)

List of Wellington Dead

Lee J. Ahern, 25
Richard M. Barnhart, 40
Ella A. Beck, 30
Emma Beck, 4
George L. Beck, 40
Harriet Beck, 6
Leonard Beck, 2
Grover W. Begle, 24
Earl Edgar Bennington, 29
R.H. Bethel, 44
John Bjart, about 40
John Bjerenson, 28
Arthur Reed Blackburn, 33
Richard C. Bogart, 36
Fred Bohn, 20
Albert Boles, 34
William E. Bovee, 26
John Brockman, 45
Peter Bruno, 40
Alex C. Campbell, 28
J.O. Carroll
H.D. Chantrell, 50
Alex Chisholm, 60
G. Christy
Solomon Cohen, 50
William Corcoran, 45
Sarah Jane Covington, 69
George F. Davis, 35
Thelma Davis, 3
William N. Dorety
Anthony John Dougherty, 27
H.J. Drehl, 40
William A. Duncan, 45
Archie R. Dupy, 23
Harry Elliker, 40
Charles S. Eltinge, 50
Earl Fisher, 19
John D. Fox, 42
Inigi Giammarusti, 45
Donald Cameron Gilman, 33
Mike Guglielmo, 23
George A. Heron, 26
M. Milton Hicks, 25
George Hoefer, 28
Benjamin F. Jarnagan, 31
G.R. Jenks
Charles William Jennison, 28
Sidney H. Jones, 25
John Edward Kelly, 23
William Kenzal, 38
Charles F. LaDu, 26
Libby Latsch, 30
J. Liberati
Sam Lee, about 25
Gus Leibert, 25
Ada Lemman, 39
Edgar Lemman, 47
Stephen Ernest Lindsay, 33
Earl R. Longcoy, 19
John Mackie, 24
Francis S. Martin
Archibald McDonald
Nellie Sharp McGirl, 26
James McNeny, 59
Albert G. Mahler, 55
Bert Matthews, 37
William May, 54
James Monroe, 26
Peter Nino, 37
Catherine O'Reilly, 26
T.L. Osborne
Harry Otto Partridge, 35
John K. Parzybok, 24
Joseph L. Pettit
Antonio Porlowlino, 35
William E. Raycroft, 31
L. Ross, 25
Carl Smith, 50
Francis Starrett, 8 months
Lillian Starrett, 9
Andrew Stohmier, 30
Vasily Suterin, about 35
Benjamin G. Thompson
Rev. James M. Thomson, 57
Edward W. Topping, 29
Giovanni Tosti, 30
Hiram Towslee, 36
John C. Tucker, 37
J.R. Vail, 60
Lewis George Walker, 53
Julian E. Wells, 19
G.R. Yerks, 24
Donato Quarante

six unidentified laborers

www.ingramcontent.com/pod-product-compliance
Lightning Source LLC
LaVergne TN
LVHW060623110826
845147LV00015B/927

* 9 7 8 1 4 6 7 1 0 2 7 3 5 *